Five percent of the author's book royalties, matched by the publisher, is being donated to Montana Partners of the Americas for fisheries conservation in Argentina.

ARGENTINE
TROUT FISHING

A FLY FISHERMAN'S GUIDE TO
PATAGONIA

Frank Amato Publications
Portland, Oregon

Cover Art: "Spawners" by Argentine artist Alejandro del Valle of Junín de los Andes, Neuquen Province, Argentina.

Oil Paintings: Parks Reece: 10

Cover Photograph: A typically spectacular Patagonian sunset over Lago Nahuel Huapi from the Hotel Correntoso.

Frontispiece: The author seeking salmon on the Río Traful.

Back Cover Photograph: A lone fisherman tries his luck in the fabled Boca of the Río Chimehuin on an unusually calm day.

Frank Amato: 17, 20, 21, 23, 25, 45, 46, 86 bottom left.
Jorge Trucco: 79, 98, 113, 115, 118, 119, 147.
Roland Turney: 100 bottom right, 105, 122, 129.

Published in 1991 by Frank Amato Publications, P.O. Box 82112, Portland, Oregon 97282.

Softbound: ISBN 1-878175-06-8
Hardbound: ISBN 1-878175-07-6

Design: Tony Amato

Typesetting: Charlie Clifford

Maps: Tony Amato

Printed in Hong Kong

For Allan Fraser
1923 - 1991

He gathers the river around him,
he draws the mountains into a circle.
The trees and rocks lean forward
to see him fishing, fishing...

—**From** *Bob Bagg Fishing*
—by Roberts W. French

ACKNOWLEDGEMENTS

Any readers who experience good fly fishing and good adventure as a result of this book owe, with me, a debt of gratitude to a long list of Argentines, a few Americans, a Scot, and a Welshman:

Jorge Calandra, scholar, fly-tier, owner of the largest fishing library in Argentina, who patiently guided me through the complex history of fly fishing in his country;

Alfonso Racedo, hotelier, enthusiastic fisherman, and member of the Club Norysur on Lago Meliquina, who shed further light on Argentine fly fishing;

Mauricio and Mercedes Lariviere, and Felipe and Teresa Lariviere, owners of the two estancias that embrace the Río Traful—Arroyo Verde and La Primavera, respectively—charming hosts and lifelong stewards of that remarkable river, who led me to fifty years worth of fishing data;

The late Allan Fraser, Marcelo Morales, Jose "Pepe" Navas, Carlos Trisciuzzi, and again, Jorge Calandra—men who develop and tie with consumate skill flies the rest of us lose to sloppy backcasts and big fish in the rivers of Patagonia;

Fernando and Jorge de las Carreras, men short in years and long in vision, engaged in the prickly task of making Tierra del Fuego's Río Grande the finest sea-trout stream on the face of the earth;

Rosario, Ester, and Silvano Bonaccorso, Jorge and Jacqueline de las Carreras, Ashley and Tom Carrithers, Jonas Berg, Tim Hamilton, Orlando van Heerden, Trevor apIwan, Tony Koloszyc, García Mendez, Carlos and Carmen Olsen, Roberto Sacconi, Salty Saltzmann, Ariel Semenov, Roland and Elizabeth Turney, and Hector Vérgez: hosts, guides, residents, estancia and lodge owners, fly fishermen, friends, lovers of Patagonia every one . . .

I owe a special debt to Argentine biologists and archivists whose special training and access to scientific records helped me separate fact from fancy, among them Miguel de Lourdez Baíz, Jorge Bruzone, Reinaldo Gader, Teddy Griffiths, Simon Lewis, and Alejandro del Valle.

Very special thanks are due Jorge Graziosi, Juan Lincomán, Raúl San Martín, and Jorge Trucco, four top-flight Argentine fishing guides who generously took time from busy mid-season schedules to answer interminable questions, and when necessary, set me straight.

I wish to thank the authors of the following books, each of which illuminates a different dimension of the Patagonian experience: Polo Bardín, *Hablemos de Truchas;* Jorge Donovan, *Nací Pescador;* Raul Fuentealba, *Una Provincia Llamada Neuquen;* Ginés Gomaríz, *Pescando Truchas;* García Méndez, *En Busca de la Trucha;* Werner Schad, *Los Rios Mas Australes de la Tierra;* Ernie Schwiebert, *A River for Christmas and Other Stories,* and Eric Shipton, *Tierra del Fuego: The Fatal Lodestone.*

Finally, I wish to thank Simon Lewis, of Junín de los Andes, who may one day build his own spring creek in the shadow of the Andes, John Lutz, of Emigrant, Montana, who has already built his own spring creek, Lutz's Folly, in the shadow of the Absoraka Mountains, and to biologists Wayne Hadley and Dale Miller and oceanographer Jeff Fox and entrepreneur Enrique Poodts for reviewing this manuscript and offering helpful suggestions.

Passages on South American national parks in Chapter 6 appeared in *South America's National Parks,* published in 1990 by The Mountaineers Books. Passages in Chapter 12 appeared in *The Flyfisher* magazine in fall, 1987.

Any errors, omissions, or misinterpretations that lurk between the covers of this book are of course my own responsibility.

As long as this book remains in print, a portion of its earnings will be donated by the author and by publisher Frank Amato to *Montana/Patagonia Partners of the Americas* for the express purpose of protecting and enhancing the trout fishery in the streams and lakes of Argentina's Neuquen Province.

Readers are advised that any references to specific accommodations or professional guides are intended to be descriptive, and should not be construed as recommendations.

Bill Leitch—
Livingston, Montana

CONTENTS

Note On Taxonomy And Languages   8
Note To Readers   8
Introduction   9

PART I—THE PAST

Chapter 1 — How The Streams Got There   13
Chapter 2 — How The Fish Got There   17

PART II—THE PRESENT

Chapter 3 — Patagonia's Fly Fishing Zones   27
Chapter 4 — Argentina and its People   37
Chapter 5 — Fauna and Flora   49
Chapter 6 — Parks and Reserves   63

PART III—PREPARATIONS

Chapter 7 — Regulations   80
Chapter 8 — Patagonian Guides   87
Chapter 9 — What to Take and When to Go   93

PART IV—THE WATERS, NORTH TO SOUTH

Chapter 10 — Northern Zone   99
Chapter 11 — Central Zone   159
Chapter 12 — Southern Zone   178

Fly Fishing Glossary   190
Selected Bibliography   191

NOTE ON TAXONOMY AND LANGUAGES

In June, 1988, the Committee on Names of Fishes of the American Fisheries Society changed the generic name for all native Pacific drainage trouts, previously called *Salmo*, to *Onchorhynchus*. In addition, the specific name for rainbow trout (and its anadromous form, steelhead) was changed from *gairdneri* to *mykiss*. The scientific name for rainbow trout is now *Onchorhynchus mykiss*. In order not to confuse future investigators of the origin of the Patagonian trout fishery, throughout this book I have used the older term used in early documents by the men who introduced rainbows to Argentina, *Salmo gairdneri*.

The official language of Argentina is Spanish. You need not speak Spanish to fish in Patagonia, but the more words you learn to recognize or speak, the richer your experience will be. The rewards are tangible: call your dry fly a *mosca seca* (mohs-kah SAY-kah), your first pool a *pozón* (poh-SOHN), and your first trout a *trucha* (TROO-chah), and you will provoke broad smiles all round. To help in this respect, I have included in the text and in a glossary at the back of the book translations of fishing terms and names of Patagonian flora and fauna that fishermen are most likely to encounter and remember.

Although Spanish is the language of Argentina, many geographical features in Patagonia are named for the region's earliest inhabitants, just as in the North American West. In most of Patagonia, those inhabitants were Araucanians; tall, grim, warriors who fought the Spanish invaders fiercely and were defeated more decisively by alcohol and pestilence than by force of arms. Scholars agree that the proper name of the Araucanian language is *Mapuche* (mah-POO-chey), and Araucanian Indians are commonly called Mapuches throughout Patagonia. Nearly all of the rivers and many of the lakes of Patagonia have Mapuche names that describe the character of these waters to a degree more precise than either Spanish or English. For this reason, wherever possible, Mapuche place-names are also translated for the reader.

The Mapuches have poetic imagination. Neither staid Englishmen nor no—nonsense Americans give crystal-clear rivers names like *aluminé*—("one sees [into it] very deeply"). . .

NOTE TO READERS

For all fly fishermen, there exist certain waters endowed with a form of magic—waters that enchant and exert a powerful influence upon us. These waters, of course, are different for different fishermen, but the effects are the same on everybody; mere mention of a stream, lake, or region immediately elicits a sigh, turns the mind to fishing, conjures up crisp memories of past events, and floods our imagination with astonishing experiences yet-to-come. For months prior to a trip to these waters, we are swollen with anticipation and ponder daily which flies to take, what size tippets, which rods or lines. Thousands of other details crowd our minds.

Increasing familiarity with these special waters breeds neither contempt nor indifference; the more we visit them, the more firmly we become entwined in their spell. Through each of our personal Elysian Fields flow such bewitched streams.

My Elysian Fields lie in Argentina, where a seemingly endless succession of clear rivers flow cold from the Andes eastward into the steppes, each with a unique set of characteristics, each sustaining superb populations of enthusiastic trout and salmon, each designed by nature for the sustenance and well-being of curious fly fishermen. . .

All fly fishermen need the stuff of dreams. It gets us through the seasons of snow, cheers us up when nothing goes right, and keeps us from growing old too fast. We need the knowledge that somewhere far off lies that perfect river with perfect fish that we will deceive some perfect summer evening with our perfect cast and our perfect fly.

It's down there all right, somewhere in Argentina. I hope you find it, too. . .

INTRODUCTION

In the winter of 1520, shortly after Ferdinand Magellan and his men dropped anchor off a bleak, windswept shore at the present site of San Julián, the shore crew came upon a set of enormous footprints along the beach. Spurred by their ominous discovery in this remote land, the party hastily returned to the ship and soon set sail, not inclined to meet the owner of such *patagones* (big feet). The story circulated widely, as tales of New World mysteries did in those days and the land that stretched off to the western horizon behind San Julian eventually became known as Patagonia.

At least so goes the most popular story to which the naming of Patagonia is attributed. Many scholars doubt that this is the true origin of the area's name and we may never know the precise truth, but everybody agrees that in the centuries since Magellan's visit, Patagonia has exercised an irresistible fascination on travelers, at once terrifying and exhilarating.

It is a land of dramatic contrasts, in some respects a fearsome terrain—stark, austere, perilous—and in other respects awesome—beautiful, remote, possessed of an indescribable character that lures adventurers as the flame draws the moth. Inexplicably, the perverse attraction this land holds for men does not flag as the centuries pass, but grows.

Sir Francis Drake stopped by for a short visit in 1578 in order to hang a disgruntled officer, with whom he calmly took breakfast prior to the execution. The ebullient, wide-eyed young naturalist Charles Darwin explored its shores and steppes in 1832, and in ensuing decades wondered why he so sorely missed such an inhospitable place. The indefatigable Francisco "Perito" Moreno explored its rivers and lakes during several arduous journeys in the 1870s, twice barely escaping death at the hands of Araucanian Indians. Until laid low by the long reach of the law in 1905, Robert Parker and Harry Longabaugh—we know them better as Butch Cassidy and the Sundance Kid—led a gang that plundered and murdered its way through the bleak steppes of Patagonia for several years. British author Eric Shipton was one of the earliest mountaineers to explore the mountains and icecaps of its most remote fastnesses for the first time as recently as 1960, and Bruce Chatwin brought Patagonia to the attention of a wide reading audience with his 1973 book, *In Patagonia*.

Most of the perils of travel in Patagonia have faded into the past, but the region's spell has not diminished at all. Every summer Argentines flock to a handful of tourist centers in Patagonia, but much of the region is nearly as remote, trackless, and empty as it was four centuries ago.

Patagonia is genuine frontier country, much of it wilderness. The most recent battle between Argentine troops and Mapuche Indians occurred in 1883, seven years *after* Custer's stand on the Little Bighorn. The earliest recorded visit of bonafide tourists began before this battle in January, 1879, when a group of five young English aristocrats (plus a servant) seeking an adventurous place for a vacation landed in Punta Arenas, Chile. The group, headed by 22-

Lost fish are always bigger.

The tourist hatch.

year-old Florence Dixie, hired a guide and spent nearly three months in southern Patagonia, covering nearly 1,600 miles by horseback.

Patagonia is also a land of dramatic extremes, part desert (frigid in winter and sweltering in summer), part treeless grasslands, and part forested, storm-battered mountains that cradle scores of active glaciers and apart from Antarctica, the largest continental ice-caps in the southern hemisphere. Many first-time visitors, not yet under Patagonia's spell, fail to apprehend the beauty of the arid steppes between the Andean Cordillera and the barren coast to the east; they find these featureless flatlands dreadfully monotonous. But visitors always appreciate the scenic splendor of the Patagonian Andes, for they embrace alpine features to which all travelers respond with immense satisfaction: snow-capped peaks, glaciers, verdant forests, wildflowers and wildlife, sparkling lakes, and rivers large and small.

It is these lakes and rivers that are responsible for the newest, and in some respects most excited wave of visitors to Patagonia—fishermen—for these waters support populations of trout and salmon that today sustain what is arguably the best fly fishing on the face of the earth...

This book is intended to introduce newcomers to that fly fishing, but also to enhance the Patagonian fly fishing experience for others.

It eventually dawns on all fishermen that hooking a fish is a nearly inconsequential feature of fishing. What does matter is the feel of sun, drizzle, or snow on your cheek, the sound of the river, the birds, or leaves rustling in the breeze, the sudden splash of color with which the wildflowers adorn the meadows, the breath-catching anticipation with which we approach a pool for the first time, the first icy sip of a cocktail after an exciting day on a stream, the calm conversation or shared silences with companions around the fire, and a myriad other impressions that have little to do with mere fish.

Fly fishing is an experience of the total landscape. It defies general analysis because it is so personal, but what does seem universal is that the more comprehensively we understand our total fishing environment, the more downright pleasant our fishing experiences prove to be. Some foreigners journey to Patagonia and catch plenty of fish, yet find themselves vaguely disappointed, as though something had not happened; their tales and memories of Patagonian fishing are a bit insubstantial. For North Americans, something indeed is missing, and that something is a comprehensive understanding of the fishing environment. A fisherman new to Patagonia may succeed on its streams because he has been fishing somewhere else for most of his life. But he will understand almost nothing else... He doesn't recognize the flora or fauna, has trouble with the language, isn't quite sure how to deport himself in this new land, has little idea where to go or where he is much of the time, has little idea where the fish, rivers, and mountains came from in the first place, and knows next to nothing about Argentina and its people. That sort of knowledge is an integral part of a fisherman's experience in his home waters, but is hard to come by easily in Patagonia, especially by boarding a plane in Denver, New York, Calgary, or San Francisco, deplaning in Patagonia, fishing strange rivers hard for ten days, and making the return trip almost before your waders are dry.

This book is intended to flesh out that experience, to fill in important gaps for fishermen, so that when they arrive, they will already know something about the region—something about the geological history of Patagonia and the political history of Argentina; something about Argentines and their manners, cuisine, and fishing styles; something about Patagonian trout and salmon: where they live and why, how they got there, where they came from and when, how they are managed; something about the flora and fauna that live along, in, and over the rivers and lakes; and many more of those features of the total landscape that can enhance a fishing experience, and transform an ordinary trip into an extraordinary adventure, which is, after all, what good fishing is all about. . .

Two points to remember: First, Argentina has more streams, to say nothing of lakes, than the most peripatetic trout fisherman could explore in a long, active lifetime. This book deals only with the part of Argentina called Patagonia because the highest quality fishing is found in that region. It deals with streams because of my own preference; lakes are described only in

passing. Second, although the material described in these pages will help any fishermen to appreciate Patagonia, the book is about fishing with flies, not lures or bait.

I've noticed that many first-time visitors to Patagonia expect all fish to be gigantic and abundant, along the lines of the ideas expressed by Livingston artist Parks Reece on the facing page. That is a false expectation and should be dispensed with here and now.

My intention is to help readers find *quality* fishing; that does not necessarily mean big fish or even many fish. Plenty of Patagonian trophies await the right fly, but I prefer to call a reader's attention to a small stream with real character that lies in scenic terrain rich with birds and wildlife, than to a stream noted only for its big fish. A number of Patagonian streams hold fish, but for one reason or another are simply not fun to fly fish, so one of my criteria for deciding to describe a stream in this book is whether or not it is a pleasure to fish. Appropriateness for fly fishing is another. Quality fly fishing is not served by sending a fisherman to a weed-choked, murky stream with no current, to a shallow stream that braids its way through a boring mile of gravel bars, or to a stream so broad and powerful that it is more like a lake than a river, even if these waters teem with trout.

I will describe Patagonia's trophy spots, for they occupy hallowed ground in international trout fishing lore, but they do not in general provide the high quality fishing sought by experienced fly fishermen; most North Americans will try these spots because they will simply be unable to pass them up, but before long, they'll find themselves numb with boredom if they catch fish or not, and will soon move on to the real fishing.

This book will direct you to Patagonian trout streams and help you to catch fish, but it is not a substitute for a professional guide or for twenty years experience on trout streams. Only writers wiser or more reckless than I dare tell other fly fishermen how to fish. . .

HOW THE STREAMS GOT THERE

Sooner or later, every fly fisherman who works the streams of Patagonia will take a break, find a grassy seat in the shade, gaze out over the river, and wonder how on earth the fishing got so damned good in the first place in this faroff corner of the world. What natural processes combined to set the stage for the afternoon's wonderful fishing?

If one word embodies the events that account for your presence at this river, that word is glaciation. But before exploring the relationship between long-vanished glaciers and your day's fishing, we need to make a brief visit to the deep past.

As you sit in the shade next to your Patagonian stream, you, the stream, the tree, the fish, and everything else around you are moving west at the rate of about an inch and a half a year. You and the rest of South America are passengers on a 60-mile-thick chunk of the earth's crust and underlying mantle called the South American Plate which floats cork-like on the viscous lower mantle and has been moving westward for about 200 million years. The plate broke loose from the ancient super-continent Gondwanaland, which encompassed Africa, India, Antarctica, and Australia and has since moved 3,000 miles from Africa, opening the gap now filled by the South Atlantic Ocean. When the plate began its westward drift there were no mountains where you now sit; all of Patagonia and the west coast of South America were flat, featureless plains.

The South American Plate might have continued its westward drift without complication, but 100 million years ago a change in plate boundary occurred, and it collided with another wandering piece of the earth's crust, the Nazca Plate, which was moving deep below the waters of the Pacific Ocean in the opposite direction and twice as fast—3 inches a year.

The two plates did not merely grind to a halt when they collided. Something had to give, and the Nazca Plate, composed of denser rock, was pushed beneath the South American Plate. Both plates continued then (and now) on their eastward and westward courses over the face of the planet.

But the collision of the plates had profound effects on the South American continent. Friction created by the movement of vast quantities of rock generated enormous heat and the inevitable cracking of the earth's crust created weak points through which magma from the mantle sandwiched between the plates welled up to the surface. These fissures occurred all along the west coast of South America, just east of the line along which the Nazca Plate slips under the South American Plate. These weak points became the long chain of volcanos that began to build the Andes, the southeastern margin of the so-called ring of fire that lines the Pacific Basin. About 50 million years ago, these early Andean volcanos reached their maximum intensity, pouring massive amounts of magma onto the earth's surface, slowly building a base for the Andes.

But vulcanism was not the only force which built up the Andes. The plates did not slide past one another like two pats of warm butter. They folded, buckled, and fractured, pushing huge wedges of rock upward. The movements are sometimes sudden; layers of the plates snap instead of fold, and the earth shudders, creating the frequent and often deadly earthquakes that are a common part of life in the Andes. When

Just north of the Southern Fishing Zone, the spectacular mountains and glaciers of Los Glaciares National Park.

Charles Darwin crossed the Andes from Mendoza to Santiago, Chile, he had no idea when or how the mountains were formed, but he found marine fossils several thousand feet above the sea and realized that vertical movement of titanic proportions had to have occurred sometime in the long history of the Andes.

To summarize, the mountains we see today have resulted from the effects of two geological forces: first, the deposition of successive layers of volcanic rock, called andesite, poured onto the surface of the earth, and second, the stacking up of basement rocks that were, and continue to be, compressed, buckled, and uplifted as the two plates converge and the South American Plate overrides the Nazca Plate.

The volcanos which laid down the original foundations for the Andes are not, however, the volcanos we see today. Those ancient mountains eroded away long ago. What we see today is partly a result of a second episode of vulcanism that began about 15 million years ago, when enormous volumes of ash were blown from the earth, to eventually cover 60,000 square miles of South America with layers of ash that averaged 1500 feet in thickness. These eruptions continued until about four million years ago, definitely not good conditions for trout; that would come much later.

About the same time that Andean volcanos were spewing ash across the continent, even perhaps as a result of these eruptions, the earth's climate began to change. No one knows exactly what triggered the changes, but cold spells grew longer, snowfalls deeper, and the glaciers that had formed around the high peaks began to edge further and further out of their mountain recesses. The ice ages had begun. . .

At several intervals during the last million years, continental glaciers formed and swept from the polar areas toward the equator. During the most recent of the major glaciations, 18,000 years ago, most of the northern United States, the southern tip of Africa, a portion of Australia, and *all* of present day Patagonia were covered by snow and thick, active sheets of ice. The burgeoning ice-caps of Antarctica were unable to reach Patagonia from across the sea, but the Andes were now high enough to strip moisture from the westerly winds and feed their own glaciers. The Patagonian Ice Age was severe. In the south, some ice flowed eastward across lower Andean divides, deepening them and pushing far out into the steppes.

At their maximum, some Patagonian ice-sheets were as much as 4,000 feet thick, heavy enough to depress the earth's crust near the sea by several hundred feet. The glaciers gouged deep gorges through the mountains which were invaded by the ocean after the glaciers retreated and sea level rose once again. The Strait of Magellan, which separates Tierra del Fuego from the South American mainland, is one of these ice-carved canyons; the Beagle Channel, north of Cape Horn, is another. The glaciers went into reluctant retreat thousands of years ago, but they have by no means disappeared. Over 9,000 square miles of continental ice-cap

Bizarre but beautiful formations of weathered limestone characterize the valley of the Río Traful.

Just north of the Southern Fishing Zone, the spectacular mountains and glaciers of Los Glaciares National Park.

---

lie in two sections between the peaks of the southernmost Andes, and smaller glaciers nestle in wrinkles in almost all of the higher Andean mountains, calm now and patient, quietly awaiting the next shift in climate. . .

These ice-sheets and glaciers gave the mountains of Patagonia the sculpted character we observe today, laid the basic groundwork for the trout habitat found there, and continue today to nurture the streams in central and southern Patagonia.

When the Patagonian glaciers plunged from their mountain valleys, they pushed east well into the steppes, grinding deep valleys and forming immense terminal moraines from the rock scooped from the valley floors. When the climate changed and the glaciers retreated, very little water from the moist Pacific winds reached the land east of the Andes and the once lush plains turned into the semi-desert steppes we see today, hardly good trout country.

But the glaciers had created a series of enormous lake basins along the eastern margin of the Andes from the northern edge of Patagonia south to the shore of the Strait of Magellan, and this series of lakes is the linchpin in the story of the Patagonian trout fishery.

Rivers in the part of the southern Andes north of Patagonia lack headwater lakes; they tend to be intermittent streams, dependent entirely upon snowmelt and rainfall for their flow. Their levels fluctuate widely; they can go nearly dry in late fall, and flood out of their banks in spring. It is no accident that quality trout fishing in Patagonia begins at the point at which the first large glacial lakes appear, for these

How The Streams Got There

lakes, some the size of inland freshwater seas, provide a stable physical and chemical environment for fish which is absent in watersheds that lack such headwater lakes.

Most of the Patagonian glacial lakes are large enough to function as settling basins for sediments carried from the mountains by snowmelt, contemporary glaciation, spring freshets, and other processes of alpine erosion. The lakes intercept the sediments and prevent them from reaching the rivers, where they would not only seriously interfere with our fly fishing by roiling the water, but inhibit spawning success by blanketing redds with suffocating layers of sand and silt.

The lakes are also sufficiently large to function as enormous heat sinks that protect their outlet streams from sudden changes in temperature. Lake temperatures vary between summer and winter, of course. In northern Patagonia, lake temperatures range from about 64-66° F. in summer to 42-48° F. in winter, but seasonal changes are gradual rather than abrupt. Rivers in extreme southern Patagonia (which also lack large headwater lakes) freeze over during the winter. In addition, the normal range of temperatures in most Patagonian streams corresponds closely to the optimum temperature range for salmonids—cool enough to hold plenty of dissolved oxygen yet warm enough to promote vigorous growth.

Little information is available on the chemistry of these lakes. They are all poor in electrolytes and have low levels of phosphorus, which means plant growth is relatively low. Because the west end of most of the large lakes lies within the forested Andes, it is likely that their waters receive ample amounts of nutrients that might limit some links in the food chain that leads to trout and most of the lakes are supersaturated with oxygen. Trout heaven.

The lakes provide fish with shelter from enemies and are nearly as effective as regulating dams in providing stable flows for the rivers they feed.

In a word, the lakes provide the streams with an element essential to any ecosystem: stability.

Finally, the lakes provide fishermen with an essential element of quality fishing: striking beauty. They are extremely transparent, and pass that clarity on to the rivers to which they give birth. Most of them lie in the very lap of the Andes, with volcanos, snowcapped peaks, and forested mountain slopes for backdrops. Their scenic quotient is simple magnificence.

Not only did the Pleistocene glaciers provide the trout of Patagonia with the nurturing lakes, but while grinding their way down through the Andes, they provided the rivers with an ideal substrate for salmonids. For their first few miles, virtually all of Patagonia's lake-originated rivers flow through terminal moraines, hill-sized mounds of glacial till left behind when the glaciers began their slow retreat. The moraines and often miles of downstream outwash plain are comprised of a conglomeration of weathered rocks and gravel that, when etched by rivers, form into the meandering freestone streams characteristic of Patagonia. There are drawbacks for fly fishermen, for many streambeds are paved with round, slick boulders the size of basketballs, utter hell to wade through. But most streams also have long stretches of gravels nearly ideal for spawning salmonids, usually located at the very point where they are most advantageous for the fish—at the lake outlets.

When you've finished rummaging through your fly boxes and leave your seat in the shade, take a glance up and down the valley, try to imagine it filled with a rumbling river of ice, and murmur a small prayer of thanks to those vanished Pleistocene glaciers, for you owe them a great deal.

And while you're at it, you might give a mental nod to a small group of men—the determined biologists who first brought the fish to these remote, sparkling waters—for as we are about to see, you owe them a great deal, too.

HOW THE FISH GOT THERE

In Hurlingham, a quiet, aging suburb of Buenos Aires, Sunday strollers may hear the pop of bat on ball or the drumming of horses' hooves as they pass the meticulously groomed grounds of the Hurlingham Club. The games are not baseball or horseracing, but cricket and polo, and if the strollers wander into the club around five o'clock, they will be served tea and crumpets—all very British.

At the turn of the century, the British presence and influence in Argentina was even more pervasive than it is today and Hurlingham was an enclave more reminiscent of London than Buenos Aires. A small stream, Arroyo Morón—today little more than a conduit for industrial wastes—meandered

through the suburb and this stream loomed large in the history of trout in Argentina, for along with their love of tea, cricket, and polo, the British brought with them their passion for trout fishing.

The earliest recorded introduction of trout into Argentine waters occurred in Hurlingham several years prior to 1893, when with more enthusiasm than forethought, an unnamed English "angling enthusiast" introduced rainbow trout into Arroyo Moron. The unfortunate trout did not survive long, for the sluggish Moron, a small stream, becomes very warm during the hot pampas summer. But the ill-fated experiment lodged in the Argentine mind, and at about the same time, a young, ad-

venturous Argentine who was also thinking about fish set into motion a series of events that would have far-reaching effects on Argentine trout fishing.

Francisco "Perito" Moreno, a surveyor and enthusiastic explorer, fell under the spell of Patagonia early and occupies a pre-eminent place not only in the annals of Argentina's national park movement, but also in the story of its fresh water fishing. Sent by the Argentine government to Patagonia when he was only 23 years old to explore the region and survey the Chilean frontier, Moreno visited most of the large lakes and traveled extensively along the many rivers that flow out of the Andean Cordillera. During a series of trips beginning in 1875, Moreno noted that relatively few fish populated the lakes and streams in the area and observed that the potential for a freshwater fishery was enormous. Moreno suggested to the government that introduction of fish to the area for commercial and sporting purposes would be a wise venture and in 1892 he invited a Frenchman, Ferdinand Lahille, to undertake a study of Patagonian waters in order to see if the proposal was worthwhile.

While Lahille explored and analyzed the headwaters of the Río Neuquen, the Argentine Minister of Agriculture hired an Italian scientist, Felipe Silvestre, to explore the headwaters of the Río Santa Cruz for the same purpose. The results of both explorations were inconclusive and the Minister, now Ambassador to the United States and weary of Europeans and uncertain studies, hired the foremost fisheries biologist in the United States, John W. Titcomb, to go to Argentina, and get on with the job.

Titcomb arrived in Argentina in 1903, took a train to the frontier town of Neuquen and then set off for Lago Nahuel Huapi, a rugged 19-day trip by horseback and wagon (the same trip today is a four-hour drive). He spent a few months sampling water quality and making fluvial measurments near the lake, concluding that conditions were ideal for a variety of freshwater fish. He set about building temporary hatchery facilities at the eastern end of Lago Nahuel Huapi and returned to Buenos Aires with his findings.

At the turn of the century, Patagonia was still little more than primitive wilderness, populated by bandits, a few police and soldiers, reluctantly pacified Mapuche Indians, and half-wild gauchos only recently become *estancieros* (ranchers). Titcomb and several other American fishery biologists who assisted and later succeeded him lived lonely lives of relative privation during the decade they devoted to their fisheries work. Dusty copies of their letters to families in the United States (still filed in the archives of the Virgen de las Nieves Hatchery near Bariloche) are fascinating reading, full of accounts of dangerous adventures, illnesses, and poignant messages to loved ones.

In his initial enthusiasm, Titcomb recommended that the Argentine government introduce into Patagonia nearly every species of fresh-water fish then popular in the United States, among them black bass, crappies, rock bass, and shad. The rigors of a trip down the Río Limay enroute to Buenos Aires cooled his ardor somewhat, but he nevertheless cabled an order to the United States for several species of fish.

E. A. Tulian received the cable and was given the task of escorting the eggs safely to Patagonia. He assembled his shipment, seven large boxes, but at the last minute discovered to his horror that no American steamships had refrigerated compartments large enough to accommodate the containers in which the eggs had to be shipped. To make matters worse, the voyage from New York to Buenos Aires required about fifty days, far too long to permit the eggs to be packed in ice rather than be refrigerated.

Tulian, not a man easily discouraged, worked out an ingenious solution. The voyage from New York to Southampton, England required only ten days and British steamships, designed to ship

Argentine beef to England, did have refrigerated compartments large enough to receive the egg boxes. So Tulian had the boxes packed in ice, and on January 19, 1904, shipped them to England, to be transfered to British refrigerator ships and sent on to Buenos Aires. (Tulian's solution was repeated several times with subsequent shipments, doubtless the source of the belief that Argentina's trout originated from British rather than American stock.)

The eggs arrived in Buenos Aires safely, were put on a train to Neuquen and then transfered to ox-drawn wagons for the harrowing three-week trip to Lago Nahuel Huapi. On March 4, after a journey of 50 days, Tulian reached the temporary hatchery. His seven boxes contained the following cargo:

Whitefish
   Coregonus clupeaformis 1,000,000 eggs

Brook Trout
   Salvelinus fontinalis   102,700 eggs

Lake Trout
   Salvelinus namaycush   53,000 eggs

Landlocked Atlantic Salmon
   Salmo salar sebago   50,000 eggs

Losses during the trip were extraordinarily low—about 15 percent. The shipment was a success, and the eggs soon hatched.

The entire batch of whitefish alevins was put into Lago Nahuel Huapi, where (thank God) they disappeared without trace. The brooks, lake trout, and salmon were distributed among several nearby lakes—Espejo, Nahuel Huapi, Traful, and Gutierrez. Some fish were kept at the hatchery for brood stock and successfully spawned three years later.

The delighted biologists immediately requested rainbow trout eggs. This shipment, accompanied by another American, a Mr. Ormsby, was sent out the same year, but was a star-crossed cargo. Slowed by poor roads and delayed by unseasonal blizzards, the eggs began to hatch, and rather than lose the entire shipment, Ormsby put them into a small lake when he was still in the steppes 200 miles short of the hatchery at Nahuel Huapi.

The next six years comprised the golden age of salmonid introduction in Patagonia. Six more shipments of eggs were sent to the Americans toiling away in their remote hatchery on Nahuel Huapi, and to other newly constructed facilities elsewhere. Some arrived safely, others suffered heavy losses. They included large numbers of eggs of the following species: rainbow trout *(Salmo gairdneri)*, brown trout *(Salmo trutta)*, sockeye salmon *(Oncorhynchus nerka)*, silver salmon *(Oncorhynchus kisutch)*, chinook salmon *(Oncorhynchus tshawytscha)*, freshwater codfish *(Gadus morrhua)*, and more brooks, lake trout, and Atlantic salmon.

The rainbows, brooks, and Atlantic salmon were planted widely and indiscriminately throughout Patagonia during these years, and flourished in almost every lake and stream into which they were introduced.

The cod disappeared.

The Pacific salmon were planted in several rivers in expectation of establishing runs in the Atlantic drainages. They dutifully migrated to sea, found themselves in the wrong ocean, and were never seen again.

The early shipment of brown trout was also a failure, for most of the eggs did not survive the trip; their day was yet to come. . .

The last major shipment of eggs arrived safely in Buenos Aires on February 17, 1910, an assortment of salmon and lake trout which were forwarded to a new hatchery at Santa Cruz.

From 1904 to 1910, eight major shipments of salmonid eggs from the United States (and later from Europe) had been sent to Argentina and hatched, the offspring introduced into nearly every drop of water in Patagonia. In 1910, the shipments suddenly stopped. The remaining Americans went home, their job done, and the golden age was over.

Several hatcheries had been established, however. Stocks had been built up and the hatcheries were self-sustaining. Record-keeping fell off and little is known about the hatcheries' activities during many of the years that followed. It is safe to assume, however, that the hatcheries continued with an aggressive stocking program.

The importation of salmonids was halted for twenty years, during which the hatcheries continued to raise and plant their fish throughout Patagonia. Several incidents occurred during these decades which complicate the story and make it difficult to unravel the sequence of events. Once, a plane laden with alevins destined for a large lake in the extreme south of Patagonia was forced down near remote Lago Cardiel. The pilots, faced with the loss of their entire cargo before help could arrive, decided to release the fish into this alkaline steppeland lake without an outlet, judged by biologists to be completely unsuitable for salmonids. To everyone's surprise, the fish not only survived, but flourished. Stories abound of fish intended for one location being deposited in another because wagons broke down, horses ran away, ice melted too fast, and so on.

The perca *is a native fish but it has become rare as trout species continue to populate the streams.*

Because of these incidents, and because private landowners were by now initiating their own stocking programs, an accurate record of what fish were deposited where and when is not likely ever to be reconstructed.

In 1930 Argentina made an arrangement with the Chilean government to import eggs of several salmonid species introduced to Chilean waters, one of which would have a profound effect on Patagonia's fresh water fishery. Argentina requested and received from Chile Atlantic salmon, rainbows, and for the first time in large numbers, 175,000 eggs of a trout new to Argentina—brown trout *(Salmo trutta)*.

This brief review of salmonid introductions to Patagonia (complete data on the first nine shipments is provided in Appendix 1) will help fishermen to understand why they can conceivably catch a landlocked salmon, rainbow, brook, brown, or some very strange hybrids from nearly any lake or stream in Patagonia. The fish were planted everywhere, and the processes of ecological succession are still working themselves out. Today brown trout are the dominant species in some streams, rainbows in others, and brooks in still others, but in the long term, these are only temporary positions. A state of dynamic equilibrium among these species is not likely to be achieved for decades. In the meantime, fly fishermen will continue to be able to look forward to an occasional surprise fish at the end of their line, a circumstance that adds a pleasing tang to fishing in Patagonia.

A maxim of ecology holds that one cannot introduce a new species into an ecosystem without in some manner affecting the other elements of that system. In Argentina, the abrupt introduction of salmonids into Patagonia's aquatic ecosystem indeed affected other elements of the system. For Patagonia's native fish, the arrival of the salmonids was not a minor nuisance, but rather a major catastrophe. . .

Little is known about the productivity of the native Patagonian fish

Ten pound sea-run brown. This hen was caught and released while on her spawning run. Scale samples showed she had spent two years in fresh water before smolting. Fish this size normally spend two or three years in the ocean.

before the introduction of salmonids, but indirect evidence suggests that while widespread and abundant, Patagonian lakes and streams did not exactly teem with fish. Most of the natives are small, vulnerable to predation by larger fish, and their numbers are known to have fallen off drastically when pitted against the aggressive and larger trout, salmon, and char. The principal native fish are the *trucha criolla* or *perca* (creole trout, trout-perch, or perch), *pejerrey patagónico* (Patagonian kingfish), *puyen* (a Mapuche name), and the *peladilla.*

The trucha criolla *(Percichthys trucha)* is the largest of the native fish, reaching weights in excess of six pounds and about 18 inches. It resembles a black bass, although somewhat more fusiform. Its body is covered with rough, bony scales and it must be handled with care, for like the bass, its anterior dorsal

and pectoral fins are spined. The trucha criolla inhabits both lakes and rivers, takes lures and wet flies readily, and occasionally rises to a dry fly. Many Argentines consider the trucha criolla a palatable sport fish. It can tolerate lower oxygen concentrations and higher salinity than most salmonids and some authorities consider it to be a grouper which has adapted to fresh water. Its numbers have nonetheless dwindled as salmonid populations increase.

The Patagonia pejerrey *(Basilichthys microlepidotus)* attains a foot in length, and a half-pound in weight. It looks like a small, slender shad, but is darker and has tiny scales and a protractile mouth. Pejerreys are abundant in those rare waters not inhabited by salmonids, but do not survive long once trout arrive. They are usually found in vegetated shallows along lakeshores. Their diet is insect-based,

How The Fish Got There

but they are only rarely taken on flies.

The long, thin puyen *(Galaxias maculatus* or *Atherina speciosa)* is also an insect-eater. Most of its fins are near its tail and it lacks scales. Adult puyens, seen but rarely, are dark brown and can reach about seven inches, but the most commonly seen fish are two to three inch minnows. When developing, puyens are nearly transparent and school along lakeshores, where they are eagerly picked off by large trout. A few Argentine streamer flies have been designed to imitate these translucent minnows.

Peladillas *(Haplochiton taeniatus)* are silvery brown fishes that resemble small trout in silhouette and even have an adipose fin. They lack scales, however, and seldom exceed six inches in length. The fish spawn in the middle of the austral winter, a highly unusual ecological characteristic. This South American genus—along with some Patagonian plankton and aquatic crustaceans—is also found in New Zealand and Australia, indirect evidence that the three land masses were once joined. Peladillas are not faring well since the arrival of the salmonids and are found principally in the troutless lakes of Perito Moreno National Park. Most of the lakes in this extremely remote park drain into the Pacific and were somehow overlooked when trout were being introduced with such abandon into Patagonian waters.

From the purely ecological perspective, and certainly from the perspective of native fish, the sudden and widespread introduction of salmonids into Patagonian waters was a horrific mistake. The derangement of aquatic Patagonian ecosystems has been profound and permanent, and many native fish are likely to disappear altogether. Many modern Argentine biologists still resent the decisions of their predecessors to introduce exotic fish into Argentina. This resentment, tinged perhaps with a bit of anti-British sentiment (many of the private stocking programs were carried out by British and Anglo-Argentine landowners), emerges today in philosophical and managerial conflicts between the Argentine Park Service and provincial authorities or commercial interests.

The Argentine National Park Service, somewhat like our own, adheres to a policy of maintaining (and if possible, reestablishing) a pristine ecosystem, as much as possible unaffected by human activities. Park service officials do not look kindly upon any stocking programs that would tend to drive animals under their jurisdiction toward extinction and that includes fish. As a result, parks protect native species and promulgate regulations for salmonids that are judged by some to be too liberal and not sufficiently protective. A few fishermen even suspect that the regulations are designed to rid the parks of salmonids and reestablish native species.

Provincial and private interests, however, recognize that the native fish have no significant commercial value. They are less interested in preserving native species than in both exploiting and protecting salmonids. For this reason, and because of traditional and deeply ingrained conflicts between federal and provincial officials in Argentina, dinner conversations among fishermen often involve damning one authority or the other—or both.

The introduction of salmonids may well have been a disaster for the native fish, but it has been a godsend for fly fishermen. The whitefish, cod, and three species of Pacific salmon vanished long ago, but the Atlantic salmon and lake trout have held on in a few places and the rainbows, brooks, and browns not only survived, but flourished, and have moved into virtually all waters which have suitable habitat.

All fishermen who visit Patagonia

Sea-run brown trout range from three pounds to over 20.

eventually ask themselves why the trout have done so well there. What are the factors that are so favorable for them?

In Chapter 1, I suggested that the Pleistocene glaciers set the stage for trouts' success by gouging out the enormous lakes that lie along the east margin of the Cordillera. The presence of the lakes, however, is only one reason that trout do so well in Patagonia.

Within any ecosystem, every organism occupies a distinct, well-defined place. We call this place an ecological niche, which may be broadly defined as the relationship of an organism to its biotic and abiotic environment – that is, plants or animals that comprise its food, shelter, or habitat, and such attributes of its physical environment as temperature, essential minerals, oxygen, pH, and so on. Another maxim of ecology holds that all organisms tend to completely fill their ecological niche, or put another way, tend to to maximize their biotic potential. Thus locust populations increase until they run out of food or are checked by the arrival of insecticides, hungry pigeons, or winter.

When the salmonids arrived in Patagonia, they were introduced into an ecological niche that was for all practical purposes vacant. The native fish did not seem to be limited by food, and more important, were not troubled by significant predation. Yet they were small in size, and apparently not abundant – in other words, they failed to efficiently utilize their environment, fill their ecological niche, or maximize their biotic potential. The introduction of the aggressive, efficient, cannibalistic salmonids was like the arrival of hungry wolves at a sheep pen. The salmonids not only made efficient use of available food supplies, but augmented their menu with the native fish themselves. A few dangerous predators were present – herons, kingfishers, cormorants, and otters – but not threatening to large populations. Only upon the arrival of relatively large numbers of trout fishermen in recent decades could

predation be considered significant in some streams.

Patagonia has a diverse variety of habitat for cold water fish: large, deep rivers and small, shallow, high energy streams, large and small lakes. With a few notable exceptions, Patagonia's lakes and streams are still as unpolluted as they were a century ago. Few large scale logging or mining operations, agricultural or industrial developments, or construction projects threaten entire watersheds, indeed drainages, as they do in North America.

This is *not* to say that Patagonia's trout are unthreatened. Effects of overgrazing by domestic livestock are beginning to show up on Patagonian rangelands, and before long will begin to show up in the rivers and lakes. Hydroelectric projects have already destroyed much of the Río Limay, and threaten several other rivers. A large dam has also converted a chain of productive mountain lakes in Los Alerces National Park into a single large reservoir of dubious value to fishermen.

The arrival of large numbers of fishermen has been a mixed blessing; the depredations of greedy, ignorant fishermen can be serious, but other fishermen can bring about the development of protective measures. Heavy fishing pressure is a relatively recent and localized phenomenon. By North American standards, only a few of Patagonia's streams are under heavy pressure. For most of their tenure in Patagonia, salmonid populations have therefore been able to develop virtually free of fishing pressure. And that is one of the most pleasant aspects of fishing today in Patagonia...

There is great satisfaction in fishing waters in which trout populations develop undisturbed that is altogether missing in put-and-take waters. The source of this pleasure is difficult to identify; it relates somehow to a fisherman entering into a relationship with creatures that are pristine, as yet uncorrupted by humans. All fishermen who stalk the trout of Yellowstone National

Park experience this extra measure of subtle but palpable pleasure. Trout did not evolve in Patagonian waters, of course, and Yellowstone's trout were thoroughly manipulated during the early days of the park's history. But in Patagonia the trout were basically undisturbed for so long after their introduction that scores of generations of fish have worked their way along nature's paths with little interference from men.

In this sense, Patagonian streams have been created by a happy collaboration of nature and history for the pleasure of fly fishermen. . .

Although male brook trout don't have the spirited fighting energy of the rainbow, they more than make up for it in beauty.

Part 2—THE PRESENT

PATAGONIA'S FLY FISHING ZONES

Patagonian trout are a long, long way from North America. . .

Direct flights to Buenos Aires from Miami pass through two time zones and take eleven grueling hours to cross the Caribbean, Amazon Basin, and Gran Chaco before reaching the capital of the Pampas. Unfortunately, Buenos Aires constructed its international airport, Ezeiza, nearly 20 miles from the center of town. Jorge Newberry Airport, which handles domestic flights, is near the center of the city. Airborne fishermen must therefore tote luggage and rod cases to downtown Buenos Aires to make connecting flights onward to Patagonia—still 800 miles southwest at its nearest point. (Wise travelers rest up for a night or two in Buenos Aires before continuing on to Patagonia.)

Moreover, Patagonia is also larger than you think; you can't fish it all in a couple of weeks.

For scale, suppose you decided to fish several Patagonian rivers to get a feel for the region, beginning with the northernmost good river, the Río Trocoman. If the Trocoman was in the far western United States, on the Canadian border, and your next stop was the Río Traful, you'd have to travel the width of Washington state to the Colombia River. If the Río Senguerr was next on your list, you would move on to about Sacramento, California. To get to the Río Gallegos, you would have to continue to Los Angeles. And to reach the Río Pipo where it enters the Beagle Canal, you would make for the Mexican border.

Small wonder that Patagonia's fishing grounds are so diverse; as the crow flies, from north to south they are spread over the distance from Bell-

ingham to San Diego, or New York to Miami. Add a sparse network of remote and rough roads, infrequent public transportation, widely scattered public accommodations and gas stations, poor communications facilities, and you can see how a wide-ranging Patagonian fishing trip can easily convert to an exciting adventure, like it or not.

These vast distances tend to mask Patagonia's diverse character. Three or four jarring days spent bouncing over gritty roads can blunt the senses of the most keen observer, and the entire Patagonian landscape soon acquires a timeless, endless character; it all begins to look and feel the same. From the perspective of fly fishermen, however, these enormous fishing grounds actually comprise three zones, each with unique characteristics, each with something different to offer wandering anglers. The zones are sufficiently distinct that should a a fly fisherman spend one week in a different zone for three succeeding years, he would have a experience different fishing each year.

Each zone is described in general terms in this chapter; following chapters fill in the details. From this point forward, please think about Patagonian fly fishing in terms of these three zones—North, Central, and South—and you will find it much easier to grasp the character of the entire region.

NORTHERN ZONE

The northern zone is most familiar to foreign and Argentine fly fishermen. They go there to fish the following rivers, listed roughly north to south: Trocoman, Aluminé, Ñorquinco,

---

The astonishing clarity of the water is only one of the technical problems successful fly fishermen must solve at the boca. Here Bebe Anchorena, one of the Grand Old Men of Argentine fly fishing, drifts a fly through the boca of the Río Chimehuin.

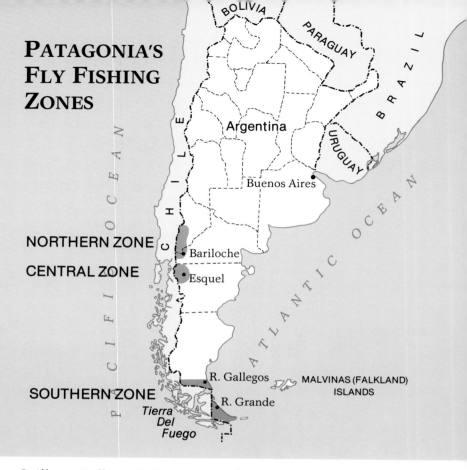

PATAGONIA'S FLY FISHING ZONES

BOLIVIA

PARAGUAY

BRAZIL

Argentina

URUGUAY

Buenos Aires

P A C I F I C O C E A N

A T L A N T I C O C E A N

NORTHERN ZONE

CENTRAL ZONE

Bariloche

Esquel

SOUTHERN ZONE

R. Gallegos

MALVINAS (FALKLAND) ISLANDS

R. Grande

Tierra Del Fuego

Quillen, Malleo, Collon Cura, Chimehuin, Curruhue, Quilquihue, Caleufu, Meliquina, Filo Hua Hum, Traful, Correntoso, Limay, and Manso. Lake fishermen who visit this zone seek out one or more of the lakes that follow, also listed north to south: Aluminé, Moquehue, Ñorquinco, Quillen, Tromen, Paimun, Huechulafquen, Epulafquen, Curruhue, Lolog, Lácar, Meliquina, Falkner, Traful, Espejo, Correntoso, Nahuel Huapi, Gutierrez, Mascardi, Hess, and many, many others.

The northern zone is the most accessible and busiest of the three; hundreds of thousands of tourists, mostly Argentines and Chileans, visit the region's parks every summer. But few of these tourists are fishermen, and hundreds of miles of trout streams wind through the zone on which the few fly fishermen among the tourists can lose themselves. Some reaches of a few streams may be relatively crowded, and a common complaint of old-time fly fishermen, both Argentine and foreign, is that, alas, the streams have become much too crowded, and the good old days are gone forever.

The good old days—like all good old days—are indeed gone forever: thirty years ago I was frequently the only fly fisherman on a river, for that matter, an entire watershed. It was nice, and it's still nice. . .

It is true that the number of fly

fishermen on Patagonia's streams has increased dramatically in recent years, but the claim that the streams are too crowded these days is a subjective judgement, to my mind generally overstated. During the 1989-1990 season, I waded miles of streams for hundreds of hours without another fisherman coming into sight.

The towns and villages in this zone are, in order of size, San Carlos de Bariloche (called simply Bariloche), on the south shore of Lago Nahuel Huapi; San Martín de los Andes, at the eastern end of Lago Lácar; Junín de los Andes, on the banks of the lower Río Chimehuin; Aluminé, on the upper Río Aluminé; Villa La Angostura, on the northern shore of Lago Nahuel Huapi; and Villa Traful, on Lago Traful.

Tourist accommodations (hotels and restaurants) and services (stores for provisions, travel agencies, currency exchange shops, gas stations, and so on) are plentiful enough in the northern zone, and range from good to excellent. At this writing, however, quality fly fishing equipment, including flies, is available only in San Martin Junin, and Bariloche.

Most of Patagonia's best known fly fishing lodges are in the northern zone: Estancia Arroyo Verde, Estancia La Primavera, Estancia San Huberto, Estancia San Ignacio, Hostería Chimehuin, and Hotel Correntoso.

Six of Patagonia's most famous but not necessarily best fishing spots are also in this northern zone: the boca of the Río Chimehuin, at the eastern end of Lago Huechulafquen; the boca of the short, spirited Río Correntoso, linking Lagos Correntoso and Nahuel Huapi; the boca of the Río Limay, at the east end of Lago Nahuel Huapi; the legendary Río Chimehuin; the Río Malleo, which flows east from the araucaria forests on the flanks of Lanín Volcano; and the Río Traful and its landlocked Atlantic salmon, which flows from Lago Traful to the Río Limay. (*Boca*—BOH-kuh—is Spanish for the point at which a river either enters or leaves a lake or another river.

All of the fish for which Patagonia is noted—except sea trout—are abundant in the northern zone: browns, rainbows, brooks, landlocked salmon, and an occasional lake trout.

Nahuel Huapi, Argentina's oldest and most popular national park, attracts a quarter million annual visitors and encompasses several streams and lakes of the northern fishing zone. Nearby Lanín National Park is less developed and embraces headwaters and upper reaches of several more good streams. Laguna Blanca National Park, west of Zapala, is of no interest to fishermen, but is one of the best places in Argentina to see large numbers of typical Patagonian birds. Hot spring buffs will want to visit the Lahuen-Co thermals, not far from Junín de los Andes.

Patagonian scenery is determined by one's location with respect to the mountains. The headwaters of nearly all the streams in the northern zone lie in forested Andean valleys, where scenery is usually spectacular. Within the mountains, the fishing environment is splendid. However, the lower reaches of these streams—often the best waters—flow out onto parched, treeless steppes. These plains, exposed to harsh winds and covered with low, thorny scrub, extend eastward all the way to the beaches of the South Atlantic. The steppes have an austere beauty of their own and the scenery can be dramatic, but it is an acquired taste for most travelers; first time visitors often find the landscape bleak and unappealing. Roads along the eastern front of the Andes vary from excellent, high-speed paved highways to rough, rocky tracks.

The northern zone is poor in terrestrial wildlife compared to the other zones. Several interesting species have been introduced to Lanin and Nahuel Huapi National Parks, but are seen rarely by fishermen: European red deer, *Cervus elaphus*, called *ciervo rojo;* dama deer, *Dama dama*, called *ciervo dama;* axis deer, *Axis axis*, called *ciervo axis,* and wild boar, *Sus scrofa*, called *jabalí).* Bird life along the streams is varied and relatively abundant in this zone.

The climate is temperate. Summers are moderate to hot. At low elevations, the average annual temperature seldom reaches 50° F., but can reach 85° F. in summer and dip to 20° F. in winter. Fishermen must be prepared for rain even in summer, for microclimatic differences are extreme in this zone. Average annual rainfall on a river which has reached the edge of the steppes may be as little as 16 inches, but a few miles upstream, rainfall in its mountainous headwaters may be 160 inches. May and June are the rainiest months. Thunderstorms are uncommon, but when they do occur, rain (or hail) can be torrential and temporarily spoil streams for fly fishermen. Under these circumstances, knowledgeable fly fishermen head for streams lacking tributaries that pass through erosive terrain, fish streams near their bocas, or depart for the central zone, where this problem is rare.

Throughout Patagonia, winds are a serious matter for fly fishermen, not to be dismissed lightly. Midday and afternoon winds can be very strong in this zone, not as fierce as in southern Patagonia, but stronger and more incessant than those to which North Americans, including western fishermen, are accustomed. Strategies for dealing with wind will be discussed in a following chapter.

CENTRAL ZONE

By Patagonian standards, the heart of the Central Zone is not far south of the Northern Zone—about 200 air miles—but from the perspective of fishermen, it is a different universe.

Most of the streams of this zone flow through deep, densely forested mountain valleys. Powerful, high-energy streams for the most part, they are often difficult to wade and are several degrees colder than the northern streams. But they are gin-clear, and fly fishermen will work the waters in the midst of stunning scenery, often in the shade of dense streamside forests, a rare and welcome experience on Patagonian streams.

The principal streams in the Central Zone are the Río Chubut, Río Carrileufu, Río Rivadavia, Río Menéndez, Río Arrayanes, Arroyo Pescado, Río Grande, And Río Corcovado. The main lakes are Lago Cholila, Lago Rivadavia, Lago Verde, Lago Menéndez, Lago Futalaufquen, and Lago Amutui Quimei.

The Central Zone feels more like true Patagonia than the Northern Zone. The mountains and steppes are more remote and considerably wilder. Most rivers and lakes are concentrated in a single area in this zone, but the population is much lower, towns are widely separated, facilities scarcer and more rustic, and good roads at a premium.

Three towns lie within the zone, in order of size: Esquel, gateway to Los Alerces National Park; El Bolsón, which has attracted many Argentines seeking alternative life styles; and Trevelin, a community of Welsh descendants. The only other communities in the fishing zones are tiny villages with limited facilities and supplies: Cholila, Tecka, and Villa Futalaufquen.

Accommodations for fishermen range from good to excellent, but are plentiful only in a few places. Choices are more limited than in the Northern Zone, distances between fishing grounds are longer and are also slower because the mountain roads are rougher. More careful planning is required of fishermen traveling on their own in this zone. Quality flies and other equipment are not available.

Three relatively well-known fishing lodges lie in the zone: Hostería Quimé Quipán and Hostería Cume Hue, a few kilometers apart on the eastern shore of Lago Futalaufquen; and on the western shore of the lake, Hotel Futalaufquen, a charming inn frequented by fishermen.

The most notable fishing spots in the Central Zone are the rarely fished waters of the upper Río Chubut; the Arroyo Pescado, one of Patagonia's few true spring creeks; and the series of rivers and bocas that link the chain-

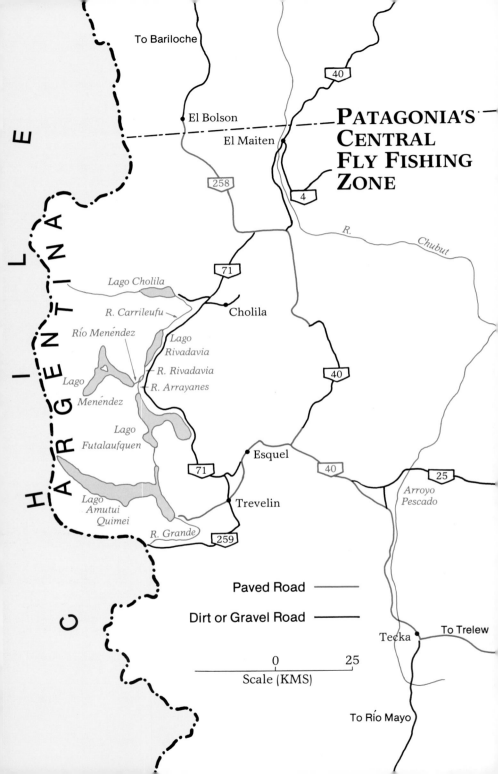

To Bariloche

40

El Bolson

El Maiten

PATAGONIA'S CENTRAL FLY FISHING ZONE

258

4

R. Chubut

71

Lago Cholila

R. Carrileufu

Cholila

Río Menéndez

Lago Rivadavia

R. Rivadavia

R. Arrayanes

40

Lago Menéndez

Lago Futalaufquen

Esquel

71

40

40

25

Arroyo Pescado

Trevelin

Lago Amutui Quimei

R. Grande

259

E

L

A R G E N T I N A

H

C

Paved Road

Dirt or Gravel Road

Tecka

To Trelew

0   25

Scale (KMS)

To Río Mayo

lakes of Los Alerces National Park, the Carrileufu, Rivadavia, Menéndez, and Arrayanes.

The Central Zone's waters support all of Argentina's trout and char species except sea trout and in recent years Pacific salmon have begun to appear in a few streams that drain into the Pacific from this zone.

Los Alerces National Park encompasses most of the streams of the zone and is one of Argentina's most scenic mountain parks. Nearby Lago Puelo National Park is of little interest to fishermen.

Fishermen will find scenery in this zone far superior to the Northern Zone because most of the rivers are in the very lap of the Andes. They flow through steep-sided valleys that within the park are densely forested and outside the park are carefully cultivated, verdant and distinctly pastoral in character. The steppes of the Central Zone, site of the Arroyo Pescado and Río Chubut, are as bleak and treeless as the more northern plains, but their more rugged and broken terrain is a dramatic prelude to the wild and remote landscape to the south. The finest forests in the southern Andes lie within this zone.

Patagonian wildlife is far more abundant in this zone than in the Northern Zone. You are likely to see otters in the rivers within the park, and if you range far enough from main roads in this zone, you may see a few ñandus or guanacos. Streamside birdlife is abundant.

The climate during fishing season is about the same as the Northern Zone, though somewhat cooler. Microclimatic differences are extreme here, too, so good raingear is a must, but summer thunderstorms seem to be less frequent, a boon to fly fishermen. Wind can be a problem for fly fishermen in this zone, as everywhere in Patagonia, but because many streams lie in densely forested valleys that are oriented north to south, it is often possible to maneuver so as to avoid the wind or escape it altogether.

SOUTHERN ZONE

To reach the northern edge of this large and distant zone, visitors must somehow travel about 600 air miles south from the Central Zone. You can fly or drive. If your time is limited, unfortunately you must fly, for it is a long and arduous journey by land (about 1200 miles of mainly dirt roads). But it is also one of the world's most interesting land journeys, for it passes through the empty heart of Patagonia. It is no place for travelers with tight schedules or for chronic worriers, for it is a truly remote region in which a mechanical breakdown or punctured fuel tank could force a delay of a week or more into a carefully planned itinerary.

A few good places to fish are tucked into the hundreds of miles between the Central and Southern Zones, but they are not end-of-the-road hot spots, but rather end-of-the-world fishing holes. I will describe them later only in passing on the unlikely chance that some of you find yourselves there for purposes other than fishing. They are so scattered, and the effort, expense, and risk required to reach them so great in the endless expanses of central Patagonia that it would be irresponsible to send a reader to them when other good fishing is more readily available.

I wish to re-emphasize, however, that any fisherman who could journey to the Southern Zone by land (along the Andes, not along the coast) should by all means do so, for it is a trip as fascinating as it is difficult, not likely to be soon forgotten.

The Southern Zone is much larger than the other two zones because many of the rivers are widely scattered, the road network is less dense, and the zone includes terrain almost in sight of Cape Horn, the island tip of the southern hemisphere.

The rivers include the Río Rubens, Río Penitente, Río Gallegos, Río

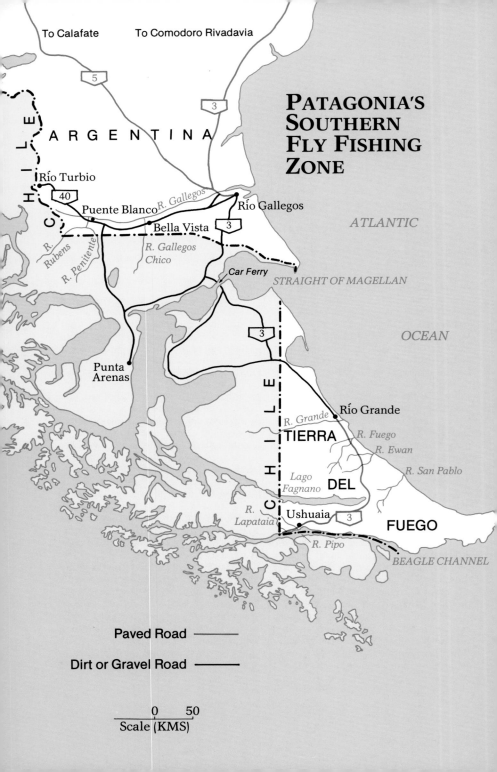

To Calafate   To Comodoro Rivadavia

5

3

A R G E N T I N A

PATAGONIA'S
SOUTHERN
FLY FISHING
ZONE

C
H
I
L
E

Río Turbio

40

Puente Blanco

Río Gallegos

R. Gallegos

Bella Vista

3

Río Gallegos

ATLANTIC

R. Rubens

R. Peniente

R. Gallegos Chico

Car Ferry

STRAIGHT OF MAGELLAN

OCEAN

3

Punta Arenas

C
H
I
L
E

R. Grande

Río Grande

TIERRA

R. Fuego

R. Ewan

R. San Pablo

Lago Fagnano

DEL

R. Lapataia

Ushuaia

3

FUEGO

R. Pipo

BEAGLE CHANNEL

Paved Road ———

Dirt or Gravel Road ———

0   50
Scale (KMS)

Gallegos Chico, and on the island of Tierra del Fuego, Río Grande, Río Menéndez, and several smaller streams, the Turbal, Fuego, Ewan, San Pablo, Claro, Irigoyen, Pipo, and Lapataia. The only noteworthy lakes are Lago Fagnano and Lago Yehuin.

The Southern Zone is, of course, the least crowded of the three zones. In some parts of the region, services are so far apart on roads that are often appalling that a *full* tank of gas is required to get from one service station to the next. Although distances between gas stations may not seem great, an extra gas container is advisable, for the stations frequently run out of gas. If you intend to get off the beaten track in this zone, you must plan fishing explorations with great care.

Most of the zone's population is concentrated in three small communities: from north to south, the town of Río Gallegos, at the mouth of the Río Gallegos, and on Tierra del Fuego, the town of Río Grande, at the mouth of the Río Grande, and on the north shore of the Beagle Canal, Ushuaia, southernmost city in the world. Accommodations in towns range from adequate to excellent, but are limited. Two towns on the margins of the fishing zone, Calafate and Río Turbio, provide a few more hotels and restaurants. Outside of these towns, however, what few accommodations exist are rough, and services are practically nonexistent. All prices are distinctly higher than other parts of Argentina, even other tourist areas.

At this writing, only two true fishing resorts are established in the Southern Zone, and they are relatively new: Kau-Tapen and Truchaike. They are, however, firmly dedicated to keeping fly fishermen comfortable and happy while they pursue one of Patagonia's primary attractions, sea-run brown trout.

The primary fishing spots in the Southern Zone are the famed Río Grande, the lesser known Río Gallegos, and the small rivers of Tierra del Fuego.

Fish in the zone include browns, rainbows, brook trout, lake trout in a few lakes and rivers, and the extraordinary sea trout that draw most of the fishermen to this area.

The only park within the Southern Zone is Tierra del Fuego National Park, a reserve with outstanding flora, but difficult access save near Ushuaia, and of marginal interest to fishermen. On the margins of the zone, however, lie two of the most interesting and spectacular Andean parks in South America, Los Glaciares National Park, near Calafate, and Chile's Torres del Paine National Park, across the Argentine border not far from the town of Río Turbio.

Do not come to the Southern Zone for scenery. The sea-trout rivers, for most of their length, wind through absolutely treeless grasslands; not even willows line their banks. Beech woods of the rolling, forested portion of the zone are a pleasant contrast to the flat plains, but the forests of the other two zones are just as pleasant and more diverse. The birds and wildlife of this Southern Zone, however, are among its primary attributes for fishermen. In parts of the zone it would not be unusual for fishermen to look up between casts to see rheas, guanacos, flamingos, hundreds of sheldgeese, and, of course, the ubiquitous sheep wandering along the shore.

With a single exception, the few roads in the Southern Zone range from poor to appalling. Vehicles must be in top running order and an extra spare tire is a wise investment.

The weather of the Southern Zone is highly variable, and can be harsh even during the relatively short fishing season. Midday temperatures can be hot enough for shirtsleeves, but rainstorms and cold spells are frequent in summer, so fishermen need to be prepared for cold and wet weather at any time during the season.

Fly fishermen who visit the Southern Zone face a truly daunting technical problem—wind. These winds are not the troublesome gusts that spoil casts, and occasionally last for several hours, as occur on streams of the

Patagonia's Fly Fishing Zones

western United States. The winds of southern Patagonia can be terrestrial gales that reach 100 mph, and can last for weeks. I have had 60 feet of nine-weight floating weight-forward line abruptly plucked from the surface of the Río Gallegos and either blown straight onto shore, or draped about me like Christmas tree trappings.

Curse the wind if it makes you feel better, but keep in the back of your mind an adage heard in fishing circles throughout Patagonia: *Cuando no hay viento, no hay pesca,* "When there is no wind, there are no fish. . ."

Be prepared, however, for these Patagonian gales, for they impose a stiff psychological toll on the calmest of fly fishermen. When the wind raises two–foot waves and blows their tops into your face, making it impossible to read the water, and in turn soaking and freezing you, when it keeps you from being able to talk to your companion, hold a camera still, or reel across a meadow without great effort, when it scatters the contents of a fly box over a hundred yards of frantically waving grass, it is too easy to shout curses into the eye of the gale, retreat to your car, and return to town to calm yourself in comfort and shelter as you wait it out. And if you awake the next day to find that the wind has picked up some, you can contract a colossal case of fishing frustration.

Frame of mind is important. You can avoid a great deal of this before you even arrive by accepting the wind as a fact of fly fishing life in southern Patagonia. The wind is a function of climate and terrain (since the flat and treeless landscape rarely offers adequate shelter), and there is nothing you can do about it. Rather than rail against nature, prepare yourself for wind, and save some of your strength for those days on which the wind is gentle or absent. A sturdy, warm windbreaker, a good sweater, and heavy tackle are requirements for fishing in this zone. Don't invite trouble by finding yourself on a gale-lashed river with nothing but a five-weight outfit when the sea trout are running. Patagonian winds are merely a new dimension of the fly fishing experience. Accept it, prepare for it, and you'll be fine.

A summary of the zones' characteristics from the fisherman's perspective may be helpful.

Northern Zone. Largest selection of streams and resorts, but also the most popular and most developed of the three zones, in this respect the least Patagonian. Towns, services, and accommodations plentiful. Best roads of the three zones. Three interesting national parks in or near zone. Poor in wildlife. Access to streams good to fair. Wind can be troublesome. All species but sea trout. Guides available.

Central Zone. Fewer streams and resorts, but less crowded than the Northern Zone, and more scenic than either of the other zones. Getting to be real Patagonia. Fewer towns, services, and accommodations. Roads good to poor. One outstanding national park in zone. Wildlife fair. Access to streams excellent. Wind seldom a problem. All species but sea trout. Guides available.

Southern Zone. Remote and has a fearsome climate, but offers the best wildlife show to fishermen of any of the zones and has the only sea-trout fishing in Argentina. One of the most remote regions of the populated world. Few towns and accommodations, services only in towns. Roads fair to appalling. One national park within the zone, two outstanding parks nearby. Access to streams good to fair. Winds can be murderous. All species but landlocked salmon. Guides available.

Don't expect these criteria to indicate that one zone is somehow better or fishier than the others; it won't work. Each zone has its own attractions and a character that will appeal more to some of you than others. Selecting among them is a matter of style in fishing or traveling. All three zones offer quality flyfishing, good to excellent. . .

ARGENTINA AND ITS PEOPLE

I have indicated elsewhere that quality fly fishing is an experience of the total landscape. That landscape includes people, wherever you fish—guides, storekeepers, your fishing partners, fishermen you meet on the stream, and hosts, be they innkeepers or your in-laws. Cordial, two-way contact with these people is an important part of your fishing day, especially important when you fish the waters of a foreign country.

A comprehensive characterization of Argentines is well beyond the scope of this book, but a brief introduction to manners and mores will not only augment your fishing experience, but help you to avoid some of those unintentional gaffes that may offend an Argentine you hope to befriend.

In general, Argentine fly fishermen like North American fly fishermen. They appreciate the angling ethics we have developed and in the sincerest form of flattery, have adopted many of them. They marvel at the physical energy we put into fishing and the skill with which we fish, and they admire our deep appreciation of the outdoors. But on at least two other matters, we fall somewhat short in their eyes. . .

First, Argentine fly fishermen are a sophisticated lot, well-educated and often well-traveled. Most of them know a great deal about the geography, history, and politics of the United States and they are dismayed at how little we know about their country. Second, they are invariably taken aback when North Americans express such surprise that

The lower Río Gallegos, near the town of Río Gallegos.

Argentines are far more similar to North Americans than they had expected.

Accordingly, this chapter discusses a few topics that address these shortcomings: a smattering of Argentine history, a description of the Argentines, how they behave, and what they eat and drink. Finally, we'll take a brief look at how some of them fish.

HISTORY

Many of the main streets in Argentine towns are named after one or another of the country's many presidents—Rivadavia, Mitre, Avellaneda, Sarmiento, Yrigoyen, Perón, and so on. In order to go fishing in Argentina, it is not necessary to know what these men did, but a few historical highlights may help you understand the many social contradictions so apparent in modern Argentina.

Argentina is the second largest country in South America, about one-third the size of the contiguous United States. Patagonia occupies about a third of the country, an area about equal to Texas plus Ohio. Spaniards first landed near Buenos Aires in 1516 and Magellan landed there briefly in 1520 before continuing south down the coast. The first attempts to establish settlements along the Río de la Plata failed miserably because of fierce Indian resistance. Spanish attention in early centuries was focused on the riches of Peru and later expeditions from the north and west were able to establish the first Argentine settlements, but in the northwest of the country—Salta, Mendoza, Jujuy, and others. Buenos Aires, a tiny fortified settlement, languished unnoticed and unimportant until about 1776.

As in the rest of South America, native-born colonists, called *criollos,* grew restive under the heavy-handed and inept Spanish administration. So on July 9, 1816, forty years after the United States broke with England, a Revolutionary Congress formed in Tucumán to declare Argentina's independence from Spain. The event was important, of course, and explains why so many Argentine city streets (and a small Patagonian town) are named *Nueve de Julio* (Ninth of July). A brief civil war led by one of South America's principal heroes, José de San Martín, freed Argentina from the Spanish grip.

In the meantime, Buenos Aires had become an important commercial center and port for beef and hides being produced on the grasslands of the Pampas. Commercial interests in Buenos Aires sought to impose strong centralized control on the rest of the country, but the large landowners and their gaucho employees (gauchos were essentially nomadic herders of livestock, Argentina's cowboys) who reigned in the provinces had developed a strong sense of independence and were not interested in being ruled by soft-skinned city dwellers. Tensions grew and finally flamed into armed struggle between federal forces and large landowners leading unruly bands of armed gauchos. The first round of the struggle was won by provincial forces and led to the brutal dictatorship of Juan Manuel de Rosas, a bloodthirsty tyrant who ruled the country for nearly twenty years.

Rosas was overthrown in 1852 and political power seesawed between the rapidly growing capital and the provinces for the next 40 years. Federal forces eventually won out and in 1880 Buenos Aires was organized as a federal district somewhat after the fashion of Washington, D.C. Relations between Buenos Aires and the provinces have been uneasy at best for over a century, however, and even today policies, and often employees, of the federal government are regarded with suspicion or derision in the provinces. Virtually every political conversation you find yourself part of—and politics is a favorite Argentine topic—will eventually get around to this subject.

From 1878 to 1883, a military campaign was mounted to clear the Pampas of Indians and open even more land to

Gauchos enjoying the "Fiesta del Puestero".

settlers. As was the custom in those days, successful military leaders were rewarded with portions of land they had wrested from the Indians and many officers received land grants in excess of 130,000 acres, a policy that helped to perpetuate the modern Argentine pattern of huge ranches, or *estancias,* found in the hands of a few extremely wealthy landowners.

Following up on the success in clearing the Pampas of Indians, the Argentine army initiated the infamous Campaign of the Desert. Argentina had not taken vigorous steps to develop Patagonia and in fear of growing Chilean hegemony in the area, asserted its sovereignty by sending an army into the area. Led by General Julio Roca, mounted troops made a series of bloody incursions into the Patagonian homelands of the Mapuche Indians. Once regarded as a legitimate struggle to pacify bloodthirsty savages, the campaign is now considered by most scholars to have been a blatantly genocidal invasion.

The following decades were a period of consolidation for Argentina. The agricultural riches of the pampas were developed, railroads were built, oil was discovered in Patagonia, several presidents, ranging from democratic idealists to right-wing demagogues, served their terms, and the military began to increase its meddling in political affairs. Argentina's indelible European character was established during the decades 1860 to 1930, when upwards of six million Europeans migrated to the rapidly developing farms and factories, setting the stage for unprecedented prosperity for the nation.

As World War II approached, Argentina was already prosperous. The Pampas had been developed into an extremely productive agricultural resource and Argentina had become one of the ten wealthiest countries in the world. It now stood to gain even more by selling its beef, wool, wheat, and other foodstuffs to the combatants and their allies. The simile "as rich as an Argentine" had made its way into the languages of the world and Argentina's future looked sunny indeed. Unfortunately, at that moment an Argentine army colonel was absorbing many of the ideas he saw being put into practice in fascist Italy, where in 1939 he was serving as a military observer. His name was Juan Domingo Perón. . .

Perón's influence on Argentina's history cannot be overstated. His memory still evokes strong passions in a people who discuss politics from the moment they learn to speak. Very little disinterested middle ground devolves about Perón; he and his equally famous wife, Evita, are either loathed or revered by Argentines. Together, they are either blamed for all of the country's present woes or credited with establishing a middle class that until recent years had been the most prosperous in Latin America.

Not long after Colonel Perón returned to Argentina from Italy, a military junta overthrew the government of a corrupt and inept president, Ramón Castillo, and set an ominous precedent by placing military officers at the head of federal ministries. Perón was put in charge of the Ministry of Labor in 1943 and shortly afterwards took up with a young and pretty aspiring actress named María Eva Duarte. Eva, soon to be known to the world as Evita, was of humble origins, but probably not, as Perón's many detractors insist, a prostitute. She was, however, energetic, charismatic, ambitious, and politically astute, a true *eminence grise*.

Together, they recognized that Argentina's vast pool of laborers, nearly ignored by previous administrations, would be a powerful political springboard, and Perón and Evita set about sponsoring progressive labor legislation,

bolstering the unions, and making the workers their own. The military soon recognized the threat they had unwittingly created from within their own ranks and arrested Perón, but it was too late. The labor unions organized massive demonstrations and Perón, now married to Evita, was swept into power in 1946.

Perón and Evita instituted massive public works projects and built schools and hospitals, but to maintain the support of the unions also encouraged the growth of huge industry in a country notably lacking in basic industrial resources. They also began to convert Argentina into a welfare state for the middle class at a time when prices for agricultural products was dropping and droughts were drastically reducing Argentina's productivity. About the time that Evita died of cancer in 1952, Argentina simply could not pay the bills it had incurred and the economic roof collapsed. Perón was overthrown by the military in 1955, fled to Paraguay, and went into exile in Spain.

During the next 20 years, a succession of presidents struggled unsuccessfully to reverse Argentina's declining economic fortunes and to cope with the tide of left-wing guerrilla activities that increased as the country edged closer to economic chaos. Military repression of such urban militants as the Montoneros grew increasingly brutal and jails began to fill with political prisoners. In this tense climate, Perón returned from exile and was returned to power in 1973. He died only a few months later and his second wife, Isabel, took over the reins of government. Isabel was not Evita, however, and her tenure was a catastrophe for the country. The military, impatient with civilian attempts to restore normality, deposed her in 1976 and took power themselves. And so began the darkest period in the history of modern Argentina. . .

For the next seven years, a series of generals ruled Argentina and instituted, in collaboration with police and elements of the political right wing, a campaign against dissidents so barbaric that it was quickly labeled the "dirty war." Opponents of the regime were not merely imprisoned without charge or even given mock trials and then shot; they were simply made to disappear. An estimated 20,000 to 40,000 Argentine men, women, and children, often entire families, were picked up, usually in early morning hours, by nameless men, taken away, raped, tortured, murdered, and buried in unmarked graves. Fathers, mothers, sons, daughters, brothers, or sisters who tried to find out what happened to their relatives met an official wall of absolute silence; those in authority professed not to know anything about it and thousands of dissidents continued to vanish without trace. They were given a grim name: *desaparecidos,* the disappeared ones.

By early 1982, the foreign debt approached 50 billion dollars, inflation raged unchecked, Argentine currency plummeted in value, unemployment had skyrocketed, and the military had lost all moral authority in the eyes of the nation and the world. In a classic attempt to acquire prestige and divert the attention of the populace from failed policies and bankrupt morals, the military junta, led by General Galtieri, chose this moment to invade the Falkland Islands, over which Argentina had long claimed sovereignty.

England did not, as hoped, abandon the distant islands, but after brief and bloody combat, inflicted a humiliating defeat on Argentina's ill-trained and poorly supported armed forces.

The military, unable to solve the country's problems, and now thoroughly discredited, withdrew from power, and in 1983 a civilian, Raúl Alfonsín, was elected to the presidency by a majority of Argentine voters. The long nightmare was over and democracy had been restored in Argentina.

One of Alfonsín's first actions after assuming the presidency was to begin an investigation into responsibilities for the dirty war and the fate of the *desaparecidos,* an unprecedented act of enormous courage. With the full support of the Argentine people, nine generals and admirals were eventually put on trial. A few were acquitted, but others received life sentences. Light punishment, perhaps, for crimes against humanity (Argentina does not have capital punishment), but the first time in the history of Latin America that military dictators had been held accountable for crimes against their own people. The Argentines had recovered not only their democracy, but their moral stature within the community of nations.

Alfonsín inherited a country that was once again free and proud, but what had once been one of the wealthiest of nations was hopelessly in debt, and in economic ruins. The road to recovery will be slow, but in my view sure, for Argentina has an astonishing potential for agricultural productivity, and as the population bomb slowly explodes, the world will once again turn to Argentina for the foodstuffs the country can so easily produce. And having lost and recovered their freedom at such great cost, the Argentines are not likely to let it slip away again and will overcome the present adversity.

WHO ARE THE ARGENTINES?

A glance through a telephone book for an Argentine city suggests that Argentines are the Americans of South America. You'll find such names as Sanchez, Pizzini, Voroshovsky, Van Hooten, Schilling, and Smith. Like the United States, Argentina is a melting pot, a land of immigrants.

Unlike the United States, however, the 32 million Argentines lack a strong sense of national identity and incessantly bemoan the fact. All Argentines speak Spanish, but ask a man where he's from, and the answer is as likely to be Italy or Spain as Argentina. Sociologists still debate the reasons for the failure of the nation to achieve the social cohesion which forged American immigrants into a single cultural unit. Immigration to Argentina took place in massive waves and over a relatively short span of years, factors which may have contributed to the identity problem.

Nearly half of these immigrants were Italian, another third Spanish, and most of the rest were from northern Europe. By the early 1900's, one-third of Argentina's population was foreign-born and in some cities foreigners nearly crowded out native-born Argentines.

On inspecting the crowd at an Argentine airport, North Americans find themselves wondering if they haven't somehow deplaned in Rome, Madrid, or London rather than Buenos Aires, Córdoba, or Mendoza. Argentines look and act far more like Europeans (or Americans) than the "South Americans" they had anticipated seeing. Argentines are more like Europeans or Americans than citizens of any other Latin American country. In fact, Argentines *are* Europeans. . .

The ethnic composition of modern Argentina is predominantly white and European—a full 85 percent. About 12 percent are Asians and Arabs and the remaining 3 percent is made up of a mixture of Indians and *mestizos* (mixed Indian and European blood).

The massive influx of Europeans into Argentina has created confusing social currents that have complicated the country's self-image for decades. Rather than emulating and forging alliances with neighboring nations or North America, Argentina looked back to Europe for cultural, commercial, and intellectual inspiration. As a result, Argentina became somewhat isolated in South America and earned a good deal of contempt from its neighbors. Even today, many citizens of neighboring countries regard Argentines as arrogant, aloof, and self-important sophisticates who rank themselves a cut above the

Jose "Pepe" Navas, Argentina's first fly-tier.

rest of the South Americans.

To an extent, the charge is true, for Argentines do identify more closely with Europeans—and these days, North Americans—than with other South Americans, but the notorious Argentine aloofness is greatly exaggerated, as visitors soon discover. In my view, a major reason for this reputation is that Argentines are primarily an urban people; 80 percent of Argentines live in large cities. City dwellers the world over have idiosyncracies that others find peculiar or infuriating, and so do many Argentines. Imagine judging all Americans by those who live in New York City. . .

Patagonia, on the other hand, is anything but an urban milieu and Patagonians do not fit neatly into the Argentine cultural mold. Patagonia is much like Alaska is to the rest of the United States, and Argentines move there for the same reasons Americans move to Alaska. Argentina's Last Frontier, its residents have a strong sense of independence and self-reliance, a pioneering spirit. The region is remote and has few of the niceties of the large cities to the north. Prices are higher, but so are wages. Winters can be miserable, but summers are wonderful. The area is uncrowded and the fishing's great. . .

HOW DO ARGENTINES BEHAVE?

We North Americans experience Argentines as more formal than ourselves. Formal does not mean stuffy or stiff, however, and they do not make us uncomfortable, for they are warm and considerate hosts, genial and quick to laugh, not nearly as unapproachable as citizens of many other South American countries. It quickly becomes clear, however, that a rigid system of courtesies and customs governs their public behavior.

The importance of physical contact is immediately apparent; Argentines constantly reassure one another of their good will with their sense of touch. Salutations and farewells invariably involve touching. Men shake hands upon meeting and upon taking their leave. They often slap each other on the arm or back and hug each other at ceremonial events or if well acquainted. Argentines appear to North Americans to kiss one another at the drop of a hat, so don't be surprised when a woman you've never seen before offers you her cheek. Men kiss women on the cheek when meeting and again when departing. Women kiss both men and women at introductions and chance encounters as well.

So how do you behave? You just get right in there with everybody else and kiss away. You won't offend anybody and you'll discover what a nice custom it is.

In North America, we customarily thank our hosts when we leave a party and say good night to whomever we meet on our way out. In Argentina, one never leaves a dinner table or a party without shaking the hand or kissing the cheek of virtually every person present, even if a score of people are in attendance. It takes time to leave a large gathering in Argentina, but only because they observe basic good manners we often overlook in our own country. Should you fail to meet this obligation, you may be regarded as uncultured at best, at worst a rather unfriendly, frigid sort of fellow.

This courtesy reaches to some extent into public facilities, indeed into the outdoors. When, for instance, most Argentines enter a restaurant or hotel dining room and make their way to a table, they do not ignore fellow patrons as we do, but rather nod and give a smile and pleasant greeting to whatever other diners catch their eye, even if they are total strangers. And on nearing a house in the country, you approach it slowly—at a walk if on horseback—and clap your hands loudly. The gesture does not merely replace a doorbell (which the house will not have), but rather avoids surprising the residents, and gives them an opportunity to prepare for your arrival with equal grace by washing up, combing their hair, putting on the coffee, and so on. (It also prevents you from being surprised by the gigantic, foul-tempered watchdogs that are usually just around the corner of the house.)

Most North Americans quickly check out of a hotel or motel without a second thought, but to leave a hotel or inn without personally saying goodbye to the host and/or hostess is considered a grave discourtesy in Argentina. Only under the most extreme circumstances can you do this without being considered a serious boor.

At first, these mannerisms seem rather elaborate to North Americans, but we soon discover that the courtesies are more genuine than ceremonious. Patagonia, for example, is to the rest of Argentina much as the American west is to North America: more informal, open, casual, helpful, friendlier than the rest of the country. Yet even in Patagonia, good manners are never ignored. As you travel about Patagonia, you will often see gauchos ride by on roads and through streamside fields. They will look, see that you are a foreigner and uncertain of your customs, may not always wave first. If you wave, however, your greeting will invariably be returned, usually with a broad smile, for gauchos are very friendly. In fact, all Argentines smile a lot and you would be wise to reciprocate.

As it is considered rude to leave a social gathering without saying goodbye to every other guest, it is considered insensitive to greet an Argentine acquaintance without asking how life has been going, even if you've seen him or her just an hour ago. That is, you do not greet an acquaintance or even a stranger by saying "Hi," and continuing on your way. Rather, you say "Hi, how are things going, how are the wife and kids, how is work, and so on." You do not have to speak Spanish fluently to accomplish this; in Argentina, the simple phrases *qué tal* or *como anda* usually convey this extra bit of consideration. Argentines insist that even with your house in flames, it would be ill-mannered to let arriving firemen unroll their hoses without first asking about their work, family, and lives in general.

Another story illuminates a curious flaw in Argentine courtesy that every visiting fisherman needs to be aware of. It is said that if two Argentines arrive at an elevator at the same moment, it may take an hour for them to reach their destination, for courtesy requires that each let the other enter the elevator first. But put the same two men on the street behind the wheels of their cars and they become implacable adversaries who gladly risk death and dismemberment in order to get through an intersection first.

For some reason, courtesy is banished the moment an Argentine steps into a car. Anyone who drives in Argentina needs nerves of steel, perfect reflexes, eyes in the back of his head, and a very laid-back attitude, for Argentine driving is sheer dog-eat-dog and Argentines are among the most aggressive and inconsiderate drivers on the face of the earth. I'll have more to say about this later.

You will also find that like other Latin Americans, Argentines are not as punctual for meetings as North Americans normally expect. It is not considered discourteous to arrive late to a meeting or a cup of coffee, or unusual for a store or office to open quite later than its posted hours. The pace of life is slower in Argentina than in North America and Latins in general are far more relaxed about such matters than their frenetic northern cousins. Further, phones don't always work, buses don't always run on time, the subway may fail to arrive, or one's taxi may get caught in a traffic jam, quite plausible reasons for being late, so why dwell on the matter?

To summarize, you will find most Argentines amiable companions and gracious hosts. They are likely to be more relaxed and far more polite than your own countrymen—except when in their cars—in short, thoroughly good company. . .

Roast lamb is always a treat.

ARGENTINE FOOD AND DRINK

Argentines eat and drink well and one of the best reasons to go fishing in Patagonia, apart from the fishing, is the opportunity to join Argentines at table.

Argentines don't eat—they dine—a custom most of us long ago lost to fast food chains. A meal is not a hurried affair, but a social event, a gathering of the clan, a marvelous excuse for spirited conversation and convivial gossip. One lingers over dinner and savors every dish and every story. Argentine food is not so foreign to the North American palate that we suddenly have to adjust to a broad range of exotic tastes, like it or not. In fact, in my view the cuisine suffers from a lack of variety—too much meat, too much pizza, too much pasta, not enough soup, not enough vegetables.

But what Argentines do eat is prepared with loving care and meals are delicious.

North Americans will recognize, and can eat, most of what they are served anywhere in the country (Argentina is the only country in South America in which fresh salads may be eaten regularly without risk). Most Americans will find Argentine breakfasts skimpy, but only two other major adjustments are called for—meat and meal hours.

The first adjustment is to the amount of red meat you will be served. We all know that Argentines eat a lot of meat, but we don't realize how much. We Americans, for example, are well-fed and on a per capita basis we eat about 75 pounds of beef a year; each Argentine eats about *220 pounds* of beef a year! A rare day passes when an Argentine does not eat a steak and many eat a meat dish twice a day.

Beef is raised to the level of culinary art in Argentina. Steak lovers will be able to fulfill their fondest fantasies several times over in a week or two. A steak is called a *bife* and is ordered to taste. *Jugoso* means rare, *a punto* medium, and *bien hecho* well done. A head-spinning variety of cuts which only approximate our own confront the visitor, but North Americans will usually be happy with a *bife de lomo* (sirloin), *bife de costilla* (T-bone), or *bife de chorizo* (rump steak). Many restaurants, called *parrillas*, specialize in *parrilladas*, meals the British call mixed grills, which consist of an enormous platter of several cuts of meat, including roast, kidney, sausage, intestine, udder, and other curiosities few North Americans will recognize and are probably best left unrecognized. The meal is sometimes grilled at your table, is much better than it sounds, and is usually generous enough to feed two Argentines or four or five North Americans. An *asado* is a roast, as well as a style of meal. If you are invited to an *asado*, it will usually be outside and you'll be fed meat sliced from an entire calf or lamb roasted on spits before an open fire.

You will eventually tire of so much meat, but not before you've had some wonderful meals. After a hard day on the river, few meals are as restorative as a huge steak, accompanied by an *ensalada mixta* (lettuce, tomatoes, onions, oil, and vinegar) and washed down with a bottle of good *vino tinto* (red wine).

Waiters are respected professionals in Argentina. They are well-attired, usually provide excellent service throughout your meal, and never rush diners. A typical meal in a good restaurant starts with a basket of fresh baked bread or rolls served with butter *(manteca*, which does *not* mean lard in Argentina) or a piquant butter/cheese mixture, followed by an appetizer. Typical appetizers are *ensalada rusa*, a sort of potato salad, *tomate atún*, a tuna-stuffed tomato, or *matambre surtido*, assorted cold cuts and cheese slices. The main course follows, often accompanied by some sort of salad. Potatoes and vegetables are ordered separately.

Desserts are usually ice creams, fresh fruit of the season, or *flan* (scrumptious caramelized custard) and the meal is topped off with a cup of fresh-ground espresso coffee.

Argentines understand coffee, to my palate the best in the world. It is fresher and stronger than that served in North America and a cup or two for breakfast, with your customary croissants (called *media lunas*, half-moons), will wake you up in a hurry. A *cortado* is a demitasse of espresso cut with cream (ask for a *cortado doble* if you want a large cup) and a *café con leche* is half espresso and half steamed milk.

No Argentine meal is considered complete without wine and Argentina is the fifth largest producer of wine in the world. Yet Argentine wines are almost unknown outside the country. The reason is not that they are mediocre wines, but rather that the Argentines themselves consume nearly all of the nearly 50 varieties of wine they produce, to the annual tune of about 16 gallons per capita.

The two types of wine are *vino de mesa* (table wine) and *vino fino* (fine wine). Both types come in red *(tinto)*, white *(blanco)*, and rose *(rosado)*. You will recognize most of the varieties on the wine list and on the shelves: Merlot, Chardonnay, Cabernet Sauvignon, Riesling, Chenin Blanc, Pinot Noir, and so on. Table wines range in quality from good

Food you will not forget!

to bad and are served by the glass, or in quarter-liter or half-liter decanters. Bottles of table wine are liters. Wine, however, is so inexpensive in Argentina that at every opportunity you should indulge yourself with *vino fino*, (also called *vino reserva* or *vino tres cuartos*), served in 3/4 liter (750 cc) or 1/2 liter (500 cc) bottles and always corked. When you buy a good bottle of wine, ensure that it is uncorked at your table so you may be certain of your purchase.

Most of Argentina's fine wines come from the province of Mendoza and considerable time is spent arguing about which wines are best. I have no intention of joining that argument, but if you order a wine produced by one of the following wineries *(bodegas)*, you are not likely to be disappointed: San Felipe, Lavaque y Mattei, San Telmo, Santa Sylvie, La Rosa, or Michel Torino.

The several brands of Argentine beer are good and usually served cold enough to suit North Americans. Beer and cocktails are often served, at your request, with *picadas*, generous snack-plates of cheese cubes, nuts, crackers, and sausage chunks that Argentines munch as they indulge in the pastime for which they are renowned—conversation. Be cautious about mixed drinks; they are very strong, usually doubles.

Throughout Argentina, but especially in the north and in Patagonia, you will see men and women sipping something with metal straws from orange-sized gourds, often furnished with tiny tripod legs and partially encased with silver embellishments. They are drinking *yerba mate*, usually called *mate* (MAH-tay), an infusion of the leaves and stems of a shrub grown in northern Argentina and Paraguay. *Mate* contains about the same amount of caffeine as coffee and is drunk for the stimulation it provides. Very popular, almost the national drink of parts of Argentina, Uruguay, Paraguay, and southern Brazil, *mate* tastes peculiar to most North American palates, rather like extremely strong green Chinese tea. Like martinis, retsina, and haggis, a taste for *mate* is ac-

Old World elegance characterizes the interior of the Hotel Correntoso. Note the old espresso machine.

quired rather than bestowed and most foreigners find their first taste unpleasant. If you persevere, however, you will soon find the drink as refreshing as regular tea or coffee. The ritual by which *mate* is drunk is as interesting as the beverage. Several batches of water are steeped in the same gourdful of *mate* and each drinker empties the gourd handed to him before passing it on to be refilled and handed to the next drinker. Since succeeding infusions diminish in strength, it is something of an honor to be given the first—and strongest— gourdful of *mate*. Do not fail to try it.

The second major adjustment North Americans must make to Argentine dining is the dinner hour. You will soon discover why Argentines are in the habit of having a light snack in mid-afternoon, for by our standards, Argentines eat dinner incredibly late in the day. Few restaurants open before 9:00 p.m. and some restaurants in small Patagonian towns are not even ready to serve dinner until 10:30 p.m.; many patrons do not even arrive until nearly midnight. Meals in private homes are served somewhat earlier, but seldom before about 9:00 p.m. It takes time to get used to a heavy meal so late in the day, but the custom is made to order for fly fishermen, for you can fish until dark and be assured of a good meal when you get back to town.

ARGENTINE FLY FISHERMEN

Fly fishing is still relatively new in Argentina, but today it is in a logarithmic stage of growth. In the 1950's, there were fewer fly fishermen in Argentina than suitable streams for them to fish. Perhaps 30 enthusiasts met on weekends to practice casts on the lawns of the Palermo Gardens in Buenos Aires, where most of them then lived. Over the years, fly fishing has caught on among the sporting public and while nobody knows how many people have since taken up the pursuit, guides believe it to be somewhere over ten thousand, or about one of every 3,000 Argentines.

The first Argentine fly fishermen were wealthy aristocrats. Well-equipped and proficient casters, over the years they have become excellent fly fishermen by any standards. However, those members of the Argentine middle class who have since adopted fly fishing have not had the same opportunities for stream experience as their predecessors. This fact, along with certain social customs, has led to a style of Argentine fly fishing that visiting fly fishermen should be aware of.

Well-to-do Argentine fly fishermen have good equipment and cast well; poorer fishermen have spinning gear or use tin cans in an ingenious fashion I will describe later. What both types of fishermen seem to lack are the decades of stream experience that many North Americans have been fortunate enough to acquire. As a result, while Argentine fishermen may be technically proficient, many of them are not skilled at reading water. In general, Argentines tend to fish only the most obvious places for trout. As they move up or down a stream, they move from hole to hole, walking around intervening reaches. Consequently, they often pass up productive holding waters or feeding territories that do not look like classic fishing holes. So despite the fact that many streams get considerable pressure, that pressure is almost exclusively restricted to a few places. More experienced fly fishermen who work these heavily fished waters almost always find fish that have been missed.

Argentines are also inclined to fish relatively accessible stream reaches. As a general rule, they don't like to walk far. If you avoid the more readily accessible stretches and walk some distance up or down a stream from the car, as in this country you will find water that receives significantly less fishing pressure.

Further, when Argentines take vacations, they customarily stay up late at night and get up quite late the next morning. Many hotels, in fact, do not serve breakfast until nine or ten in the morning. Argentines will fish late, but they tend to be middle-of-the-day anglers and they do not hit the streams early. At seven or eight in the morning, you are very likely to be the only fly fisherman on the river.

Finally, many Argentine fly fishermen are more patient than their North American counterparts, perhaps to a fault. Less experimental in their approach to fly fishing, they are reluctant to change flies often. I have often watched fishermen work a small pool with a fly and returned an hour later to find the same fisherman working the same pool with the same fly, without having had as much as a flicker of interest from a trout.

These are, of course, general observations. There are plenty of excellent Argentine fly fishermen, but from the perspective of many North American fly fishermen, most Patagonian streams still receive very light fly fishing pressure.

In summary, North American fishermen who journey to Argentina can expect a number of surprises—nearly all of them pleasant. They will find themselves in a country surprisingly similar to the United States, in the company of courteous people of diverse European background who eat well, take a calm, relaxed approach to life, drive like maniacs, and get just as excited about fly fishing as the rest of us.

FAUNA AND FLORA

A few days ago, I stood behind a giant willow watching my hair-wing caddis bob toward the head of a riffle on the lower Yellowstone, when I heard a light splash just upstream. I peered through the willow, hoping to see a ring on the water within casting range and instead saw a white-tail doe standing stockstill in the water, ears high and straining. She had not seen me nor heard me over the riffle's susurration, so I froze. She soon moved further into the river, looked back toward shore and a tiny spotted fawn gingerly stepped from the brush into the water. The pair moved out into the current, swam for several strokes in the center of the stream, regained footing on the other side, and disap-peared into the willows. Preoccupied with the crossing, they never noticed me and I returned attention to my drenched caddis. A half hour later, a trio of deer crossed the river fifty yards downstream. The same day, I watched a pair of Canada geese court at the tail of an island of cobbles, saw a great blue heron stalk minnows in a quiet backwater, watched several kingfishers hover and rattle, and listened to the raspy croaks of sandhill cranes as they wheeled about over nearby meadows. I did not catch many fish that day, but had a thoroughly good time. . .

The wildlife sightings that common-ly spice fishing trips in Yellowstone Park are even more dramatic, occa-

The Patagonian Fox, zorro colorado, *is especially abundant on Tierra del Fuego.*

Shoreside willows usually shelter fío-fíos in Patagonia.

sionally hair-raising—elk, bison, bear. On streams of the western U.S., with which I am most familiar, wildlife is an important part of every fishing trip. A trip with plenty of fish and plenty of wildlife is a resounding success. A trip with no fish but lots of wildlife is still a resounding success. But a trip with neither fish nor wildlife? Well, several hours with a good novel might have been better. . .

Fishermen who make their way to Patagonia, however, can look forward to discovering a whole new community of interesting wildlife, some familiar, but most new. A review of all of Patagonia's wildlife is not appropriate in this book, but a description of birds and animals that fishermen are likely to encounter along Patagonian streams will help to enhance the fishing experience, and that is a primary objective.

I have indicated that for fishermen the Southern Zone is richest in wildlife, but many animals, especially birds, are common along streamsides in all three zones. Many of the birds are boisterous, even raucous characters, whose cries grow so familiar and so firmly etch into your memory that their absence along a stream becomes noteworthy.

You will hear the first of these long before you see it, for it is a shy creature, quite small, and can drive you nearly mad. Argentines have given the bird the onomatopoetic name *fío-fío*, English-speakers call it the white-crested elaenia, and ornithologists call it *Elaenia albiceps*. Shortly after you step into any willow-lined stream in Patagonia, you will hear a high-pitched peep, a short pause, then a repeated peep. At first you are likely to ignore them, but you soon notice that the odd, sad peeps continue for quite a while and as the day passes, you realize that the damned peeping almost never stops. *Fío-fíos* are flycatchers about the size of small sparrows, olive green birds that flit silently about in willows and other brush that line streams and are very difficult to spot. They are irritating at first, for they can sing their short song without pause for hours on end and the incessant peeping can be distracting, but you eventually learn to tune it out. Ultimately, they become welcome companions, and the river seems strangely silent without them.

The second bird you notice is the *tero-tero*, or southern lapwing, *Vanellus chilensis*. The *tero* is a large bird—adults are over a foot long—with big reddish eyes, long red legs, and a pert black crest at the back of its head. The bird is green to black with white underparts and has distinct black and white wings. *Teros* are ground-nesters, which explains why they so persistently scold fishermen. As soon as you start across a meadow, every *tero* within a hundred yards pops into the air and wheels overhead, diving and calling as if the world were about to end. The birds never try to peck, but they are so abundant, loud, and irascible that they become part of every fisherman's streamside experience.

If the meadow is not full of *teros*, it will likely be full of another bird abundant along Patagonian streams, the *bandurria* or buff-necked ibis, *Theristicus caudatus*. Because of its size, appearance, and raucous call, the *bandurria* is one of the most conspicuous birds of Patagonia. Found from the savannas of Venezuela to the steppes of Tierra del Fuego, it is seen in largest numbers in spring and summer in and around the marshes of Patagonia foraging through

Clockwise from top left: tero-teros; *black-necked swan;* torrenteros, *or torrent duck;* bandurrias.

Fauna And Flora

meadows and wetlands in search of bugs and frogs. Adult birds stand nearly two feet high and have a long, black decurved bill. They have a gray body, males have white wing coverts and both sexes have the distinctive rufous-orange head and neck that gives them their name. *Bandurrias* travel in flocks and their metallic honking is another of those unforgettable sounds that forever invoke memories of a certain region.

All Patagonian birds are not as raucous as *teros* or *bandurrias*. On slower stretches of the rivers and on many lakes in all three zones, you will see many stately black-necked swans, *Cygnus melanocoryphus*, which Argentines call *cisne de cuello negro*. One other swan is native to South America, the coscoraba swan *(Coscoroba coscoroba)*. The distribution of the two swans overlaps, and you may see both birds, but you are not likely to confuse the two species: the smaller coscoroba has black-tipped primary wing-feathers and a pink bill; the more common black-necked swan has a distinctive ebony neck and a prominent ruby–red caruncle at the base of its bill. Chilean poet Pablo Neruda described the bird in definitive terms:

Above the swimming snow
A long, black question mark.

You will see a host of ducks and other waterfowl along Patagonian streams and on the lakes, many of which will be familiar—coots, widgeons, pintails, teals, shovelers. Two common birds you will not recognize, however, are the torrent duck, *Merganetta armata*, and the neotropic cormorant, *Phalacrocorax olivaceus.*

Flyfishermen would do well to keep an eye out for the torrent duck, called *pato torrente* or *torrentero*, for they feed almost exclusively on stonefly larvae and are found only in habitat appropriate for these insects: clear, rocky, swift-flowing streams. They are small ducks and you will recognize them by their red bill, a conspicuous black stripe that runs down the neck from their eye, and by their distinctive habitat. They are shy birds, invariably seen in pairs, always in the midst of whitewater cascades or swift boulder-studded runs, which they negotiate with ease. They are difficult to stalk with a camera, for they swim underwater as easily as fish, upstream or down, and once they dive may not reappear again for a hundred feet or more.

The neotropic cormorant, called *biguá* or *cormorán*, is a type of bird that North Americans are more accustomed to seeing on seacoasts than small inland rivers, but they are frequent companions to flyfishermen in Patagonia, zipping in a whir of wings up and down streams at eye level like shiny black bullets. This sleek cormorant has a long, straight bill hooked at the end and holds its head and neck extended when in flight. It is glossy black and may be distinguished from other cormorants by the small tuft of white feathers at each side of its head.

Three species of kingfishers inhabit Argentina, but only the ringed kingfisher, *Ceryle torquata*, called *martín pescador*, is common in Patagonia. Adult birds are a foot long and look, sound, and behave much like the belted kingfisher common on the rivers of western rivers of North America.

Along high lakes and headwater reaches of streams in the Northern Zone, fishermen will see an unexpected sight—seagulls. The bird is usually the Andean gull, *Larus serranus*. The only gull that frequents the high Andes, it is easy to recognize in summer with its jet-black head and wingtips, and white body.

Raptors are common in fields and forests throughout Patagonia, including such familiar forms as peregrine falcons and sparrow hawks. The most common hawk seen on the fishing grounds is probably the *chimango caracara (Milvago chimango);* a small, brownish hawk with prominent white wing bars often seen scavenging along roadsides. Occasionally, especially when fishing headwater

Chimangos *are one of the most common small raptors in Patagonia.*

reaches in the mountains, you will see the gigantic Andean condor *(Vultur gryphus)* soaring far above on rising thermals. It looks like an eagle, with primary wing-feathers held open at the end of its wings like the spread fingers of your hand, but is readily distinguished from eagles by its size and cream-colored neck ruff.

Woodpeckers are called *carpinteros* (carpenters) by Argentines and when you fish streams that flow through mature beech forests, you are likely to see one of the most spectacular of them all, the Magellanic woodpecker, *Campephilus magellanicus.* They are large birds, up to 17 inches long, and are black with white wing bars. Males, with bright scarlet head and crest, are unmistakable. Like the perhaps extinct ivory-billed woodpecker of the southern United States, they require snags and older trees for food and nesting sites, so watch for them in stands of the oldest and largest beeches you can find. Try tapping on trees to attract their attention and listen for their calls, which are raspy squawks.

The most jarring sights for fishermen who also watch birds are the noisy flocks of 16-inch-long burrowing parrots, *Cyanoliseus patagonus,* called *loro barranquero,* that create huge rackets in stands of poplars and stream-side forests of the Northern and Central Zones. These birds and the smaller olive green austral parakeets, *Enicognathus ferrugineus,* called *cachañas,* are the only parrot or parakeet-like birds in Patagonia. The *banqueros* prefer the savannas and wooded steppes, while *cachañas* are most common in the dwindling Araucaria forests of the Northern Zone.

Fishermen who travel to the Southern Zone will have the best chances to see large numbers of three fascinating birds of Patagonia—flamingos, sheldgeese, and rheas.

Of the three species of flamingos that live in Argentina, only one, the Chilean flamingo, *Phoenicopterus chilensis*, called *flamenco austral* by Argentines, lives in Patagonia. It is the widest ranging of the flamingos, found in lakes, marshes, and along muddy riverbanks at all elevations from Ecuador to Tierra del Fuego. They are easy to recognize, splotches of pink or salmon against the drab tones of the grassland steppes in which they are most abundant. Every fly fisherman who gets to the steppeland streams will from time to time round a bend to see several flamingos strutting about in the muddy shallows.

Sheldgeese or upland geese are collective terms for five species of South American birds that resemble geese but are more closely related to ducks. Four of the five species spend most of their lives in the extreme south of the continent. Called *cauquen, kaiken,* or *avutarda* by Argentines, they are one of the unforgettable wildlife sights of southern Patagonia and Tierra del Fuego. One species, the kelp goose, is exclusively marine and not seen by fishermen, but the rest are land birds that only occasionally make use of the sea. These land birds are incredibly abundant; flocks may contain thousands of birds and it is not uncommon to see hundreds of thousands of birds during the course of a day's drive in southern Patagonia or Tierra del Fuego. They are most abundant from November through May, feeding in every meadow in sight and raising their families on nearby watercourses. The most common is the Magellan goose *(Chloephaga picta)*, with white head and rump, and the rest of its plumage barred black and white. The rarest—and most beautiful—is the colorful ashyheaded goose, *Chloephaga poliocephala*, the only species of sheldgeese with a distinctly gray head.

Millions of sheldgeese or kaiken, considered a plague by sheepmen, inhabit the grassy steppes of southern Patagonia and Tierra del Fuego.

The ruddy-headed goose, Chloephaga rubidiceps, is the smallest of the sheldgeese and is native to Tierra del Fuego.

The geese have managed to survive despite the organized efforts of sheepmen to reduce their numbers. In a classic example of ecological mismanagement, Patagonian and Fuegian sheepmen drastically reduced the numbers of the geese's principal predators, the Patagonian and Fuegian foxes, at the same time clearing land to encourage growth of the short grasses of the steppelands, the primary food source of the geese. The population of grass-eating rodents soared, of course, and with plenty of food and few predators, the population of sheldgeese skyrocketed. In due course, they became the principal competitors of the sheep for the grass. Appalled, the sheepmen, claiming that from two to eight geese ate as much grass as one sheep, had the geese declared a national plague in 1972 and instituted a campaign to eliminate them. Hunters were paid 5 cents for each egg, gosling, or pair of legs brought in, and in the early years of the program, hundreds of thousands of birds were killed in this manner. Populations have since stabilized, but the birds are still considered to be nuisance species by sheepmen.

The last of this trio of Southern Zone birds is the rhea, the so-called South American ostrich. You may occasionally see rheas far out into the steppes of the Northern and Central Zones, but only in the Southern Zone are you apt to see them while you are actually fishing. Rheas have a host of common names in English and Spanish. There are two species of rheas: the greater or American rhea, found on the plains of southern Brazil, Uruguay, Paraguay, and northern Argentina, and the lesser or Darwin's rhea of the southern Andes and Patagonia.

The Patagonia rhea, *Pterocnemia pennata,* called *choique* or *ñandú* (pronounced CHOY-kay and nyahn-DU, respectively) by Argentines, is only a distant cousin of the African ostrich and is more closely related to the flightless birds of Australia—kiwis, emus, and cassowaries—further evidence that South America and Australia were once united.

Choiques are smaller than ostriches, about 4 feet high, weighing from 40 to 60 pounds, but they appear enormous to anyone who sees these birds for the first time. They are ungainly in appearance, but their periscope-like neck is well adapted to life on the flat plains; they can outrun a horse and maneuver cleverly over broken terrain. Their camouflage is flawless; when they freeze, they appear to vanish. They invariably flee when threatened, but can be dangerous when cornered because of the sharp claws on their powerful legs. Avoid being kicked by a choique.

They have a curious social structure. At nesting, males defend a harem

Rheas, called choique *or* ñandú *by Argentines, are especially common in southern Patagonia.*

of from four to six females, who all lay their eggs in the same well-hidden nest, which can contain as many as 50 eggs. The male then drives off the females, incubates the eggs, and guides and defends the chicks until they can manage for themselves. Their predators are mountain lions, foxes, feral dogs, and of course, man. Choiques were once hunted for sport, feathers, and food (imagine the drumsticks) and their populations were in serious decline. Their eggs, up to 6 inches long, were considered great delicacies. Under protection, they appear to have made a remarkable recovery, especially in certain parks and reserves, and their populations have stabilized.

Armadillos are among the most common terrestrial animals along steppeland reaches of streams in all three zones, where they forage along sand and gravel bars. The nine-banded armadillo, *Dasypus novemcinctus*, called *peludo*, is the most abundant. They are over a foot long and have good hearing, but they do not see well, so if you freeze, you can observe them at close range. When they spot you, however, they will dart away at surprising speed, scurrying along smoothly on tiptoe like tiny animated hovercraft, much faster than you can

The harmless piche ciego *takes the form of an armored softball when threatened.*

run. In the south, you may also see the tiny three-banded armadillo, *Zaedyus pichy*, called *piche-piche* or *piche ciego* by Argentines. This is the armadillo that can, and will, roll up into a well-protected sphere about the size of a softball when cornered. If you must see armadillos and haven't seen any along the streams, keep an eye out for dead sheep along the roadsides. When you spot a sheep, flip it over, and chances are good that one or two armadillos will be under it, taking shelter in the pungent shade, with lunch handy.

The European hare has been introduced to Patagonia, has flourished, and is very abundant. You will see them everywhere. If lucky, you may see the true, but rarer Patagonian hare, *Dolichotis patagonum*, called *mara* or *liebre patagónica*. It is a native rodent, the ecological equivalent of the jack rabbit, and looks much like a hare, but with shorter ears.

What we call an otter, Argentines call a little river wolf, *lobito de río*, or *huillín*. The species you may encounter in any of the three zones is *Lutra provocax*. They have been ruthlessly exploited, but are making a comeback in rivers that are within parks or reserves. You may spot them in the Quillen,

When alarmed, the nine-banded armadillo, or peludo, *scurries along on tiptoe faster than a man can run.*

Darwin marveled at the guanaco, "an elegant animal. . .with long slender neck and fine legs."

Malleo, Arrayanes, or Gallegos Rivers. Do not confuse them with the common, but much smaller muskrat-like nutria, *Myocaster coypus*, called *coypu* or *nutria criolla*, which has a naked tail. You will usually see a *coypu* swimming along with a mouthful of reeds or grass on which it feeds and constructs its nests.

Larger animals are more abundant in the southern zones. Foxes are hunted relentlessly by herders, but are often seen along roadsides, and are remarkably tame: the Grey fox, *Pseudalopex gracilis*, called *zorro gris*, and the more abundant Patagonian fox, *Dusicyon culpaeus*, called *zorro colorado*.

When Darwin landed in Patagonia in 1832, he was greeted by the sight of "an elegant animal...with long slender neck and fine legs" in herds that reached the size of several hundred individuals.

The tawny brown and white animals he saw are the most typically South American animal fishermen will see in the Central and Southern Zones—guanacos, *Lama guanicoe*.

Guanacos are the tallest South America mammal and are closely related to camels. The ancestors of the guanaco and its cousins, the vicuñas and domesticated llamas and alpacas, reached South America by crossing the Panamanian Isthmus thousands of years ago. They died out in North America, but were very successful immigrants to South America. Their only enemy, except for man, was the mountain lion and their range once extended from Bolivia to the Strait of Magellan, including most of the Pampas and Patagonia.

From the moment the first Spanish colonists and their 72 horses landed on the shores of present-day Argentina in

1535, the huge guanaco herds were doomed. The animals had been hunted by Indians for food, skins, and bones for implements, but rifles, increased hunting pressure, and competition with sheep and cattle for habitat proved to be too much, and the herds dwindled. By 1900, only a few family bands survived in remote corners of forests and mountains. The animals have received protection in recent decades, however, and like rheas are making a dramatic comeback, especially on Tierra del Fuego.

Guanacos are about the size of pronghorn antelope, mostly caramel to cinnamon brown, with a creamy white breast and belly. They have long necks, long ears, and long eyelashes over enormous liquid eyes. In motion, they are fleet and graceful, with a hobby-horse-like gait. They are shy animals, but curious, and fishermen are most likely to see them wandering along the forest edges in the Southern Zone. In some parks, where they have been protected for many years, they are quite tame and permit humans to approach closely. Keep your eyes on their ears. Ears flattened against the skull indicate displeasure; if you get too close, you may be splattered with a noxious gob of half-digested grass, for guanacos, like llamas and alpacas, spit when irritated.

The last creature worthy of mention is only an inch or two long, but its significance with respect to fishermen is enormous. Its common name in Argentina is *pancora*, a member of the genus biologists call *Aegla*. The *pancora* is a crayfish, a freshwater crustacean extremely abundant in most rivers of the Northern and Central Zones; it probably accounts for the lion's share of the outstanding physical condition and rapid growth rate of the fish in those streams. In the water, *pancoras* look like tiny blue-black lobsters, but with a broader, somewhat rounded carapace and a shorter tail with fewer segments. They lack sharp spines, but keep fingers clear of the pincers on their first pair of legs. You can find them by looking along shore near the water for empty cases, which dry tan to pale orange in the sun, or by turning over rocks in the shallows. They dart backwards quickly and if they head into deeper water won't get far without attracting the lethal interest of the nearest trout. A third place to find them is in the stomachs of trout. You don't have to kill the fish, for adults are two inches long, and you can easily feel the knobby stomach of a fish with a belly full of *pancoras*.

In all three zones, some parts of fishing streams flow through dense forests and other parts meander either through grasslands or gravelly plains too arid to support trees. Few of the trees will be familiar to North Americans.

Most of the forests of the southern Andes are beech or *Nothofagus* forests, which make their first appearance in this zone. The zone, however, is also the only region in which fishermen see extensive stands of a striking tree that Argentines call *pehuén* or *araucaria* and English-speakers call the monkey-puzzle tree, *Araucaria araucana*. The English common name derives from the stiff, spiny leaves that encircle its twigs and branches. These branches arch upward and their concentration near the top of mature trees lend the trees the appearance of giant parasols (Chileans indeed call them *paraguas*—umbrellas). The *pehuén* is a primitive conifer, little changed from the forms that have been identified from fossil remains elsewhere. The thumb-sized seeds, rich in carbohydrates were once a basic food of the Araucanian or Mapuche Indians. The tree is becoming rare, and as a living relic, is completely protected within the national parks. Several pure stands *(pehuenales)* are found at higher elevations in this zone, especially along upper reaches of the Aluminé, Quillen, Ñorquinco, and Malleo rivers. Smaller isolated groups are scattered throughout the zone and since the *pehuén* is a favored decorative tree, it is the main species planted in the squares of Junín de los Andes, San Martín de los

Lanín Volcano is the backdrop for this monkey puzzle, or araucaria tree.

Andes, Bariloche, and other Patagonian communities.

The beech forests of Patagonia appear at first to comprise a bewildering variety of trees that are similar in appearance, but there are only five principal species, each generally found at different elevations. In lower, more humid areas, the tall evergreen beech, *Nothofagus dombeyii*, called *coihue*, is the dominant tree. A tall, relatively straight tree, it is the largest of the beeches, sometimes exceeding 100 feet, and its dense upper canopy of leaves creates a cool, dark, and open understory. The *ñire*, or Antarctic beech, *Nothofagus antarctica*, another low elevation tree, prefers moist sites, and often lines the shores of rivers and lakes. Most fishermen will spend a good deal of time plucking fishing flies from the branches of *ñires*. It is often associated with the false beech, *Nothofagus obliqua*, or *roble*. At higher elevations, the *coihue* is often associated with the *raulí*, *Nothofagus alpina*, distinguished from other beeches by its enormous leaves, some 4 to 5 inches long. At highest elevations, the high beech, *Nothofagus pumilio*, or *lenga*, predominates. It is the *lengas* that herald the approach of winter, for they are deciduous trees whose leaves begin to splash the highest Patagonian hillsides with red, gold, and orange in March and April.

Before you set foot into a stream, indeed as your plane lands, your attention will be drawn to the long rows of graceful column-shaped trees that are so abundant in the Northern and Central Zones. The trees are *álamos*, which we call the Lombardy poplar, *Populus nigra italica*. They are not native to South America, but were introduced by immigrants who appreciated their stately appearance as much as their effectiveness in breaking the fierce Patagonian winds. Quite often, they are the only trees in sight on the steppelands, orderly patches of green on an otherwise bleak plain. Most cultivated fields, orchards, and farmhouses in northern and central Patagonia are bordered with tight rows of *álamos,* appropriately named *cortinas* (curtains) in Argentina. Lombardy poplars are deciduous trees and they line the orchards and fleck the fields and streams with gold in the austral fall. Fishermen are likely to spend many pleasant hours in the welcome shade of streamside *álamos* in Patagonia.

One of the rarest of trees that fishermen will see is a myrtle-like tree called the arrayán *(Myerceugenella apiculata).* The bark of the arrayán is pale orange and it curls into parchment-like scrolls on older trees. The tree produces a profusion of pure white flowers and shortly thereafter bears tiny edible blue berries. Individual trees are not particularly striking, but their rarity invests them with a peculiar appeal. The charm of the arrayánes reveals itself in the pure stands, for trunks of mature trees are severely contorted and with little strain of the imagination fishermen find themselves wandering through the groves of Vincent van Gogh's twisted cypresses. The Río Arrayán in the Central Zone is named for the trees, which line both of its banks and transform the river into a colonnade lined with creamy-white blossoms in late February and early March. Arrayán forests were once found in Argentina and Japan, but the Japanese forests perished with the population of Hiroshima and the sole surviving forests are in Argentina. Pure stands of arrayán exist on the northern tip of Isla Victoria and the southern tip of the Quetrihue Peninsula in Nahuel Huapi National Park in the Northern Zone. Argentines take pride in the fact that these stands are said to have been adopted by Walt Disney as the model for the forests through which Bambi wandered. The stands are not large—40 acres or so—but they are truly unique and have been given extraordinary protection by the Argentine government.

The last tree of special interest is the *canelo,* or Winter's bark *(Drimys winteri),* whose name derives from historical events. When 33-year-old Francis Drake entered the Strait of Magellan in 1578, scurvy customarily decimated the ranks of all sailors on long voyages and often led to disaster. Upon learning that Patagonian Indians used *canelo* for medicinal purposes, Drake's Captain, John Winter, insisted that his crew use the bark of the tree in their food and to make tea, in an effort to stave off the ravages of scurvy. The effort paid off for both men, for Drake went down in history as the second man to circumnavigate the globe and Winter's name will forever be attached to this tree. Look under beeches for shorter trees with 3- to 4-inch-long lance-shaped evergreen leaves, white flowers with six petals, and spicy bark and seeds. The tree is found in all three fishing zones.

Fly fishermen who rush headlong through the brush to reach the stream will acquaint themselves quickly with a pair of formidably armed shrubs. They are not to be ignored, for they poke holes in both skin and light waders. The shrubs are called *chacay (Discaria serratifolia)* and *calafate (Berberis sp.)* by Argentines. *Chacay,* especially abundant along streams of the upper Río Limay drainage, not only pierces fingers and waders, but catches sloppy backcasts as well. Extricating a tiny fly from these spiny thickets is a delicate job that all fly fishermen will undertake from time to time. *Chacay* bears white flowers and is a damned nuisance, but *calafate,* also a nuisance, has a vital redeeming feature. *Calafate,* which we call barberry, bears fragrant yellow flowers that in fall transform into semisweet, rather seedy blue-black berries. Its importance to visitors is neither its spines nor its beauty (the red-flowered *notro* and Magellanic fuchsia are far more attrac-

Clockwise from top left: Amancay; mutisia; reina mora; fuchsia.

tive) but rather its power. Centuries ago, the legend says a lonely Tehuelche Indian medicine man seeking company taught birds that the berries of the shrub were good to eat and would even sustain them over the cold Patagonian winter. The birds ate the berries, stayed with the shaman, and from that moment forward the fruit acquired magical properties. Today, whoever eats the berries of the *calafate* will be unable to forget the sights and sounds of Patagonia, and when away, will experience an irresistable urge to return. To ensure your prompt return, try some, but be advised that the berries temporarily stain lips and teeth rather deep blue.

Several hundred flowering plants have been identified in the three zones, but four are in such colorful contrast to their surroundings that they inevitably draw the attention of fishermen. The *amancay* or *liuto (Alstroemeria aurantiaca)* is a bright yellow or orange flower, common in the Northern and Central Zones along forested stream and roadsides. It is usually a foot or two high and can be recognized by four to ten six-petaled flowers supported on an umbel-like structure. Two or three of the petals are flecked with dark brown or black striations. Cooked rhizomes of this plant are edible and infusions of tea are said to cure liver ailments. *Mutisia* or *reina (Mutisia decurrens)* is another bright orange flower abundant in these zones. It looks somewhat like a large orange daisy—the flower can be four inches wide—but is a vine-like plant that climbs shrubs and low trees. This flower and its purple look-alike cousin, the *virreina* or *reina mora (Mutisia retusa)*, are the most common roadside flowers in the Northern and Central Zones. The last and most spectacular of fishermen's flowers is a familiar one, the fuchsia *(Fuchsia magellanica), called chilco* in Patagonia. The fuchsia, actually a small shrub, evolved in the Southern Andes and the lovely pendant flowers that blanket a shrub in bloom are among the most memorable sights of Patagonia. The flower has four red sepals and four purple petals. The plant is always found near water and infusions of its leaves are used to treat fever and as a diuretic.

As you explore the banks of rivers that reach the steppelands, the mirror-image relationship of Patagonia to the Rocky Mountain west of the United States becomes striking. The plant that contributes most to this imagery is *neneo*, Patagonia's ecological equivalent to sagebrush. From a distance, low, rounded *neneo* shrubs *(Mulinum spinosum)* look exactly like sagebrush and you'll have no trouble imagining yourself in Montana, Wyoming, or southern Idaho. At close hand, however—and you will walk through *neneo* to reach virtually every steppeland stream in the Northern and Central Zones—you will see that the soft sagebrush leaves have been replaced by stiff, pale green spines. The entire plant is a lattice-work of these spines. Although *neneo* covers millions of acres of precordilleran hills and plains, it is considered a weed by sheepmen, for its fruits impart a strong taste to the meat of sheep that eat them. Most *neneo* shrubs that fishermen will encounter are about knee-high, but in some areas, the shrubs are taller than a man. Their spines actually look more formidable than they are. They will scratch bare ankles if you wade wet, but won't hurt waders. Two other plants, however, will instantly attract the full attention of careless fishermen.

The Spanish word for burr is *abrojo* and in Patagonia the term takes on a whole new meaning for fishermen. The first and least onerous of these plants is the *cadillo (Acaena ovalifolia)*. From mid-summer through fall, this low shrub produces a round seed-case about the diameter of a quarter that clings with stubborn tenacity to socks, shoelaces, shirt-tails, soft wader material, and nearly any other fabric brushed against

it. The burr can be removed without peril, but it tends to break into pieces when you grasp it and it can take an interminably long time to rid clothes and equipment of this irritating burr. The real troublemaker is a small, diabolical plant called *pimpinela* or *cepa de caballo (Acaena pinnatifida)*. This fiendish plant seems to have been scattered about to remind fishermen that even in Patagonia they have not reached paradise. Innocent in appearance, it takes the form of a low green mat about a foot across. As fall approaches, it sends two or three foot-long shoots up from the center of the mat, and the trouble starts.

Several seed-cases form on these shoots and quickly grow short, hooked spines. The summer sun dries the peppercorn-sized burrs and the needle-sharp spines acquire the strength of spring steel. You'll first find them in socks and boot-laces. On your first attempt to remove them, you'll find them stuck firmly and painfully into your thumb and forefinger. Naturally, you forget about your socks and try to get them out of your fingers with the other hand.

You now have burrs stuck in the fingers of both your hands. . .

Your first experience with these burrs will be a bitter, but good lesson. You'll have broken-off spines festering in your fingers, but you'll quickly learn that it's easier to watch for and avoid these damned things than to get them out of your clothes. You'll also learn that if you somehow missed the one that stuck in your sock, it will find some soft skin, and you'll have to clamber out of your waders again.

As if to offset these minor hassles for fishermen, nature, in her wise way, has also furnished Patagonia with a variety of plants that will make Americans feel right at home. As you puzzle over these bizarre new plants, you will begin to see lots of familiar old friends: flannel-leaf mullein, yarrow, wild strawberries, goldenrod, bull thistles, violets, and even good old dandelions.

PARKS AND RESERVES

A fortuitous combination of geological history and climate have fashioned a landscape in the southern Andes that encompasses much of the world's most dramatic scenery. Fortunately for visiting fishermen — and the rest of humanity — the Argentine government has established a chain of national parks along the mountains to protect and perpetuate these priceless scenic resources. The parks are among the finest on the South American continent and every fly fisherman will find occasion to wet a line in one or more of them.

Now and then, when fishing grows dull, when poor weather settles in, or when you simply need a change, take the opportunity to visit some of these parks, for in each of them you will find some very pleasant surprises. And do not leave your rod behind. . .

Six national parks lie within or near the fishing zones described in this book; a thumb-nail sketch of each park will help you enjoy them. They are, from north to south, near the Northern Zone, Laguna Blanca, Lanín, and Nahuel Huapi; in the Central Zone, Los Alerces; and near the Southern Zone, Los Glaciares, and Tierra del Fuego.

LAGUNA BLANCA

Until recently, only two reserves had been set aside in the western hemisphere for the express purpose of protecting swans. One is Red Rock Lakes National Wildlife Refuge in southwestern Montana, established to protect the trumpeter swan and the other is Parque Nacional Laguna Blanca in northern Patagonia, established in 1945 to protect the black-necked swan.

Laguna Blanca (White Lake) is a large shallow body of water that provides the combination of features essential for the survival of the swans: ex-

cellent habitat and a location sufficiently remote to ensure that the birds are not unduly disturbed. Situated on austere highlands just east of the Andes, the park is in a region typical of Argentina's precordilleran steppes, a harsh land from the perspective of humans, but admirably suited for swans wherever water can be found.

A short but high mountain range — the first intimation of the Andes — lies to the west, but a few parched hills provide the park with its only vertical relief. The park's volcanic origin is somewhat masked by sedimentary strata laid down in ancient seas, but evidence of more recent vulcanism is plentiful. The sandy ground is strewn with cobbles of pumice and basalt and outcrops of black basalt to the south of the lake are practically unweathered. The lake itself may have been formed when a lava flow blocked two small streams that flowed through the area.

The swans feed on vegetation, including algae and small arthropods. No fish live in Laguna Blanca, probably because of its high alkalinity, but the lake is rich in plankton. The bizarre alga nostoc is the most noticeable phytoplankton; the lake is often filled with round pale green colonies of this plant, some nearly the size of golf balls.

Swans are the most conspicuous birds on Laguna Blanca, but other waterfowl are more abundant. The swan population varies from a few hundred to over 2,000, but several thousand coots (Fulica spp.) are usually also in residence. At least three species of grebes visit Laguna Blanca, of which the silvery grebe (Podiceps occipitalis) is the most common. Ducks and sheldgeese are abundant. Several species of gulls and herons frequent the lake and a few dozen flamingos are usually wading in the shallows. The best month to visit the park is February, when the largest number of birds are on the lake.

Vegetation is typical of Patagonian steppes. All plants are xerophytes; there are no trees in the park. Shrubs are low and formidably spined. Sturdy boots, not tennis shoes, are required footwear.

A formation of yellowish limestone that outcrops in several parts of the park is of special interest because it is rich in marine fossils. Bivalves and ammonites of the Upper Jurassic Period are the most common remains.

Archaeologists have confirmed that the northeast shore of the lake was once the site of intensive pottery manufacture. Shards of pottery—Mapuche in origin—are strewn along shore in this area. Artifacts of pre-ceramic origin may also be found, including arrowheads, fleshing tools, and pestles manufactured from bone splinters, obsidian, and flint. Look, but leave them for the next visitor.

Laguna Blanca is remote, with few signs of human life in the vicinity of the park. No overnight accommodations are available at Laguna Blanca. The nearby town of Zapala has several suitable hotels, however. The park lies 20 miles southwest of Zapala in the province of Neuquen. Ruta 46, a well-maintained dirt road, connects Zapala with Aluminé, a small town near the northern tip of the next park we will discuss, Lanín National Park.

LANIN

Lanín National Park is dominated by an immense mountain of the same name. Lanín, a 12,380 foot volcano with the classical symmetry of Mount Fujiyama, is perpetually snowcapped. Indians of the area avoided Lanín, believing it to be the abode of a powerful evil

The architecture of Lanín National Park's headquarters, or intendencia, is typical of park facilities in Patagonia.

spirit, but modern travelers seek out the volcano and its striking surroundings.

Lanín National Park bears strong resemblance to neighboring Nahuel Huapi National Park, but important differences lend each park a distinct character. Lanín, for example, is not uniformly covered with dense forests. Although its terrain is mountainous, Lanín impresses the visitor as spacious, open country. There are no towns or villages within the park and in comparison with Nahuel Huapi National Park, has few developed facilities for tourists. As a result, Lanín is seldom crowded, and although ranching is permitted in some areas, it retains a pristine character. Lanín has several natural features that Nahuel Huapi lacks, such as hot springs and araucaria trees. Finally, although fishermen the world over have heard about the fishing in Nahuel Huapi, the true fishing meccas are the streams born in the lakes of Lanín National Park.

Lanín is an outstanding park for campers. Over two dozen campsites at various levels of development are established in the park, but undeveloped campsites are available on nearly all of its lakes and streams.

The park can be divided into six regions, each associated with at least one major lake *(lago)*. From north to south, they are:

Lagos Ñorquinco, Rucachoroi, and Quillen. This is a forested zone in which two trees of striking aspect make their appearance, the raulí and the pehuén. Excellent campsites lie alongside all of the lakes in this region, but Lago Quillen is especially recommended because of the spectacular profusion of fuchsias along its shores, and because of the large numbers of raucous austral parakeets and austral blackbirds *(Curaeus curaeus)* that live in the shoreside thickets. Fly fishermen should pay particular attention to the Río Ñorquinco, Río Quillen, and somewhat to the east of this zone, the upper Río Aluminé.

Lago Tromen. Lanín Volcano dominates this zone. The volcano is accessible to hikers and climbers, for a dirt road that becomes a major route between Argentina and Chile in the summer crosses the shoulder of the mountain at Paso Tromen (Tromen Pass). Eastward from the pass, the road passes rapidly through the transition zone from forest to dry steppes. The higher slopes of Lanín are covered with pehuén forests and for several miles the road passes through stands in which these rare trees predominate, with lenga or ñire growing in the understory. As travelers move east, more clearings appear. Several good campsites lie along the road, which then drops to the drier lowlands, passing through fields of volcanic rock and ash. For several miles, the road follows the valley of the fabled Río Malleo, which has cut through several layers of columnar basalt — remains of old lava flows. Evidence of the volcanic origin of the park is evident in this zone. Many mountaintops, mesa-like, are capped with resistant layers of black basalt or andesite laid down by old lava flows. Volcanic outcrops are common. Lago Tromen is typical of most lakes in Lanín National Park: large and clear, set in steeply rising forested mountains.

Lagos Curruhue and Huechulafquen. Huechulafquen is the largest lake in the park; it also supports some of the largest trout in the world. Its outlet is the famous boca which gives birth to the Río Chimehuin. The road on the north shore of Lago Huechulafquen passes through diverse countryside — dense thickets of bamboo, forest, and open meadows; vistas of the lake and mountains are splendid. Near the end of the road, massive Lanín Volcano heaves into view and soon dominates the entire northern horizon. Campsites are plentiful and first-class accommodations are available on the narrow strait that connects Lago Paimun to Lago Huechulafquen.

To the south of Huechulafquen, a different road leads past Lago Curruhue and several other lakes to the Lahuen-Co

Hot Springs, considered by locals to have highly therapeutic properties. The popularity of the hot springs is regional, so visitors are unlikely to encounter other foreigners. The spot is well off the beaten tourist path—a delightful hidden gem. The nearest town to this zone is the tiny town of Junín de los Andes, the principal destination of most visiting fly fishermen.

Lago Lolog. This wild region is almost totally uninhabited. The scenery is a combination of large wilderness lakes set in high mountains that are typical of Lanín. Lago Lolog is the source of the short, riffly Río Quilquihue, a tributary to the Río Chimehuin.

Lago Lácar. Lago Lácar is a long, narrow lake popular for recreation, but not noted for its fishing. Large tour boats ply its water, hauling passengers from the town of San Martín de los Andes to the westernmost end of the lake and on to Chile. San Martín, a modern, prosperous town set at the eastern end of Lago Lácar, is the jump-off point for fishing grounds to the south. Although the town relies on tourists summer and winter, it is not nearly as boisterous as Bariloche. Hotels for every budget and several excellent restaurants are found along its quiet, tree-lined streets. The park's headquarters *(intendencia)* is located in San Martín.

Lago Meliquina. Lago Meliquina is the principal natural feature in this zone of varied forests. Three excellent trout streams, the Río Caleufu, Río Meliquina, and Río Filo Hua Hum flow through the zone. Club Norysur, on the southwest shore of Lago Meliquina, is an internationally known private fishing club and the only place in the zone to obtain well-tied fishing flies.

Located immediately north of Nahuel Huapi National Park, Lanín National Park is accessible by road from Bariloche, Neuquen, or from Chile via Paso Tromen. Frequent bus service is available on all of these routes. Chapelco Airport, midway between Junín de los Andes and San Martín de los Andes, is served by frequent domestic flights.

NAHUEL HUAPI

When the Pleistocene glaciers retreated from the steppes into the fastnesses of the Andean Cordillera of northern Patagonia, they left behind an enormous, irregularly shaped lake. The lake is deep, but the vagaries of glacial sculpture left a narrow island anchored in the center of the lake. Centuries ago, Mapuche Indians gave this island a revealing name: Nahuel Huapi (Tiger Island). Much later, a man named O'Conner rechristened the island, giving it a much less imaginative name: Isla Victoria (Victoria Island).

O'Conner's name stuck; the island is still called Isla Victoria. But the original name also stuck, and has been given to the entire park of which this lake is the main feature.

Today Nahuel Huapi is one of the oldest and most popular national parks in South America. It has something for everyone and is to Argentines as Banff National Park is to Canadians: a honeymoon destination that offers summer music festivals, winter ski races, elegant Old World hotels and restaurants, and regional museums, all set against a backdrop of breathtaking mountain scenery.

Nahuel Huapi's rugged mountains, alpine glaciers, and well-established trails attract hordes of high country backpackers every summer. Serious anglers from around the world come to fish in the park's plentiful streams and clear, cold lakes, seeking trout and salmon. Nahuel Huapi's dense, silent forests beckon those who seek respite from the frenetic business world of Buenos Aires. And Bariloche, a sophisticated resort community, attracts those who seek to be seen in fashionable places.

The park encompasses a variety of landforms and vegetative communities because it extends from the highest

San Carlos de Bariloche is built along the shores of immense Lago Nahuel Huapi, centerpiece of Nahuel Huapi National Park.

peaks of the continental divide to the beginnings of the parched plains—an instructive cross-section through temperate South American ecosystems.

The highest mountain in the park is the extinct 11,722 foot high volcano, Tronador (Thunderer). Its name refers to the frequent rumbles caused by ice falling from the face of several glaciers *(ventisqueros)* that cling to the mountain's three peaks. According to an ancient Mapuche legend, the rumbling is a warning sent by pigmy-like creatures who are the mountain's custodians and who will slay with tiny arrows those who venture too close to Tronador.

The park contains six large lakes and dozens of smaller ones, but immense Lago Nahuel Huapi dominates the entire region and even moderates Bariloche's climate. Sixty miles long, with more than 200 square miles of sur-

face, the lake has several major arms *(brazos)* and boats regularly cross it on the way to or from Chile. In fact, Lago Nahuel Huapi is the final link in one of the most unusual short journeys in South America: travelers can cross the Andes by taking a series of ferry trips across alpine lakes and bus trips over mountain passes.

The western part of the park is the region between the Chilean border and the western margins of Lagos Nahuel Huapi, Traful, Mascardi, and Gutierrez. Annual rainfall is high in this zone—120 to 160 inches per year—and vegetation is lush and dense. Xerophytic shrubs predominate in the dry eastern zone, at the edge of the plains. The *Valle Encantado* (Enchanted Valley) lies within this arid zone. The valley extends for 25 miles along the Río Limay, the powerful river that drains Lago Nahuel Huapi.

Tertiary limestone formations loom over this valley, transformed by wind and rain into bizarre shapes given such names as *Castillo* (Castle), *Dedo de Dios* (God's Finger), *Cangalla Chilena* (Chilean Packsaddle), and so on.

A wide variety of wildlife is found in the park, but few of the animals are easily observed, except on Isla Victoria, where deer—including the cocker spaniel-sized pudú—are common.

As we have seen, trout and salmon were introduced into the waters of Nahuel Huapi just after the turn of the century and the fishing is now world renowned. Virtually every lake and stream in the park contain brown, rainbow, or brook trout, and several contain landlocked salmon. Trolling is the preferred method of fishing in the larger lakes, but fly fishing is effective in the smaller lakes and in the streams. Each major stream will be described in following chapters.

Nahuel Huapi is one of the few national parks in South America with a well-developed network of good trails and alpine refuges, so backpacking and mountaineering are popular activities. Principal hiking areas are Puerto Blest, Tronador, Cerro Catedral, and Cerro López. Many hiking maps distributed in the park are not up to date, but current information is available from the Club Andino Bariloche in town.

The history of Nahuel Huapi National Park is intimately associated with the development of trout fishing in Patagonia. On November 6, 1903, Francisco "Perito" Moreno—the same man who pressed the Argentine government to introduce salmonids into Patagonian waters—decided to donate about 75,000 acres of land he owned in the vicinity of Laguna Frías to the government of Argentina. He made his offer contingent upon a single condition and that condition altered Argentine history and firmly established Perito Moreno as the father of his country's park system. He insisted that the land be set aside for the enjoyment of all Argentines. . .

Such a notion was unheard of in those days and the government took several months to think it over. Eventually the offer was accepted and in 1904 Nahuel Huapi—the first national park to be established in South America and the third in the western hemisphere—was born.

Nahuel Huapi National Park is situated in the Andean region of Neuquen and Río Negro Provinces, well into northern Patagonia, and with Lanín National Park, in the heart of the Northern Fishing Zone. Although the park is nearly a thousand miles southwest of Buenos Aires, it is decidedly not off the beaten track, for it is not only readily accessible from within Argentina, but equally accessible from Chile. One of the most pleasant ways to reach (or depart) the park is to cross the Andes from Chile via the glacial lakes. Those who make this trip usually begin in the Chilean city of Osorno, from which they travel by bus to Chile's Vicente Pérez Rosales National Park. Passengers are delivered to Lago Todos los Santos, where they board ferries that take them to the eastern end of the lake. Another bus then transports them to Chilean customs and on winding mountain roads across the border into Argentina. The road drops steeply to the shores of Laguna Frías, where passengers complete Argentine customs formalities and board yet another boat that ferries them to the opposite end of the lake. Another two-mile bus ride brings them to Puerto Blest, on the shore of Lago Nahuel Huapi. A final boat ride brings passengers to Puerto Pañuelo, a short bus ride from Bariloche. The trip is remarkably comfortable and winds through one of the most dramatic mountain landscapes on earth. It is a journey for lovers and dreamers. . .

LOS ALERCES

About the time Greek masons first set chisels to the stones they would fashion into the Parthenon, a gust of wind swept through an Andean glade, freed a tiny seed from its cone, and spun

Alerces, South America's equivalents of the sequoias, are tucked away in remote recesses of Los Alerces National Park.

it to the forest floor. The seed lodged in a warm, moist spot, and soon sprouted and began to grow. Gautama Buddha was born and died while the tree grew. Alexander the Great marched to India, Julius Caesar was assassinated, and Christ was born; the tree grew on. The Crusaders tramped to Jerusalem, Pizarro invaded Peru, men learned to fly, and still the tree grew. . .

It still grows today in Los Alerces National Park and is one of the oldest living things on the face of the earth. Argentines call this ancient species of tree *alerce;* botanists call it *Fitzroya cupressoides.* Alerces are the sequoias of South America, ancient and massive. They are conifers that may exceed 150 feet in height, with trunks more than 12 feet in diameter. These largest of these dignified giants are located in remote sections of the park, but a well developed system of transportation by boat and trail has made them accessible to all visitors who wish to see them.

Like Nahuel Huapi and Lanin, Los Alerces National Park is situated in the Andes, in a setting of extremely rugged snowcapped mountains, large lakes, and nearly pristine forests. Small glaciers are commonplace, wildflowers profuse, and the park supports a rich admixture of forests.

Los Alerces is very nearly an ideal national park. Scenery is magnificent, accomodations are attractive as well as comfortable, museums and nature trails assist travelers in interpreting the park's natural features, and crowds seldom offend the pensive visitor. The park is the core of the Central Fishing Zone and fishing, as you will later see, is outstanding.

The best starting point for a visit is the village of Villa Futalaufquen at the southern tip of the lake of the same name. Tour the visitor center, for it contains a small but well-designed natural history museum that illustrates features of regional forests, insects, paleozoology, and paleobotany, as well as exhibits of Indian artifacts, small mammals, and the region's birdlife.

After a visit to Villa Futalaufquen, visitors should take the boat tour that enters the heart of the park, ultimately reaching the hidden world of the alerces. The trip begins at Puerto Limonao, where smartly attired crews welcome visitors aboard one of three comfortable, park-owned passenger launches. Spectacular sightseeing begins the moment the launch pulls away from the dock and brings the Andes into full view. Forests to the east of the launch show signs of exploitation,

Immaculately groomed grounds are typical of Los Alerces National Park, heart of the Central Fishing Zone.

but the dense forests to the west are untouched by human activities. As the launch rounds Punta Brava, *Cerro Químico*, an imposing mountain that drops abruptly into the lake, comes into view. In the distance, the series of granite peaks called *Cordón Pirámides* can now be seen. Most of the sharp spires of this chain of peaks are flanked by alpine glaciers.

Soon after rounding Punta Brava, the launch pulls up to a primitive dock at Playa Deseado, where passengers may disembark for lunch in a building of burnished knotty pine set in a dense grove of lengas. From Playa Deseado, the launch continues northward to the narrow strait that separates Lago Futalaufquen from Lago Verde. The two-mile strait, called Río Arrayanes, is one of the more exciting stages of the trip, for the skipper must avoid rocks and snags and

wind through shallows to stay in the channel. The strait has no rapids, but the current is fast and the launch is often forced to pass so close to shore that passengers can pluck leaves from overhanging branches. In some years the strait's water level is too low to permit boats to pass through.

After clearing the strait, the launch enters small Lago Verde, actually more blue than green. To the east is a low stretch of wooded land—a terminal moraine—beyond which lies Lago Menéndez, hidden from sight. The launch heads toward the moraine and shortly pulls up to a dock at Puerto Lago Verde.

Passengers disembark here and walk along a gentle half-mile trail to Lago Menéndez. Near the end of the walk, the path enters a dark grove of beeches, turns sharply and dips to a

Mount Torrecillas (7, 490 feet) and Torrecillas Glacier, seen from the wind-sparkled waters of trout-rich Lago Menéndez.

covered boathouse at Puerto Chucao. The boathouse holds more launches and just outside the cove, whitecaps dance where the lake is exposed to the 12-mile fetch of Lago Menéndez.

Passengers settle into a new launch and as soon as it leaves the cove, *Cerro Torrecillas*, the park's major peak, looms into view. The mountain is an upthrust massif whose broad south-facing wall is covered with ice and snow. The ice splits into two glaciers that grind their way down opposite sides of the mountain's weathered face. As the launch nears the mountain, passengers get a view down the length of *Brazo Norte* (North Arm) to the distant snowy peaks that mark the continental divide and the border with Chile. The launch continues northward under the brow of Torrecillas until it reaches the dock at *El Sagrario* (The Sanctuary).

This remote dock is the starting point for one of the finest nature trails in temperate South America. In just over a mile, the trail passes through cool green tunnels of *chusquea* (bamboo), dips under enormous windfallen logs, passes immediately alongside roaring waterfalls and cataracts, overlooks hidden lakes, and winds through groves of ancient alerces. A variety of flora is identified for hikers along the trail: ferns *(helechos)*, several species of native shrubs, including the Magellanic fuchsia, and such trees as coihues, arrayanes, and Winter's bark are placarded. The star of the show, of course, is the enormous alerce, named *arbol milenario* (thousand-year-old tree) or *el abuelo* (grandfather), near the end of the loop.

Botanists agree that the alerce is a species in decline. The tree is well adapted to the cooler, moister climate that once prevailed in the southern Andes, but is unable to flourish successfully under the ecological conditions of the present temperate climate. The alerce is a vanishing species. Park authorities indicate that the tree featured on this trail is neither the largest nor oldest alerce, but it is nevertheless impressive—nearly 200 feet tall,

El Abuelo—the Grandfather—an alerce *that took root 2,600 years ago in what is now Los Alerces National Park.*

and over seven feet in diameter at its base. Through the use of carbon-14 dating techniques, the tree has been determined to be 2,600 years old!

Park launches stop at the trailhead for just over an hour, so visitors cannot dawdle long on the trail. Backpackers or overnight campers can be dropped off at the trail and be picked up by a later boat, but only with written authorization from the *Intendencia* in Villa Futalaufquen. In order to return passengers to Puerto Limonao before dark, the launches leave El Sagrario *promptly* at the announced time. Do not be late.

Several inns, from simple to elegant, are located within the park. Most of them are situated on the eastern shore of Lago Futalaufquen and cater primarily to fishermen. Several campgrounds are established within the park. Hotels and restaurants for every budget are also available in nearby Esquel, a small picturesque town established by Welsh immigrants. Travel agencies in town offer tours of the park; check at the friendly and efficient tourist office near the bus terminal.

Los Alerces is primarily a sightseeing park, but well known to fishermen as a park whose lakes produce giant fish. All of the major lakes in the nor-

Lakes, mountains, trees and glaciers are the prominent features of Los Alerces National Park, heart of the Southern Fishing Zone.

thern half of the park—Futalaufquen, Menéndez, Verde, Rivadavia, and Cholila—are linked by streams large enough to permit easy passage of fish from one lake to the next. The largest fish are consistently caught in Lago Menéndez, from which, in a single memorable day several years ago, three rainbows weighing 23, 24, and 27 pounds were caught.

Los Alerces National Park is in the northwest corner of Chubut Province. It is readily accessible, but lies at the northern edge of the truly remote part of Patagonia. North of Los Alerces visitors are never far from towns; trappings of civilization are relatively commonplace. But to the south begins true Patagonia: one may travel for hours (and on back roads, for days) without seeing a sign of human habitation or another vehicle. Impressive names on maps turn out to be no more than a windswept crossroads or a lonely gas station and small country store. It is several hundred lonely miles to the next real town.

LOS GLACIARES

At the latitude equivalent to that of Vancouver, B.C., Paris, and Munich, a vast sheet of ice covers much of the southern Andes. Over 200 miles long and from 25 to 40 miles wide, the ice covers 5,500 square miles of mountainous terrain, in area the size of Connecticut. No fewer than 47 major glaciers flow from this massive ice field. Most flow toward the Pacific, but 13 of them flow eastward into Patagonia. The part of Argentina into which these glaciers descend is remote, nearly at the tip of the continent, but those who make the trip are well rewarded, for it is one of the great glacial regions of the world and since 1937 has been set aside as Los Glaciares National Park. Los Glaciares means "the glaciers," and the park's three major natural features are majestic mountains, immense lakes, and of course the glaciers themselves.

The park is not within any of the fishing zones described in this book. It lies several hundred miles south of the Central Zone, but is not far from the northern edge of the Southern Zone. There is some good fishing within the park, but Los Glaciares is too remote to warrant the long trip for the fishing alone. However, fishermen who travel to the Southern Zone and find some spare time away from the streams are well advised to take the opportunity to see this park.

Los Glaciares is huge, 2,300 square miles and is conveniently divided into two zones: north and south. The attributes of the northern zone are mountains, especially Mount Fitzroy and adjacent peaks, and is best suited for hikers and climbers. Accommodations are more rustic, fewer are available, and the area is somewhat more difficult to reach. The principal attractions of the southern zone are glaciers and lakes. The south is particularly well suited for sight seeing, for access is easy from the nearby town of Calafate and boat tours into remote sections of the park are available.

Los Glaciares North. Vast Lago Viedma and its stunning backdrop, the Mount Fitzroy chain of peaks, dominate the northern half of the park. Lago Viedma is so large that it lies within several biotic regimes. Nearly 50 miles long and

The spectacular mountains and glaciers of Los Glaciares National Park.

about 10 miles wide, it covers over 400 square miles of Patagonia. The eastern portion of the lake lies in the steppes. Along the dusty road that leads toward Fitzroy, visitors are likely to see guanacos, rheas, armadillos, and rabbits. Before long, however, Fitzroy comes into view and Viedma Glacier, which spills into the eastern end of the lake, appears. The road passes through an abrupt transition zone between plains and mountains, and on crossing the Río de las Vueltas (Twisting River) the visitor has unmistakably crossed back into the mountains and their beech forests.

The scenic quality of the Fitzroy complex of peaks is matched perhaps only by Wyoming's Grand Tetons. Like the Tetons, these peaks are suddenly and sharply thrust up from flatlands lacking significant foothills. Broad pink streaks are visible in the expanse of gray

granite that makes up the peaks and the immediate visual impact is stunning. Also like the Tetons, a flat plain stretches eastward from them, so that they are struck directly by the first rays of morning sun that breach the horizon and they are high enough to be backlit by the setting sun as well. As a result, the peaks undergo a kaleidoscopic variation of alpenglow from dawn to dusk. A day can be well spent at a single vantage point, watching the peaks cycle through these vivid transformations.

The highest and most imposing peak is Cerro Fitzroy (11,073 feet), first climbed in 1953. Neither Fitzroy nor its neighbors are lofty in Himalayan terms, but because Lago Viedma is only 800 feet above sea level Fitzroy leaps nearly two miles into the sky in, so to speak, a single bound.

The most dramatic of the peaks near Fitzroy is Cerro Torre, a slender needle of granite usually topped by a treacherous cap of ice known to climbers as "the mushroom." Cerro Torre has claimed several lives, and has been climbed only a few times. Controversy swirls about the first ascents, made in 1959 and 1971 with the aid of mechanically drilled holds and anchors, and some alpinists consider the first ascent to be the one made in 1974, without these aids.

Because of the popularity of these peaks among world class mountaineers, a visit to this section of the park can be fascinating. At any time during summer, climbers from Germany, Austria, France, Ireland, South Africa, Argentina, Italy, the United States, or elsewhere may be camped near the ranger station—affable, cheerful sorts constantly shouting and hurrying to and fro, comparing equipment, climbing stories, and know-how.

Los Glaciares South. By South American standards, Viedma is a giant lake, but Lago Argentino, covering 600 square miles, is larger yet—four times the size of Lago Nahuel Huapi. The lake was not discovered by Europeans until 1873 and was given its name four years later by our old friend, Perito Moreno. Lago Argentino has at its western end a series of iceberg-strewn arms *(brazos)* that penetrate deeply into the Andes and provide access by water to the glaciers that lies in deep recesses of the mountains. Because of the many glaciers that directly enter Lago Argentino or discharge runoff streams into the lake, rock flour renders the lake chalky green to turquoise. With one exception, these glaciers are difficult to reach except by launch, a trip highly recommended.

The exception is Glacier Moreno, the best known in the park and one of the most interesting glaciers in the world. In this epoch, only a few of the world's glaciers are advancing, and Moreno is one of them; it is the only glacier in the park not in regression and is one of the most accessible glaciers of its size. It is possible, with caution, to walk to its looming face and chip a few

cubes of ice several hundred years old into your beverage. Finally, every few years Moreno faithfully brings about a violent cataclysm that endangers no one, yet is one of the great recurring natural spectacles of South America.

Fed by several subsidiary glaciers, Moreno grinds its way 22 miles eastward down the Cordillera, directly toward an arm of Lago Argentino known as *Canal de los Tempanos* (Iceberg Channel). By the time the glacier reaches the lake, it is nearly 3 miles wide and the top of its face is nearly 200 feet above the water. Across the lake, a mountain, Cerro Buenos Aires, forms an immense peninsula. In about 1944, the irresistible force met the immovable object and Moreno slowly crashed into and up the side of Cerro Buenos Aires, mowing down several hundred acres of beech forests in the process.

The glacier had now cut off two long arms of Lago Argentino—Brazo Rico and Brazo Sur. Water continued to flow into these arms, however, until the water level in these amputated arms was about 100 feet higher than in the rest of the lake, just on the other side of the glacier dam. In 1947, the water finally forced its way through cracks in the glacier where it butted up against the peninsula and formed a tunnel through the ice. At last, in classic *Götterdammerung* fashion, with the air full of ear-splitting cracks and the thunder of enormous icebergs plunging into the roaring water, the tunnel collapsed in a matter of minutes. For several hours, the excess water in the southern arms thundered through this new channel until the water levels finally equalized and calm once again returned to Lago Argentino.

Glacier Moreno, however, continued its inexorable advance...

The channel was again squeezed shut and the cycle began anew. Since 1947, the collapse of the tunnel has repeated itself with increasing regularity, periodically lowering the level of the dammed brazos from 60 to 120 feet. In recent years, the event has recurred every third austral summer. The most recent collapse was on February 18, 1988. Try to be there for the next one.

The center of activities near the park is Calafate, a small community on the south shore of Lago Argentino and one of the few true towns in southern inland Patagonia. Calafate has several small hotels and restaurants, a campground, stores, and travel agencies that arrange tours to all parts of the park. Campgrounds and overnight facilities are available near the base of the Fitzroy chain of peaks (145 miles from Calafate) as well as near the Moreno Glacier (50 miles from Calafate). Check at the travel agencies before you leave town to be sure that accommodations are available. Beds fill up quickly during the summer. Calafate's airport is served by domestic airlines.

Looking west into Chile from the slopes of Guanaco Peak, Tierra del Fuego National Park. The snow-capped peaks on the horizon are the Darwin Range, the body of water at the right is Lago Roca, source of the Río Lapataia.

TIERRA DEL FUEGO NATIONAL PARK

Look carefully at a map of South America and you will note that the sharp eastward hook the Andes make at the southern tip of South America is comprised mainly of a large, irregular island separated from the mainland by a twisting channel, the Strait of Magellan. The channel existed on maps drawn as early as 1428, but was finally named for the man credited by history with its discovery in 1520, Ferdinand Magellan. On observing numerous plumes of smoke on the island from fires set by Indians to signal his arrival, Magellan named the island Tierra del Fuego—Land of Fire—and the name has stuck for nearly five centuries.

Remote, barren, nearly unpopulated, but in a strategic location of global significance, Tierra del Fuego captured the imagination of explorers, adventurers, missionaries, and settlers of every stripe early in its history. In more recent years, the island has attracted the attention of sheepmen, oil drillers, tourists, workers, and entrepreneurs seeking high wages offered to those willing to endure its grim climate. It still attracts a disproportionate share of adventurers—and these days, fly fishermen—and a few of its most remote corners have still not been thoroughly explored. In this distant and fabled land lies the southernmost park on earth: Tierra del Fuego National Park.

Shared by Chile and Argentina, the island of Tierra del Fuego is a faithful extension of the mainland. Its western portion is a mountainous continuation of the Andean Cordillera, glaciated but lower in elevation, while the eastern part—trout country—is a continuation of the flat Patagonian steppes, treeless in the drier north, but becoming increasingly forested southward.

The park is remote because Tierra del Fuego is remote—about 2,250 road miles (1,500 air miles) from Buenos Aires, 6,500 miles from New York—and has some sections so isolated as to be nearly inaccessible. Yet the park itself can be reached easily by air, road, and occasionally by sea. Located in the extreme southwest section of Argentine Tierra del Fuego, the park's western border coincides with the Chilean border.

Western Tierra del Fuego bears striking resemblance to the Alaskan panhandle, which lies at the same northern latitude (about 55 degrees), and in many respects is its mirror image: weather—tempestuous, rainy, and foggy for most of the year—is appalling in both places, but has created dense, temperate rainforests that grow to the edge of the sea; the timberline is low; glaciers are common and evidence of Pleistocene glaciation commonplace; fjords are deep, long, and spectacular; streams and rivers flow year-round in every drainage; rugged mountains jut up several thousand feet directly from the sea; lichens, ferns, and mosses are common groundcover plants; sphagnum moss bogs develop in poorly drained lowlands; and the adjacent sea is rich in marine resources.

The resemblance carries over into the population: wages are high, as are prices of goods and services, and the residents (the islanders call themselves *Fuegians)* are exceptionally friendly, tend to be rugged individualists who scorn the easy life and consider themselves pioneers on their country's Last Frontier.

The gateway to the park is itself the southernmost city in the world, Ushuaia (oo-shoo-WYE-uh). The town overlooks the *Canal de Beagle* (Beagle Channel), named for the ship that carried Charles Darwin on his voyage of discovery in 1831-36; it has a rather delapidated, frontierish look to it. In recent years, Ushuaia has responded to the influx of international tourists who are anxious to add Tierra del Fuego to their itineraries or are on their way to Antarctica. Accommodations are plentiful but expensive, and fill up quickly in the austral summer.

Tierra del Fuego National Park is not huge by South American standards, but is still large enough in which to get

A view across Beagle Canal from the slopes of Guanaco Peak, Tierra del Fuego National Park. Guanacos have been introduced on Redonda Island, seen in the foreground. Mountainous Hoste Island, in the background, belongs to Chile.

Once near extinction, guanacos are making a remarkable comeback in the region.

thoroughly lost—240 square miles of very rugged country. The principal feature of the isolated northern part of the park is Lago Fagnano, a 70-mile-long glacier-carved lake that extends into Chile and empties into an arm of the Strait of Magellan. Trout fishing is good in the lake, but access is difficult. The southern part of the park is readily accessible; its entrance lies 8 miles west of Ushuaia. The park has only 11 miles of road, so a tour of the park by car could be completed in a short afternoon, but the park's attributes warrant a more leisurely visit. The southern part of the park encompasses rivers large and small, another large glacial lake, the shore of the Beagle Channel, and several well-marked selfguided interpretive trails, which provide the best means to experience the park.

Three short trails *(senderos)* are of particular interest. The *Sendero Laguna Negra* (Black Lagoon Trail) leads to a small lake well advanced in the process of becoming a sphagnum moss bog *(turbal or pántano). Sendero de los Castores* (Beaver Trail) winds through a series of beaver ponds. Because they are not native, beavers *(Castor canadensis)* are of great interest to South Americans. They were introduced, along with muskrats, to Tierra del Fuego in the 1940s and have flourished in many of the island's streams.

The *Bahia Ensenada* Trails wind along the shore of a bay of the Beagle Channel. Marine mammals are scarce today, but you may catch sight of some interesting flightless birds from this trail. Argentina has three different types of flightless birds. Penguins are one, rheas another, and the third is the flightless steamer duck *(Tachyeres pteneres)*, so named because of its comical method of locomotion. It can't fly, but when in a hurry it runs across the water and madly flaps its wings in circular fashion, whipping up clouds of foam and spray when underway and resembling nothing so much as an old-fashioned paddle-wheeled steamer. These big ducks (up to 14 pounds) can move faster than a man can run by this means, and dive very well.

Longer trails lead from the southern

part of the park to the Chilean border (about a two-hour hike) or north across the mountains to Lago Fagnano, an arduous backpack that requires several days.

Near the Hotel Alakush in the park is a reconstructed Indian village, designed to give visitors some idea of the life led by the original inhabitants of Tierra del Fuego. Of the four tribes with distinct languages and habits that once populated the island, only one survives.

The Haush were nomadic hunter-gatherers driven by more aggressive tribes into the extreme eastern tip of the island. They did not use boats, but lived by hunting guanacos and gathering food from forest and seashore. No Haush survive.

The Onas were the most war-like of the Fuegian tribes. Like the Haush, they were nomadic inland Indians who depended upon the guanaco for their survival. A tall people, with some men over 6 feet, they inhabited the bulk of the island, primarily the treeless steppes of the north and east. The last Ona died in 1969.

The Alacalufs were canoe Indians who lived on the straits and channels of western Tierra del Fuego and the southern coast of Chile. They seldom ventured inland for fear of the fierce Onas and survived exclusively on what they could garner from the sea and seacoasts. Because the lands they occupied were so rugged and isolated, they experienced somewhat less contact with white men than the other tribes. Perhaps for that reason, more Alacalufs have survived into modern times. About twenty Alacalufs are known to be alive, most of whom are settled in the vicinity of Puerto Eden, a tiny village on desolate, rainswept Wellington Island, 300 miles up the Chilean coast.

The Yahgans were also canoe Indians who occupied the southernmost channels and offshore islands of Tierra del Fuego and survived on the rich resources of the coast. They inhabited the coast that is now part of the park and the old shellfish middens seen along

Eerie hands were left in this cave 10,000 years ago by Patagonia's first inhabitants. Cueva de las Manos Park, on the way to the Southern Fishing Zone.

sea trails in the park were most likely created by Yahgan tribesmen. The four Indians taken back to England by Captain Robert Fitzroy on his voyage of 1830 were Yahgans. These Indians were given the Dickensian names of York Minster, Jemmy Button, Boat Memory, and Fuegia Basket, and were presented to the Queen. When Captain Fitzroy returned the three survivors to Tierra del Fuego three years later (Boat Memory had died in England), one of the other members of the ship's company was a young naturalist with an enormous destiny before him—Charles Darwin.

Facilities and services for visitors abound in Ushuaia. Every first-class hotel and any of a half-dozen or so travel agencies offer trips by bus, boat, or private vehicle to just about anywhere in Tierra del Fuego, including Cape Horn. Trips can even be arranged to Antarctica from Ushuaia, although under most circumstances they are very costly. Be advised that because of its remote location, prices of all goods and services are significantly higher in Tierra del Fuego than elsewhere in Argentina and that its hotels fill up quickily during the short summer season.

Part 3—PREPARATIONS

REGULATIONS

The thought of devoting a chapter to fishing regulations caused me several sleepless nights, for as we all know, fishing regs have inflicted upon mankind some of the dullest and most obtuse language in the history of the written word. Most of us already know the basic principles and don't anticipate that they have changed much in decades, for we learned the fundamentals when we were kids and few of us have read the fine print since. Accordingly, for each new place we fish, we browse quickly through the pamphlet to ferret out essential points, ignore the rest of the information, and get on with our fishing trip.

In the case of Patagonia, however, the regulations are instructive, for they not only lay out rules all fishermen must observe, but also provide insight into Argentine attitudes toward conservation in general and trout fishing in particular. Management of trout fisheries is a relatively new art in Argentina and is evolving rapidly in a cauldron of political, commercial, and conservation interests that are often diametrically opposed. Most fly fishermen who visit Patagonia are uncommonly well-informed with respect to trout habitat and management issues and their opinions are given careful consideration by most Argentines. For this reason, informed visitors should have more than a cursory acquaintance with Patagonian regulations.

In general, fishing regulations for Patagonia bode well for the future of trout and salmon fishing in Argentina. They hold several surprises for North American readers and in many respects are more progressive than North American regulations. They are not perfect, but are several steps up the road toward a system that is fair both to fishermen and to fish.

Patagonia, like Canada, is divided into provinces rather than states. The three fishing zones described in this book involve five provinces: Neuquen, Río Negro, Chubut, Santa Cruz, and Tierra del Fuego. In addition to provincial land, federal jurisdictions are involved, principally national park lands. As in the United States, most flowing waters are property of the federal government and a complicated, overlapping framework of laws purports to balance the interests of the public and of private landowners.

The *general* fishing regulations are hammered out in meetings attended by representatives of the four northernmost provinces (Tierra del Fuego works out its own regulations) and the national park service. At these meetings, regulations are established that are agreeable to all parties; they become the general regulations. Later, each province and the national park service promulgate specific regulations for particular waters under their own jurisdiction. The general and *specific* regulations are then published together, usually on a single sheet of paper.

Although Neuquen Province occasionally prints regulations in English, they are normally printed in Spanish, of no use to most visiting fly fishermen, who must rely on their guides for meeting the letter of the law. The regulations are slightly confusing, so take careful note of signs near trout streams. (I have unwittingly fished in closed waters and have also observed guided clients fishing in closed waters.) Avoid possible embarrassment by reminding your guide to obtain your license for you, and by asking if he knows the cur-

---

Page 79: The small and fertile Río Quillen is, in the author's experience, the best dry fly stream in the Northern Fishing Zone.

The upper Río Carrileufu, Butch Cassidy country and trout and salmon country.

rent regulations.

The following synopsis of regulations is based upon the 1989-90 fishing season, and is intended to be illustrative rather than comprehensive; do not assume that the regulations described below will be in effect when you are in Patagonia. The regulations change frequently, and it is incumbent upon each visiting fisherman (and his guide) to acquaint himself with all current laws.

GENERAL REGULATIONS

The general regulations are about what you would anticipate. Only one outfit can be used at a time, use of explosives, guns, nets, and other devices are prohibited, and so on. But several specifics, listed below, could be well employed in some parts of North America.

General Season. Opens the first Saturday in November, and closes Easter Day, about mid-April. (The season in Tierra del Fuego is generally several weeks shorter than this season.)

Fishing Licenses. Required. A license bought for any of the Andean-Patagonian national parks or any of the Patagonian provinces (except Tierra del Fuego) is valid in all of them.

Approximate 1990-1991 prices:

Foreign Non-Resident, Season
$35.00 U.S.
Foreign Non-resident, 30-day
$18.00 U.S.

Additional fees are charged for certain preferential fly fishing only waters, such as the bocas of the Chimehuim and Correntoso Rivers:

Season—$25.00 U.S.
Seven-day—$12.00 U.S.
Daily—$3.00 U.S.

General Size Limits. The metric system is used in Patagonia. Approximate lengths in inches are indicated.

Special size limitations prevail in designated waters.

Rainbow and Brown Trout — 35 cm. minimum (14 inches)

Brook Trout — 30 cm. minimum (12 inches)

Among the more interesting of the general regulations in Patagonia are the following:

1. Fishermen can use only one lure with a single, double, or treble hook (technically, this means that dropper flies are illegal).

2. In fly fishing only and catch-and-release waters, use of barbless hooks is mandatory.

3. Fishing is only permitted between sunup and sundown; night fishing is expressly prohibited.

4. Regulations apply to landlocked salmon, rainbows, browns, brook trout, lake trout, Pacific salmon, creole trout, pejerrey, and carp.

5. In all national parks, the following native species must be returned to the water: trout-perch, pejerrey, bagre, and puyen.

6. Fishing from boats within 500 meters of a river boca or 150 meters of a creek boca is prohibited (your guide can bring you closer to a boca in a boat, but you must get out of the boat to fish).

7. Poor people are expressly permitted to use "latitas" or "tarritos" to fish (an ingenious method of spinning using monofilament and a tin can, described in a following chapter).

8. Fishing from boats in streams is expressly prohibited, except in designated waters.

9. It is against regulations to "hog" a boca, enter a stream less than 100

Lanín Volcano and monkey puzzle trees, from Paso Tromen.

meters downstream from another fishermen, or disturb another fisherman (good fishing manners institutionalized).

10. Fishing derbies or similar promotions are required to observe these regulations.

SPECIFIC REGULATIONS
NATIONAL PARKS

Daily Bag Limit. Two salmonids (not including landlocked salmon) per person, not to exceed 20 per season.

Nahuel Huapi National Park.

Fly fishing only waters: Ríos Machico, Bonito, Traful, and upper Manso.

Fly fishing only *and* catch-and-release waters: upper Río Traful.

Lanin National Park.

Waters closed to fishing: Río Escorial, Lagunas Toro, Escorial, and Huaca Mamuil, Lago Hui Hui.

Fly fishing only waters: Ríos Curruhue, Hermoso, Filo Hua Hum, Quillen Verde, and Paimun; Lago Curruhue Grande.

Fly fishing only *and* catch-and-release waters: Ríos Meliquina, Paimun, Filo Hua Hum, and Malleo (within park boundaries).

SPECIFIC REGULATIONS
NEUQUEN PROVINCE

Bag Limit. Rainbow, brown, and brook trout, *not* landlocked salmon.

Season — 20 fish
Month — 12 fish
Week — 8 fish
Day — 2 fish

1. It is illegal to cause riparian vegetation to be destroyed.
2. Fishing from boats is permitted only on designated rivers—Limay, Collon Cura, Aluminé, and Neuquen. Use of motors with boats, however, is prohibited.

3. The use of boats (or tubes) is expressly prohibited on the Ríos Malleo, Chimehuin, Curruhue, and Quilquihue.
4. Camping is permitted only on islands of the Caleufu River.

DESIGNATED WATERS
REGULATIONS
Neuquen Province.

1. Upper Río Neuquen Drainage: daily limit, 2 trout, 4 trout-perch.
2. Río Limay Drainage: daily limit, 2 trout (no landlocked salmon).
3. Upper Río Aluminé: catch-and-release; use of barbless hooks mandatory.
4. Río Caleufu: fly fishing only; daily limit one trout over 60 centimeters (20 inches).
5. Río Correntoso: fly fishing only, barbless hooks mandatory; daily limit, one trout over 60 cm. (24 inches); extra daily provincial rod fee.
6. Río Curruhue: catch-and-release, barbless hooks mandatory.
7. Río Chimehuin.

Zone 1: from boca to start of *Garganta del Diablo* (Devil's Throat Rapids) [about one half mile], fly fishing only, barbless hook mandatory; daily limit, one trout over 80 cm. (31.5 inches); extra daily provincial rod fee.

Zone 2: remaining river, daily limit, one trout.

8. Lower Río Litrán: fly fishing only.
9. Río Malleo.

Zone 1: upper river: catch-and-release, barbless hooks mandatory.

Zone 2: remaining river: daily limit, 2 trout under 30 cm. (12 inches).

10. Río Quilquihue: catch-and-release, barbless hooks mandatory.
11. Río Quillen: fly fishing only.

SPECIFIC REGULATIONS
RIO NEGRO PROVINCE

Bag Limit. Two trout per day, not to exceed 20 trout per season. Limit in Río Limay is one trout per day. One landlocked salmon per day.

Size Limits. In fly fishing only waters, minimum size limit is 60 cm. (24 inches).

Rainbow and Brown Trout—35 cm. minimum (14 inches)

Brook Trout—30 cm. minimum (12 inches)

Designated waters: Boca of Río Limay fly fishing only.

SPECIFIC REGULATIONS
CHUBUT PROVINCE

Season. Same as general season, but with specific seasons for specific species in designated waters.

Fly fishing only waters: upper Río Carrileufu, Arroyo Pescado, Río Unión, upper Río Corcovado; daily limit two trout per day, same size restrictions as Río Negro Province.

Landlocked salmon: daily limit one fish, not to exceed three fish per season.

SPECIFIC REGULATIONS
SANTA CRUZ PROVINCE

Bag Limit. Trout, four fish per day; landlocked salmon, one fish per day.

Size Limits. Rainbow, brown trout, and landlocked salmon: 30 cm. minimum (12 inches).

Brook trout: 25 cm. minimum (10 inches).

Lake trout: 40 cm. minimum (16 inches).

LOS GLACIARES NATIONAL PARK

Brook trout: 30 cm. minimum (12 inches).

All other trout and char: 50 cm. minimum (20 inches).

In Chubut Province, it is illegal to enter a stream within 250 meters of another fisherman, or to troll within one kilometer (1000 meters) of a boca (inlet or outlet).

SPECIFIC REGULATIONS
PROVINCE OF TIERRA DELFUEGO

Regulations are promulgated by the provincial administration in cooperation with fishing clubs in the cities of Río Grande and Ushuaia.

Season. Usually from November 1 to March 31.

Bag Limit. Two fish per day.

Size Limits. Landlocked salmon: 40 cm. minimum (16 inches).

All other species: 35 cm. minimum (14 inches).

This summary of regulations indicates that the intention of Argentine authorities is not only to protect and maintain healthy trout populations, but by promoting fly fishing, to maintain high quality fishing as well.

The road to Hell, of course, is paved with good intentions and the real value of any regulations lies in the will and ability of a governing body to enforce existing laws. In Patagonia, people in fact fish in closed waters, kill more fish than the law permits, and routinely ignore size and tackle restrictions. This is due in part to public ignorance—not many years ago there were virtually no regulations—and in part to the lack of regulatory presence in the fishing zones.

In the economic chaos in which Argentina is currently embroiled, neither federal nor provincial authorities have sufficient resources (staff, horses, vehicles, radios, and so on) to rigorously enforce these regulations. But the economy will change and even under current restraints, enforcement of fishing regulations has increased dramatically. During the decades that I have fished Patagonian streams, for example, nobody bothered to check my license and I saw not one game warden. Yet during the last season, 2,723 fishermen were checked by provincial authorities in the area of Junín de los Andes alone. And when the economy does turn around, a good set of regulations to back up game wardens will be in place.

The lovely Río Colon Cura may soon become the bottom of a long reservoir as a result of a massive hydro-electric project.

Just because the laws are on the books, however, does not mean that the Patagonian trout and salmon fishery is safe and sound. . .

Several problems, some quite serious, threaten our future fishing trips to Patagonia: dams, poaching, introduction of new exotic fish species, overfishing, and deterioration of riparian habitat.

Dams. Hydroelectric engineers have long cast covetous eyes on the swift streams of the southern Andes and considerable damage has already been done to trout streams. In the Northern Zone, about 60 miles of the lower Río Limay and the lower reaches of the Río Traful have been converted into a reservoir by construction of the Alicura dam. Construction of the Piedra del Aguila dam now threatens the Collon Cura River, and lower reaches of the Caleufu and Chimehuin Rivers, three of the finest trout streams in the southern hemisphere. Proposed construction of yet a third dam threatens the remaining upper reaches of the Río Limay. In the Central Zone, a chain of three alpine lakes of extraordinary scenic quality (located within Los Alerces National Park) has been converted into a single large reservoir by construction of the Futaleufu Dam. The energy lobby is powerful in Argentina, and at this writing, the only active opponents to

dam construction are fishing guides, a few fishermen, and most of the residents of of the communities of Junín de los Andes and San Martín de los Andes. A few farsighted Patagonian businessmen are beginning to realize that their best long-term interests lie in preserving rather than destroying trout streams and the threat has eased for the moment since Argentina's economic difficulties have slowed dam construction projects. But when the country recovers, the hydroelectric engineers are sure to be back.

Poaching. As I have mentioned, effective enforcement of fishing regulations is beginning to improve in Patagonia. But until park and provincial authorities are able to implement a program of frequent, routine patrols of trout streams, poaching will continue to be a serious threat to the fishery. The problem is related to Argentine dining preferences. Fresh or smoked trout or salmon are considered to be delicacies as hors d'oeuvres or full meals in Argentina and command premium prices in restaurants throughout the country, particularly in resort areas. Commercial trout and salmon hatcheries have been established to meet this demand, but poachers and unscrupulous restaurateurs can profit handsomely

Trout such as this are sometimes poached and sold in major Argentine cities.

with fish taken illegally from public waters. The scale of poaching varies widely, from a few fish killed and quietly sold to restaurants in Junín, San Martín, or Bariloche to large scale efforts involving refrigerated trucks ready to carry their illicit cargo to Buenos Aires. Visiting fishermen can help in a small way to discourage this practice by refusing to order trout in any form from Argentine menus.

Introduction of New Exotics. The Argentine and Japanese governments are cooperating in an experimental program involving commercial production of a small, but fast-growing Sakura Pacific salmon *(Onchorhynchus masou)* native to northern Japan and the northeast coast of the Soviet Union. Experiments are underway in waters adjacent to well-established Patagonian trout streams and some Argentine biologists are concerned that the experiments are not monitored with sufficient care to prevent escape of these salmon into Patagonian waters, an event that could have catastrophic and irreversible effects upon the existing fishery.

Overfishing. Licit fishing pressure on Patagonian trout streams has increased dramatically in recent years and is likely to continue to increase. In my view, this pressure has not yet made significant inroads on trout populations,

Arroyo Pescado: trout waters in a putting green, with ubiquitous sheep and black-necked swans.

but if effective enforcement of regulations does not keep pace with the increase in fishing pressure, overfishing could become a significant problem in decades to come.

Deterioration of Riparian Habitat. Even under the best of conditions, with teams of range specialists, reams of baseline data, and unlimited funds, it is difficult to determine and if necessary correct degradation of range and riparian habitat, principally because annual changes in vigor and species composition of plant communities are so slow as to be nearly imperceptible. Upper reaches of most Patagonian streams in the Northern and Central Zones lie within national parks and although forest fires and cattle grazing pose some threat to these headwater streams, the habitat is in generally good condition. In the lower reaches of these streams, however, particularly in the Central and Southern Zones, adverse effects of domestic grazing, especially goats, are beginning to appear. Excessive sedimentation and loss of tall streamside vegetation (which affects habitat diversity, stream productivity, and temperature) are the most serious results of overgrazing and their negative impacts on salmonid populations are slow but sure. Conditions may not yet drastic, but the warning signs are up, and warrant the attention of appropriate Argentine authorities.

Chilean chinook salmon, like this ocean-caught 40 pounder, migrate up streams originating in Argentina to spawn.

PATAGONIAN GUIDES

It is possible to fish most of the streams in Patagonia without a professional fishing guide, but doing it yourself is not for everyone. If you have limited time (say ten days to two weeks), speak no Spanish, are a relatively inexperienced fly fisherman, are particular about the standard of your meals and accommodations, or are unprepared or unequipped to camp out, you would be wise to purchase a package fishing trip or to hire a guide.

In deciding whether or not to conduct your own fishing trip or to hire a guide, you must give careful consideration to the objectives of your trip. If you set out to do a trip on your own, this book will help, but as mentioned in the introduction, it is not intended to be a substitute for a guide.

Patagonian guides are an interesting group of professionals. They are intensively competitive among themselves and understandably secretive about the waters they frequent. On the other hand, they are a relatively small group and help one another freely when circumstances warrant. In general a jovial group, they range from urbane, well-traveled fishermen who will discuss geopolitics or fly fishing around the world while sitting at a vise tying up a batch of flies for the next stretch of water to men whose experience is limited to the few rivers on which they have spent their entire lives and with which they are supernaturally intimate. Most are familiar with modern trends in fly fishing and are accustomed to the expectations and values of North American fly fishermen. Some speak English fluently, others struggle with a few English phrases; all will see that their clients catch fish, often when nobody else is managing to hook anything.

Despite their small numbers, the influence of Patagonian guides on Patagonian trout fishing is far more important than that of their North American counterparts. Because of their constant, close contact with large numbers of North American fly fishermen, they have observed a wide variety of North American fly fishing techniques and ethics. By and large, they admire these techniques and ethics and have adopted most of them. In Argentina, many guides are viewed as role models by their countrymen and by this means exert a strong influence on the development of fishing ethics in the country. Patagonian guides are generally among the first Argentine fishermen who adopt the use of light tackle, dry flies, and barbless hooks, and who adopt personal policies of catch-and-release on all waters. Other Argentine fishermen follow suit and soon these techniques become familiar, if not popular, to the general Argentine fly fishing public.

As in North America, many Patagonian guides have been in the forefront of fierce, ongoing political struggles required to establish such progressive regulations as protective stream closures, catch-and-release rules, and fly fishing only waters. The guides have also fought hard to forestall construction of several dams on rivers which support outstanding trout populations. These tasks are no easier to accomplish in Argentina than in the United States and in many respects much more difficult. Patagonian guides deserve a great deal of credit for their role in resisting destructive development and in establishing far-sighted fisheries management policies.

Guide fees vary widely, usually depending upon the guide's reputation, standard of accommodations, number of fishermen in your party, length of stay, and in some instances, the waters you arrange to fish. In 1990, rates ranged from $150 to $350 per day, exclusive of transportation to and from Patagonia, all else included. A few Patagonian

Fly fishermen and their guide fishing the boca of the Río Arrayanes.

guides have exclusive contracts with American firms that package fishing trips, but you can contact guides directly at the addresses which follow, and work out arrangements that fit your needs by mail (unreliable), telephone, or fax.

The professional guiding industry in Argentina is expanding rapidly these days to meet a burgeoning demand and a host of relatively inexperienced Argentine fishermen are converting themselves into "guides" by merely printing up a batch of attractive cards. We all have to start somewhere, and some of these newcomers will surely become the next generation of successful fishing guides. In all my conversations with established Argentine guides, I indicated that I wished to make a list of competent *fly fishing* guides available to readers, but made clear that I would make no recommendations for individual guides (or resorts). That policy permitted

guides to discuss themselves and others freely and enabled me to compile the following list of guides with considerable confidence. The list has been reviewed by professionals who clearly command their colleagues' respect and who head professional guide associations.

Patagonian guides share a mild disdain for their Argentine colleagues who do not live in the region year round, and who come to Patagonia only during summer months to guide their clients. While the Patagonians may envy the lives of guides who enjoy the benefits of living in cosmopolitan Buenos Aires for most of the year, the attitude reflects more than envy or professional jealousy. Guides who make their homes in Patagonia know local residents very well—and in Argentina, personal contacts are everything; they know what to do and where to go quickly in case of emergencies; they know the likely effect of local weather on fishing; they know what to expect on rivers and streams as a result of the prior winter's snowfall, and so on. For these reasons, and because this book is about Patagonia, the guides listed below are all Argentines and permanent residents of Patagonia.

Most Argentine fishermen and experienced North American fishermen readily acknowledge that the best known and longest established fly fishing guides in Patagonia are Recardo Ameijeiras, Jorge Graziosi, Raúl San Martín, and Jorge Trucco, but there are many other competent and personable guides in the region and in the country. Those who are long established in Patagonia and who specialize in guiding fly fishermen are listed below. Names are arranged by zone in accordance with each guide's address. The zones are my own device; please note that a particular guide's activities and areas of expertise are *not* restricted to the zone in which his name appears. Most guides work in more than one zone.

NORTHERN ZONE — Junín de los Andes, San Martín de los Andes

Gustavo Olsen/Ariel Semenov
Safaris Especiales
Avda. San Martín 461, Oficina 4
8370 San Martín de los Andes
Provincia del Neuquen, Argentina
Telephone and Fax: 0972-27572

Carlos Trisciuzzi
Patagonian Fly fishing
Laura Vicuña 144
(8371) Junín de los Andes
Provincia del Neuquen, Argentina
Telephone: 0944-91234

Jorge Trucco
Patagonia Outfitters
Pérez 662
8370 San Martín de los Andes
Provincia del Neuquen, Argentina
Telephone and Fax: 0972-27561

BARILOCHE ZONE — San Carlos de Bariloche

Ricardo Ameijeiras
Galería Austral
Mitre 125
San Carlos de bariloche 8400

Provincia del Río Negro, Argentina
Telephone: 0944-23763

Jorge Graziosi
Safaris Acuaticos
20 de Febrero 798
8400 San Carlos de Bariloche
Provincia del Río Negro, Argentina
Telephone: 0944-25521
Fax: 944-25521

Diego Gugliemi
Casilla de Correo 1342
8400 San Carlos de Bariloche
Provincia del Río Negro, Argentina
Telephone: 0944-22314

CENTRAL ZONE — Esquel, El Bolson, Cholila

Fernando Gullino
9 de Julio 1451
9200 Esquel
Provincia del Chubut, Argentina
Telephone: 0945-2133

Raúl San Martín
Avda. Fontana 449
9200 Esquel
Provincia del Chubut, Argentina
Telephone and Fax: 0945-2024

SOUTHERN ZONE (Tierra del Fuego) — Río Gallegos, Río Grande

Fernando de las Carreras
Avenida Pte. Roque Saenz Peña 547, Piso 3
1035 Capital Federal, Argentina
Telephone: 30-1158

Juan Lincomán
Mackinlay 557
Río Grande
Tierra del Fuego, Argentina
Telephone: 0964-22570

There are relatively few fishing lodges in Patagonia; those few are very popular because of their unique charm, because they are located on or near a particular stream, or because they are the only accommodations available in a certain region. Some guides are associated with specific fishing lodges; most will arrange accommodations for their clients in some of these lodges at one time or other during a trip because they are convenient to certain streams.

Readers who wish to contact the lodges directly will find the following list of locations and accommodation addresses useful:

NORTHERN ZONE

Hostería Chimihuin
(on lower Río Chimehuin in the town of Junín de los Andes)
Coronel Suárez y 25 de Mayo
8371 Junín de los Andes
Provincia del Neuquen, Argentina
Telephone: 0944-91132
Telex: 80767 AR Hostería Chimehuin

Estancia La Ofelia
(facilities on Lago Quillen and Río Quillen)
Contact Marcelo Morales
M. T. Alvear 624, 8°, "76"
(1058) Buenos Aires, Argentina
Telephone and Fax: 72-2423

Hostería Paimun
(on narrows between Lago Paimun and Lago Huechulauf-quen)
Junín de los Andes
Provincia del Neuquen, Argentina

El Refugio del Pescador
(on northwest shore of Lago Huechulaufquen)
Junín de los Andes
Provincia del Neuquen, Argentina

Estancia Ranquilco
(on middle reaches of Río Trocoman)
8349 El Huecú
Provincia del Neuquen, Argentina
Fax: 011-54-972-27020

Estancia San Huberto
(on middle reaches of Río Malleo)
Avda. San Martín 461, Oficina 4
8370 San Martín de los Andes
Provincia del Neuquen, Argentina
Telephone and Fax: 0972-27572

Estancia San Ignacio
(on lower Río Alumine, near con-fluences of Río Malleo and Río Catan Lil)
Perez 662
8370 San Martín de los Andes
Provincia del Neuquen, Argentina
Telephone and Fax: 0972-27561

BARILOCHE ZONE

Estancia Arroyo Verde
(on Río Traful)
M.T. de Alvear 1381, Piso 4, No. 42
1058 Buenos Aires, Argentina
Telephone: 802-2346/42-8977/8799
Fax: 799-2682

Hotel Correntoso
(at confluence of Río Correntoso and Lago Nahuel Huapi)
Villa La Angostura
Provincia del Neuquen, Argentina

Estancia La Primavera
(on Río Traful)
Talcahuano 768, Piso 10
1013 Buenos Aires, Argentina
Telephone: 45-3915/46-9123

Hosteria Ruca Malen
(on westernmost shore of Lago Correntoso)
Villa La Angostura
Provincia del Neuquen, Argentina

CENTRAL ZONE

Hostería Cume Hue
(on eastern shore of Lago Futalaufquen)
Villa Futalaufquen
Provincia del Chubut, Argentina

Hotel Futalaufquen
(on western shore of Lago Futalaufquen)
Villa Futalaufquen
Provincia del Chubut, Argentina

Hostería Quimé Quipán
(on eastern shore of Lago Futalaufquen)
Casilla de Correo 73, Esquel
Provincia del Chubut, Argentina
Radiotelephone:
0944-22622/22272;
call AZG35 Quimé Quipán

SOUTHERN ZONE

Hotel Bella Vista
(on middle reaches of Río Gallegos)
Casilla de Correo 245
9400 Río Gallegos
Provincia del Santa Cruz, Argentina

Estancia Truchaike
(on lower reaches of Río Gallegos)
Contact Marcelo Morales

M. T. Alvear 624, 8°, "76"
(1058) Buenos Aires, Argentina
Telephone and Fax: 72-24233
Kau-Tapen Lodge
(on upper Río Grande, Tierra del
Fuego)
Avda. Pte. Roque Saenz Peña 547,
Piso 3
1035 Capital Federal, Argentina
Telephone: 30-1158

At the time this book was going to print, I learned about a new project. Argentine-born Enrique Poodts, a former IBM International executive now living in Bariloche and professional guide and fly-shop owner Ricardo Ameijeiras are in early stages of forming Fly Fishing Andes, a network of fly fishing lodges throughout Patagonia—three in the Northern Zone, one in the Central Zone, two in the Southern Zone, and two more planned for Chile. For further information, they can be reached at:

Fly Fishing Andes
C.C. 1549
8400 Bariloche
Provincia del Rio Negro, Argentina
Telephone: 0944-41944
Fax: 0944-60025

Finally, there are among you those who are not inclined to adventure about, and who simply prefer to worry about no more than picking up a rod and catching fish. You may consider any of a number of firms that have experience in offering international fly fishing packages, among them:

Angler Adventures
Box 872
Old Lyme, CT 06371

Destinations
Dan Bailey's Fly Shop
P.O. Box 1019
Livingston, MT 59047

Frontiers
P.O. Box 959
Wexford, PA 15090

Shoshone Wilderness Adventures
P.O. Box 634
Dubois, WY 82513

World Angler
33855 La Plata Ave.
Pine, CO 80470

Let us return to the topic of managing your own fishing trip to Patagonia. I have been doing it for nearly 30 years, but have had several advantages: I speak Spanish fairly well, have lived in Latin America for several years, have a number of friends in Patagonia, and have often had my own means of transportation (vans or cars). On my last trip, I met four other North Americans traveling and fishing without guides and heard of several others doing the same thing. The number of people fishing on their own in Patagonia has increased sharply in recent years and is likely to continue to increase as demand for the services of skilled fishing guides exceeds the supply.

Can you do it yourself? Well, some of you can, but others can not, and should not try. As mentioned, the decision depends entirely upon your personal circumstances and your fishing objectives. If your objectives are narrow that is, you wish to explore a specific stream you've heard or read about, or want to fish only for sea trout or for Atlantic salmon, or if you have only a few days—you should hire a guide, for he will take care of a host of puzzling, time-consuming details, right down to selecting the flies and wines.

There are other reasons to hire guides. According to Argentine law, all rivers and the land for 35 meters to either side of high water mark is public property. If you are within this zone, you are not trespassing, and cannot be evicted. Private land is private land in Argentina as elsewhere and without permission you cannot cross it to reach a stream. You can walk along a stream from a bridge where it is crossed by a public road, of course, but many Argentine estancias are so large that, in effect, they may control access to many miles of river. Most estancia owners readily grant fishermen permission to cross their lands to reach a stream, but some owners who have fishing lodges or business arrangements with guides do not grant permission, and the only way to gain access to streams that cross their property is through a guide. One way to beat this problem is to float the river and another reason to hire a guide is to make use of his boats. It is nearly impossible to rent a boat or inflatable for river-floating in Argentina without hiring a guide along with the boat.

Although some waters are virtually inaccessible without the services of a guide, hundreds of miles of Patagonian trout streams are readily accessible, provided you have means of transportation. All of the streams in Patagonia's many national parks are, of course, accessible to fishermen.

You should arrange your own fishing trip to Patagonia with eyes wide open. Distances are immense, back roads are rough and often unmarked, national and international communications are often unreliable, portions of Patagonia are *extremely* remote, gas stations and repair facilities are scarce in many areas, backcountry accommodations may be rough or absent altogether, and medical facilities may be primitive.

These are hardly conditions amenable to tight schedules, but on the other hand, they are the ingredients of first class adventures and are part of the reason that fishing is still so good in Patagonia. It should be clear that the most important prerequisite for setting up your own fishing trip to Patagonia is time—and plenty of it. The pace of life in Argentina is slower than that to which North Americans are accustomed; it simply takes longer to get things done there, especially when, as a stranger, you don't quite know how things do get done. A month is about the minimum time required to carry out your own trip the first time, for a good week will be taken up in learning the ropes—what to eat, how to rent a room, when the stores are open, where to change money, how

to find maps, where to rent cars, where to go, when the bridge will be fixed, how to get a flat tire fixed, buy a fishing license, and so on. Six to eight weeks would be better for a good, solid exploration and lots of fishing.

A second prerequisite is adaptability. If you are determined to fish on your own and can deal with these sorts of problems without getting uptight, you can have a fine time in Patagonia and there are a number of ways to make your task easier and cheaper. First, try to organize a small group of fishing pals, say four. You'll need to arrange transportation, and the cost of a rented van is not bad at all when split four ways. Similarly, hotel rooms are proportionately cheaper for two or more persons than for one. Second, try to ensure that one of your party can still remember a bit from his high school or college Spanish classes. It is not essential to speak Spanish to fish in Patagonia—last year I met and fished for several days with an amiable 70-year-old Connecticut Yankee who had been happily fishing by himself for a month with a rented car and who spoke not one word of Spanish. Most Patagonians are polite and patient with fishermen struggling to make themselves understood. Sign language works most of the time, but if you can speak and understand just a little Spanish, it may prevent you from taking the wrong road, ordering up broiled brains instead of an omelet, or buying a round-trip ticket to Madagascar.

To sum up, there is no simple answer to the question, should I hire a guide to fish in Argentina? Some of you, under some circumstances, will need and appreciate the services of a guide who, in Patagonia, will give you insight not only into fishing, but into many other dimensions of another country and its culture. A sizable group of experienced and affable guides are available to you.

Others of you will do just fine without a guide. It will take you longer to figure out where to go and how to get there, but you'll have a good time just the same.

WHAT TO TAKE & WHEN TO GO

The correct answer to the question of what to take with you to Patagonia is as little as possible.

I have not once been wise enough to follow this advice and invariably take far more with me than I really need; I probably always will. Few fly fishermen I know would be caught dead on a stream without some favored article of attire, some treasured gadget, or at least 300 flies. It is reasonable, then, to assume that you are inevitably going to pack away a few items that will never see the light of a Patagonian day.

On a few occasions, however, I have found that I did *not* have something I really could have used. Accordingly, I'd like to help you to avoid repeating those mistakes by listing a few indispensables

and explaining why you ought to have them. The list that follows will not be exhaustive; you've packed for fishing trips before, and I don't like long lists any more than you do. But if you find an item or two that might not have occurred to you, it will have been worth the trouble.

ODDS AND ENDS

1. *Sunscreen.* Take whatever works best for you. Good lotions are hard to find in Argentina and very expensive.

2. *Bug Dope.* One small container will do. You will only occasionally be bothered by bugs, but better to have it.

3. *American Automobile Association Card.* If you plan to drive or rent a car,

Huge portions of Patagonia are bleak, featureless, and empty.

take a AAA card. Certain association privileges are reciprocal and the Argentine Automobile Association *(Automóvil Club Argentino, abbreviated ACA)*, a large nation-wide organization, can be very helpful to foreign travelers. In many cases, a substantial discount on car rentals is offered to ACA or AAA members.

4. *International Driver's License.* Available from AAA for a few dollars, this multi-lingual, official-looking license is technically the only document that entitles you to drive in a foreign country. Take the trouble to get one only if you intend to drive. You can get by with your regular license, but I have found the international license to be very effective with police and at border crossings.

5. *Credit Cards.* Visa and Mastercharge cards are accepted at most upscale hotels and some restaurants in most cities and towns. Always ask first.

6. *Guidebooks.* Several general guides to South America are available. Most of them go out of date quickly and a few are inaccurate or misleading. The single book that is the Bible of experienced South American travelers is The *South American Handbook*, published by Trade and Travel Publications, Ltd. It is revised annually and is expensive, but for years it has been the only comprehensive and trustworthy general guide to the continent. The only guide to South America's national parks available in English is my own book, *South America's National Parks: A Visitor's Guide*, published by The Mountaineers. Both books are available in larger bookstores.

7. *Currency.* For the sake of prudence, keep most of your spending money in the form of traveler's checks. You should also, however, take a stash of dollars in small denominations. They will come in handy when entering or leaving the country, for tips in large cities, and on weekends or holidays when banks and currency exchange houses are closed and you cannot change checks.

8. *Passport.* You need a passport, of course. At this writing, visas are not required for Argentina or Chile.

9. *Sunglasses.* Take a good pair. The extraordinary clarity of Patagonian streams and the brilliance of sunlight in Patagonia's pollution-free atmosphere lend themselves well to the use of polarized fishing glasses.

10. *Business or Personal cards.* Use of cards is more widespread and more important in Argentina than in the United States. Such cards are not only convenient, but also confer a measure of social status upon their holders, if such things interest you.

11. *Snapshots.* Argentines you meet will be politely curious about you and your life. One of the most effective and sincere means of responding to that curiosity is to have a few pictures with you. A snapshot of your wife, husband, kids, house, neighborhood, or dog will warm up a social situation more than anything you might say, and you don't even have to struggle with Spanish or Mapuche to communicate.

CLOTHES

Choice of clothing should be dictated by weather and climate, not style. In most of Patagonia, the climate is benign during fishing season. Days are clear and warm, nights cool. Summer rainstorms develop, but seldom last long. Snow will seldom be a problem. Wind is the major hassle; it can chill you on the sunniest of days, so take a good, waterproof windbreaker under which you can get plenty of clothes. If your schedule permits, buy wool sweaters in Argentina; they are good quality and good bargains. Take levis, a good cap or hat to protect your head and face from wind, sun, and errant flies, and a pair of thermal underwear for inside your waders.

FISHING GEAR

Style and preference dictate one portion of this category; wind dictates

The author shows off a Traful salmon.

another. Include a light rod for small streams and a heavier rod for large rivers and windy days, say five or six and eight or nine-weight rods. Take three or four fly lines and a good assortment of leaders and tippets. Many fly fishermen take sinking lines to Patagonia; I prefer floating lines and floating lines with fast-sinking tips. End tackle should be heavier than that to which you are accustomed. Include tippets to 1X or 0X. Take lightweight stocking-foot waders with felt-sole boots. For most of the season you can wade wet in streams of the Northern Zone, so your boots should be light. Most standard fly patterns and sizes used in the U.S. (wet and dry) work fine in Patagonia, but make sure your fly boxes contain large nymphs, muddlers, and streamers as well. If you have a few salmon flies, take them.

Finally, you may hook some of the largest fish of your career, and in splendid surroundings, so bring a camera.

A note or two on driving in Argentina is warranted.

As I have mentioned, Argentine drivers are aggressive and reckless. You can drive safely there, but you *must* drive as though your life depended on it, because it does. Defensive driving is not just a catchy phrase in Argentina; it is a formula for survival. Drive as if every other driver on the road were trying to kill you, and you'll be fine.

Many Argentine highways and secondary roads are excellent, but others are not. In many parks, for instance, roads are narrow and blind curves and hills are common. "Might makes right" is an operating principle on Argentine roads and trucks and big motor homes do not shrink from asserting that right in most cases. Be ready to give your half of the road over to the larger vehicle, no matter who you think has the right-of-way.

Be cautious about road conditions on remote secondary roads in Central and Southern Patagonia. Many of the precordilleran soils contain a good deal of clay and an excellent dirt road can become hopelessly slick when it gets wet. On many secondary roads, fords rather than culverts or bridges cross small streams or gullies. They are usually well-marked with the sign *Vado*, but approach them with caution, for they are often abrupt and even if the immediate countryside is dry, distant mountain rainstorms may have brought down floodwaters. In some towns, you will see a sign *Lomo de Burro*, "Muleback." They warn you of bumps in the road intended to slow traffic, and they mean business; you won't overlook a mule-back twice.

As you drive about in Patagonia, you will notice that every other driver seems to be waving at you. Sometimes they are, but more often than not they are merely protecting their windshield. For some reason, Argentine drivers believe that if you push your fingers or fist against your windshield, you will prevent it from breaking if gravel kicked up by a passing car strikes it. So when a car approaches you on a gravel road, you will see the driver—and often passengers as well—push out on their windshields. I have no idea if the practice is effective, but I doubt it.

Finally, try to avoid driving at night. Argentine roads are not as well marked for night driving as roads to which American drivers are accustomed.

There is no perfect time to go to Patagonia. The region is just too big and you can't be everywhere at once. Even if you stay for the entire fishing season, you can't have it all; you'll miss something, no matter when you go. Two sets of dates, however, are more or less fixed: fishing seasons and spawning seasons.

Recall that fishing season in the Northern and Central Zones lasts from early November (the first Saturday of November) to Easter Sunday, about mid-April. In Tierra del Fuego the season lasts from early November to the end of March, about two weeks shorter than on the mainland.

Fishing is closed during the height of spawning seasons, of course, but some fish will be gathering at bocas or making runs up rivers in preparation for spawning near the opening or closing dates of the fishing season. Dates reported for spawning sport fish in Argentina vary somewhat according to source and location, but the general spawning seasons are as follow:

Rainbow trout . . . mid-July to mid-Sept.

Brown trout . . . . June and July

Brook trout . . . . May to mid-June

Landlocked Atlantic Salmon . . . . May to mid-June

Fishing is good in Patagonia all season long, but personal affairs aside, a good time to go can be determined by your fishing preferences or style. Are you, for example, a spring or fall fly fisherman? Since I have indicated that fishing is better in some areas early or late in the season, however, I will point out some pros and cons of these two periods.

Early Season
(November-December) — Advantages:

1. Most smaller streams, such as the Quilquihue, Curruhue, Quillen, Filo Hua Hum, and others, will carry good flows and larger fish than in late season.

2. In some places, such as the Boca Correntoso, early season fishing is better than late season fishing.

3. The spring season is in full swing in early season; flowers are blooming, and birds and wildlife are tending their young.

4. You may be in Patagonia for Christmas and New Year's, a festive and exciting season.

A Trocoman rainbow.

**Early Season
(November-December) — Disadvantages:**
1. Late spring runoff may roil some streams in early season.
2. Some larger rivers will not be as wadeable as during late season.
3. You may have to put up with spring storms in early season.

**Late Season
(March-April) — Advantages:**
1. Though I have no data to back it up, it seems to me that late season is less windy than early season.
2. Larger rivers will be lower and more wadeable in late season.
3. In some places, such as the Boca Chimehuin, Rio Traful, and sea trout rivers, late season fishing is better than early season fishing.

4. Fishing waters in the parks are less crowded in late season.

**Late Season
(March-April) — Disadvantages:**
1. Some small rivers become to small for quality fishing in late season.
2. All streams are warmer, some perhaps too warm for good fishing in late season.
3. You may have to put up with fall storms in late season.

As in North America, every fraction of the fishing season has its own particular charms in Patagonia, so don't fret too much about schedules. No matter when you arrive, you'll be catching fish shortly after you set up your rod. . .

Part 4—THE WATERS, NORTH TO SOUTH

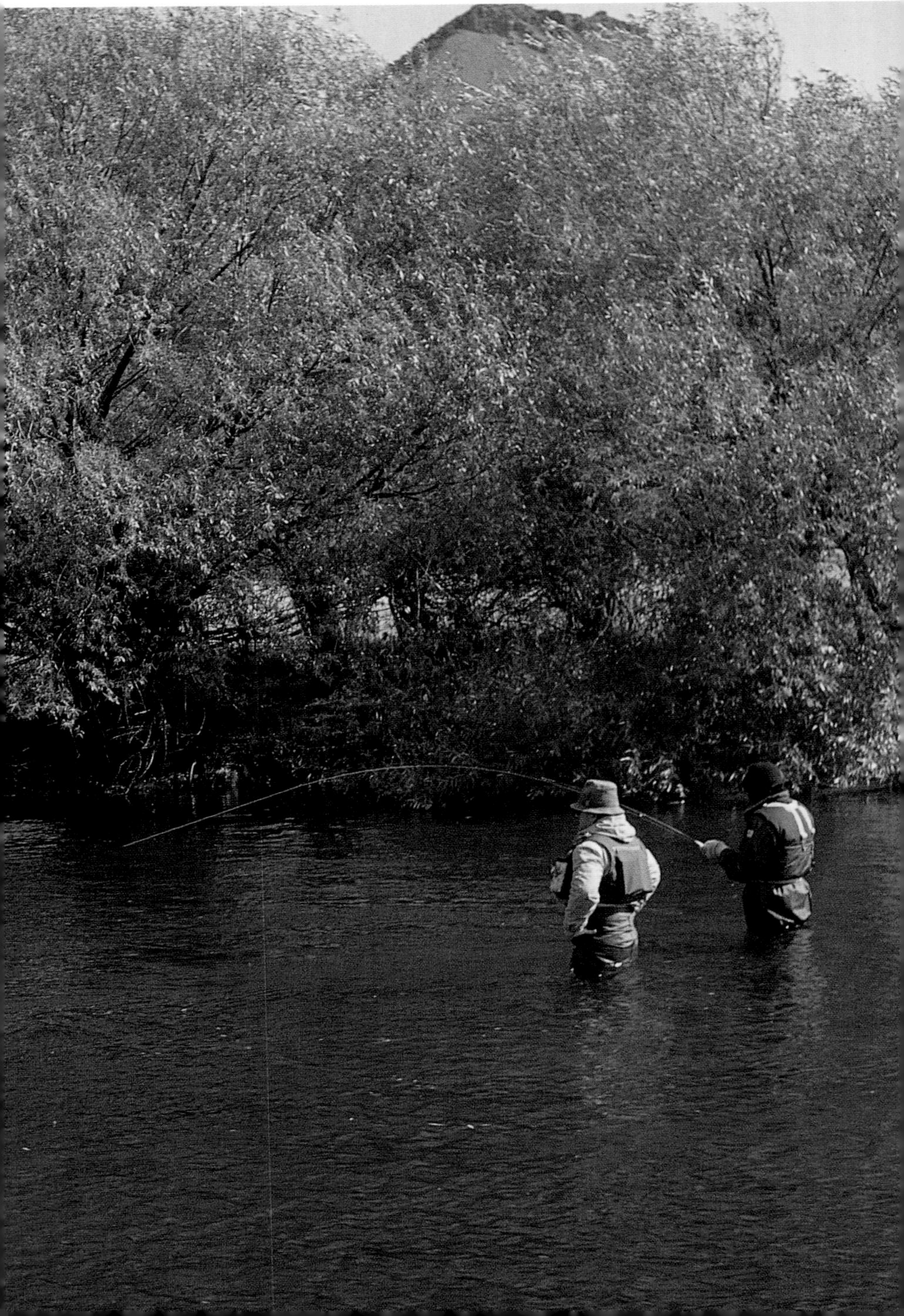

NORTHERN ZONE

The rivers that follow are organized into three Patagonian fishing zones, Northern, Central, and Southern. Within each zone, the streams are organized from north to south.

NORTHERN ZONE

The Northern Zone comprises the provinces of Neuquen and Río Negro, and Lanín and Nahuel Huapi National Parks. Most of the streams in this zone are within the watersheds of the upper Neuquen and Limay Rivers.

Río Trocoman (troh-coh-MAHN). Few, if any, Patagonian rivers are undiscovered, i.e. unfished. Some rivers, however, are fished so seldom that they might as well be unfished, or else fishing pressure is so light as to be insignificant from the perspective of a fly fisherman or biologist. The Río Trocoman is one of these rivers.

Northernmost of the outstanding Patagonian trout streams, the Trocoman is one of the few rivers in this zone that does not begin its run to the sea from a large glacial lake. The river, about 40 miles long, has been fished so seldom because until recently it has been virtually inaccessible. Born in snows of the high naked peaks of the Argentine-Chilean border, most of the river lies about 20 miles from the nearest road suitable for normal vehicles.

The steep uppermost reaches of the Trocoman comprise foaming pocket water, inappropriate in my view for quality fly fishing. In its middle reaches, however, the river acquires solid character. Deep, slow pools wind through steep-walled, shaded canyons, riffles alternate with slickwater runs, dense willow thickets and gravel bars begin to appear and the Trocoman becomes one of those rivers with physical attributes that fly fishermen dream of.

And it is full of rainbow trout. . .

The Trocoman is a delight to fish because every type of water in which experienced fishermen would expect to find trout indeed holds trout. Thigh-deep riffles hold fish as large as you would expect to catch in deep pools and in long, calm runs you can fish for rainbows as though for browns, casting under willows and in quiet, foam-streaked back-eddies; the rainbows are there and they will come out for your fly.

The middle reaches of the Río Trocoman flow through an estancia named Ranquilco (rahn-KEEL-coh), which can be reached only by horseback, tractor, or air. For 12 years the estancia has been owned by an American family who have devoted most of their efforts to building up and improving the estancia's cattle herd and operating the estancia in the time-honored tradition of Argentine ranching. But for careful stewardship, little attention was paid to the river. In 1989, however, the family decided to make the Trocoman accessible to a limited number of fishermen by flying clients to the estancia and providing services that enable them to fish without interfering with routine ranch activities. The owners of Estancia Ranquilco are determined to maintain the very high quality of fishing the Río Trocoman now offers; Ranquilco clients are expected to fish with flies and to observe catch-and-release ethics.

Facilities at this remote, self-sufficient estancia are comfortable. Firewood or propane provide for hot water and an ancient water turbine fur-

Under the appraising eye of his guide, a client plays a Malleo rainbow.

Estancia Ranquilco.

nishes electricity. The main guest facility is appointed in colonial style, rooms are spacious, and meat and fresh vegetables served at meals are raised on the grounds.

I wish to emphasize that Ranquilco is not a fishing ranch on which a few cattle are raised; it is rather a cattle ranch to which a few fishermen are invited. The Ranquilco experience is part fishing, of course, but it is also in part seeing what an estancia is really like, how it operates, and what genuine self-sufficiency is all about. Ranquilco is a working ranch, kept in operation by gauchos who live and work on the grounds and maintain the skills and independent life style for which they are renowned. The atmosphere at Ranquilco is informal and guests who tire of fishing in the river may ride to hot springs or to a pair of small trout lakes near the Chilean border, or may involve themselves in the working life of the ranch to the extent their energy, skills, or curiosity permit.

Estancia Ranquilco is for adventurous fishermen. Headquarters lie about a half-mile from the airstrip, perched at the edge of a canyon overlooking the river. Once you've landed, the only way to reach the ranch buildings or the 12 miles of river that flow through the ranch is on your own two feet, on a sheepskin saddle astride one of Ranquilco's many fine horses, or on the seat of an inflatable raft, from which you will have to return by foot or horseback. While facilities are more than adequate—a French-trained chef is often in attendance—Ranquilco is not a place for visitors who expect to be delivered to streamside in a car or van, or who demand the creature comforts of a luxury resort. They won't get them and if they did, they'd miss the whole zenny point of the estancia, its staff, and its fishing.

In the Mapuche tongue, Trocoman means "condor huddled against the cold" and the name, like so many other Mapuche names, is appropriate. Condors are common along this high Andean stream that winds through valleys separating high, rather forbidding peaks. Along the river fishermen are also likely to see Andean gulls, tero-teros, doves *(palomas)*, bandurrias, and neotropical cormorants. Dragonflies and damselflies are common along the river and though caddis-cases are plentiful on the streambed, only a few caddisflies appear during daylight hours. Pancoras are abundant, however, which probably accounts for the success of black wooly-buggers, flies that appear to select for larger fish on this river.

T.A. Carrithers beams about a Trocoman rainbow.

T.A. Carrithers plays a Trocoman rainbow.

Action on the Trocoman is nonstop. Over a three-day interval last season, during which I fished a few hours each day with two companions, my notes indicate that I released 5 fish over three pounds the first day, 15 over three pounds the second day, and 11 over three pounds the third day. Fishing through Hour-long Pool, Fast-breaking Run, Horse Swimming Pool, Five-pound Pool, and The Chute, two of us frequently had fish on at the same time, and once all three of us were dealing with large trout. The largest fish we released weighed six pounds. All were rainbows, except for a few two-pound trout-perch, which took our flies with great enthusiasm, fought with surprising vigor, and managed to stab each of us with their stiff, slimy spines.

Dry flies are not very popular, but almost any well-presented wet fly is effective; muddler patterns, small streamers, and small bucktails work very well indeed.

The Trocoman varies in width from about 30 to 50 feet and is eminently wadeable; it is easily crossed at most riffles on a firm substrate of small cobbles.

Among the few drawbacks of the Río Trocoman are creatures called *tábanos*, inch-long horseflies that literally chew a cylinder of flesh from your body if given opportunity. Fortunately, they are nearly as slow and witless as they are voracious, but the distraction spoils a good many casts and plays hell with your concentration.

On the other hand, one of the great advantages the Trocoman has over almost every other Patagonian stream is a refreshing, conspicuous lack of wind. Fresh afternoon breezes sometimes flow down the valley, but compared to the hard winds that plague fly fishermen elsewhere in Patagonia, these breezes are of no consequence.

The nearest town of any size to Ranquilco is Chos Malal, in northern Neuquen Province, but visitors to Ranquilco are most likely to arrive by small plane from Chapelco Airport, near San Martín de los Andes, just over an hour's flight south. Readers who would like more information about Estancia Ranquilco and the Río Trocoman are encouraged to send a letter or fax to the estancia at the address provided in Chapter 8, or to contact Don DeLise at (303) 923-3474.

Río Aluminé (ah-loo-mee-NAY). The Mapuches call the river *alumine:* "one sees into it very deeply." And indeed, it exemplifies a common characteristic of streams of the Northern and Central fishing zones—astonishing clarity. Except when roiled by spring freshets or rare summer thunderstorms, virtually all of the rivers in this region possess a gemlike transparence North Americans experience only in spring creeks or a few very high alpine brooks. Visiting fishermen note the quality immediately, too often the instant they step into a hole six inches deeper than their boots or waders.

The first impulse of most fishermen to these air-like waters is to tie on the lightest tippet in their supply, which brings about the prompt loss of several flies to willows, chacay, or the jaws of hefty trout. Far better to study the bottom for a few minutes, and wade about for a bit to accustom the eye and middle ear to depths and flows. Current strength can be deceiving in these crystal waters and a bit of splashing around early may prevent you from getting a good dunking later and will also help you to understand why a surprisingly small trout can so easily snap a light tippet.

The Río Aluminé springs from the northernmost of the great chain of glacial lakes sheltered in eastern slopes of the southern Andes, Lago Aluminé. A delightful river to float, it is also one of the longest rivers in Patagonia that is fishable for its entire length. From its source, Lago Aluminé, the Río Alumine flows about 100 miles south to its confluence with the Río Chimehuin, at which point the merged rivers become the Río Collon Cura. Winding through the heart of the Northern Zone's trout

country, the Aluminé is fed by several important tributaries. It is convenient to describe the mainstem Aluminé in sections: Upper, Middle, and Lower Reaches.

Aluminé — Upper Reaches (from Lago Aluminé 16 miles downstream to first bridge across river). Lago Aluminé is the immediate source of the Río Aluminé, but that lake is in turn fed by waters of nearby Lago Moquehue (moe-KAY-way). The two lakes are just outside Lanín National Park and are somewhat developed, at least by Patagonian standards, but both support trout and a brief description of them is appropriate.

Lago Moquehue, west of Lago Aluminé, is a popular site for small summer homes. Fishermen troll and occasionally cast flies for rainbows, browns, and brooks. Rainbows to 10 pounds were taken during the 1989-90 season. Several campgrounds (signs usually say *autocamping*) lie along the lakeshore, but for visitors without camping gear, only two overnight facilities are available in this entire region. One of them is the Hostería Lago Moquehue, at the west end of the lake, a small, friendly, comfortable, and inexpensive inn with a dining room. La Angostura (lahn-go-STEW-rah) is the name of the narrow strait that connects Lago Moquehue to Lago Aluminé and the name of the tiny village near the strait. Just east of the village, site of little more than a school, customs facility, and military detachment, a short road leads south to the strait—good fly fishing water, but a popular site for camping, and worked heavily by lure fishermen.

Lago Aluminé is a much larger lake that extends eastward from wooded mountainsides to dry, scrubby steppes. The Hostería Lago Aluminé, near the lake's eastern end, offers accommodations to fishermen and sightseers. It is more expensive than the Hostería Lago Moquehue, but is very pleasant and serves sumptuous meals. It is the most convenient inn for visitors who plan to fish the Río Litrán or the upper Aluminé;

there are no hotels or inns between this hosteria and the town of Aluminé, 30 miles south. Five miles west of the Hostería Lago Aluminé, the road crosses the Río Litrán, a small stream that enters the lake from the north. The mile of stream between the bridge and the lake is almost solid riffle and is fly fishing only water. If the day is not too windy, fly fishermen who enjoy fast water and are willing to walk are encouraged to fish from the bridge to the boca. Most of the trout are small rainbows, but a few reach two pounds and an occasional lunker in from the lake or sizing up the boca will keep you from falling asleep.

The boca—in this case, outlet—of the Río Aluminé is a hundred-foot-wide, steadily quickening run of smooth water about a half-mile long. Rocky points along the boca permit fly fishermen to reach casting range of patches of tall, bulrush-like reeds that surely attract cruising trout, but neither I nor any of my fishing companions have ever managed to hook a thing in this fishy-looking spot. The boca is exposed to the full force of prevailing winds and on any but light wind days gives fly fishermen a real workout.

About a mile below the boca, the Aluminé spills into a steep and narrow canyon, boiling willy-nilly through a hodgepodge of car-sized boulders, a run that sets the basic pattern for the next 16 miles of river. The upper Aluminé is a young, high energy, homogeneous stream with lots of bouncy, bubbling rapids, and few pools. The streambed is

The frustrating boca of the Río Aluminé.

Upper Río Aluminé. Note the araucaria trees. Sparse riparian vegetation may account for the low productivity of the upper river.

composed primarily of rounded boulders that range in size from automobiles to basketballs—hell to wade, for it may be two feet deep in one spot and five feet deep a pace away.

The road along the upper Aluminé is excellent if it has been graded, fine clay packed as hard as pavement. Undeveloped picnic areas and campsites are plentiful along the river and access is excellent. Good campsites are usually associated with the stands of araucaria trees that begin to appear along the river a few miles below the lake. During mid-season these campsites are often full of fishermen packing spinning rods.

Ten-inch trout, mostly rainbows, are plentiful in the upper reaches of the river, but larger fish are scarce. The largest fish I've taken from this section was a 17-inch fish that weighed 2.5 pounds. Pancoras are abundant, but there is little evidence of aquatic insect life. Periodically, this section of the river receives very heavy lure pressure, which along with sparse riparian vegetation may account for its low productivity.

Aluminé—Middle Reaches (from first bridge below lake to second bridge, near Rahue). For the next 22 miles, the river acquires a different character. The valley bottom becomes slightly broader, the stream swells as it picks up tributaries, long deep runs and slow pools become more frequent, and the banks become lined with dense stands of tall willows.

Two important tributaries enter the Aluminé from the west in this section: the Río Ñorquinco, near the upstream bridge, and the Río Quillen, near Rahue, at the downstream bridge, possibly the best dry fly streams in the zone. The town of Aluminé lies halfway between these two streams.

The abundance of willows and other riparian vegetation along middle reaches of the river adds a dimension important to fly fishermen, for they provide appropriate habitat for emerging nymphs and other insects. I've observed no hatches on Patagonian rivers as dense as those on many North American rivers, but sufficient small caddisflies hatch on this stretch of the Aluminé to provoke sporadic rises, often concentrated beneath the overhanging willows. Caddis cases are fairly abundant in the gravels and though I have never seen the adult, I have found a few shucks of large stoneflies (nearly the size of *Pteronarcys*) on willow roots and reeds.

Perhaps because of the unusual transparence of the water or the relatively low aquatic insect productivi-

Middle reaches of the Río Aluminé. The fisherman is trying to put his fly directly beneath the willows, excellent technique on this and other rivers of the Northern Zone.

ty of these waters, it seems to me that Patagonian trout seek the shade of overhanging willows to a even greater extent than their cousins do on the streams of western North America. Fly fishermen should keep an attentive eye on these shaded runs. Look for tiny pale green inchworm-like insects that live on the willows; they must be delicious, for otherwise wary trout seem to suspend their caution to get them and if you have or can make a reasonable imitation, you'll be in business. The middle reaches of the Aluminé are well-suited for exploiting this scrap of information. Where cobbles are small, footing is good, and it is possible to wade the middle of the stream, casting to willows on both banks.

Access to middle reaches of the Aluminé is easy; the road, now dusty and rough, parallels the river, and there are no fences or keep out signs. A leisurely float (taking plenty of time to stop and fish) from the upper bridge to the town of Aluminé takes two or three days and is highly recommended. In its middle reaches the river enters drier terrain, flowing through sere, rolling hills with occasional dramatic rock formations and outcrops. Araucaria trees diminish and finally disappear. The only trees in sight are now dense streamside willows and Lombardy poplars. This section of the river is easy to wade; it is seldom necessary go more than waist-deep to reach any part of the stream. The river is distinctly warmer than the Trocoman (68° F. in February) and can be waded wet. Teros and sheldgeese are common.

Small fish are still abundant, but larger fish are also more abundant. In a couple of hour's fishing, I will usually bring three or four rainbows from two to three pounds to net, and lose several more.

Middle reaches of the Río Aluminé.

Fish on! Middle reaches of the Río Aluminé.

The most convenient nearby accommodations for fishermen are in the town of Aluminé. The town has two or three small hotels, but the nicest is the inexpensive motel operated by the Argentine Automobile Club (abbreviated *ACA* in Argentina; holders of American AAA cards receive substantial discounts). Unfortunately, the concrete building has the acoustic properties of a mausoleum, but the grounds and service are pleasant, rooms are comfortable, and meals served in the spacious dining room are good. A simple, but free campground has been built on the riverside just north of town. It has a swimming beach of clean sand and is provided with *fogones* (stone barbecues).

Aluminé—Lower Reaches (from second bridge, near Rahue, to confluence with Río Chimehuin). For many years, indeed decades, fishing gossip in Junín has deemed the Río Aluminé an unproductive trout stream, not worth the effort required to fish. I am not a professional fisherman, endowed with arcane knowledge or exceptional techniques, but my own experience on the river has not borne out these these pronouncements. While I have not taken truly huge fish from the upper and mid-

dle reaches of the river, I always find the fishing worthwhile on these reaches; I often hook the largest fish of a trip to northern Patagonia in the lower Aluminé. Notes as far back as 1963 describe six, seven, and eleven pound fish and in 1988 I released a rainbow from the lower river that was literally as long as my arm.

The lower river is simply big water. Its gradient is moderate, so it does not pack the dangerous energy of the Limay or the Río Grande of Chubut Province, but by now it carries a significant volume of water and gets very deep. The lower river is accessible between the town of Aluminé and the bridge at Rahue, but downstream from this point, it enters a narrow canyon and the road is usually carved into the eastern slope of the canyon high above the water. It is only easily accessible from the road in a few places. South of the third bridge, near Pilolil, the road leaves the river and most of the river's next 25 miles are virtually inaccessible except by horseback or boat. This is the part of the river that guide Jorge Trucco calls "the fish factory. . ."

In the canyon and the inaccessible sections, the Aluminé is slow and very deep. There are riffles and stretches of pocket water at points where resistant

Lower Río Alumine at Estancia San Ignacio.

outcrops form the streambed, but they are often separated by a mile or so of uninteresting though not necessarily unproductive water. It is difficult to find places to wade across the river. This reach is lightly fished and for obvious reasons is usually fished by guided parties who float through in inflatables and commonly release 30 to 40 fish during a day's float.

Two famed Argentine streams enter the lower reaches of the Aluminé: the Río Malleo and Río Chimehuin, to which we will return. The lower river is in easy reach of Junín de los Andes and most fishing lodges in the Junín area will take clients to this portion of the stream.

One fishing lodge, Estancia San Ignacio, is located on lower Ríos Aluminé, Malleo, and Catan Lil, with access to the Collon Cura and Chimehuin. San Ignacio is a typical estancia of the Northern Zone and its transformation into a fishing lodge has followed a long and curious historical route. During the so-called Desert Campaign of the 1870's, the portion of land that comprises San Ignacio was "given" to the chief of a Mapuche tribe, presumably to encourage and ensure his continued pacific attitude. The chief eventually died and the land passed to his wife, who sold it to an early white settler. Over the years, the land passed through several hands and was gradually turned into a working cattle and sheep ranch. One enterprising owner, however, opened a general store on the ranch, at that time the only store in the entire region. In those lawless days, prudent businessmen designed their properties to withstand the depredations of bandits, so the main building more closely resembled a fortress than a general store—it had no windows through which a marauder could toss a torch or pour bullets. Within the walls of this fortified store, fly fishermen now swap stories at the bar or in the adjacent dining room, for the estancia was recently purchased by guide Jorge Trucco and several associates, and turned into a first class fishing and hunting lodge.

Estancia San Ignacio lies on the western bank of the lower Aluminé, across the river from the boca of Río Catan Lil and a few miles downstream from the confluence of the Río Malleo and the Aluminé. The old store now houses tastefully appointed common dining and lounging facilities. A building with sleeping accommodations and private baths has been added not far from the river's edge.

At San Ignacio, the Aluminé has entered the steppes. It winds through low naked hills, about to flow out onto the arid plains of northern Patagonia. Although the general character of the landscape is stark, lush grassy swales are hidden in nearly every fold of the dusty hillsides and these swales attract several score of European red deer. San Ignacio is a working cattle and sheep ranch, but future plans are to reduce the number of domestic stock, in order to sustain and improve range for these deer, and to reduce impacts on riparian habitat.

The estancia lies about an hour's drive northeast of Junín de los Andes and is accessible only by a private dirt road which leaves Argentine Route 234 about halfway between Junín and La Rinconada. Visitors who travel this road should keep an eye out for nine-banded armadillos and take note of the gigantic pale green neneo plants that grow on hilltops in this region. Most neneos (nay-NAY-oh) are no larger than small inner tubes and about knee-high; enroute to San Ignacio you will pass globe-shaped neneos as high as your head and ten feet in diameter.

About eight miles of the Aluminé and six miles of the Río Malleo flow through the estancia. San Ignacio is admirably situated for flyfishermen who especially enjoy float trips. Clients can float otherwise inaccessible portions of the Aluminé upstream from the lodge and beach rafts in front of their rooms at the end of the float, or conversely start out from their rooms to float downstream all day and be driven back to the estancia for supper.

The rather grim appearance of the landscape of the lower Aluminé may at first put off new visitors, especially those who have never fished in the western United States. Under the best of conditions, the steppes are never lush. This is dry, harsh countryside, but no more unappealling than the plains of southern Idaho, Wyoming, eastern Oregon, or central Montana, whose drab scenery has yet to blunt the enthusiasm of avid flyfishermen. Indeed, a principal attraction of lower portions of all the streams of the Northern Zone is the stark contrast with their dusty, dry surroundings. A surreal quality imbues floating limpid, cool rivers through hot, semi-desert terrain. It is a unique fishing experience, the source of fascination these float-trips hold for visitors.

The lowest portions of the Aluminé are readily accessible by road. At La Rinconada, Highway 234 crosses the Aluminé on a one-lane bridge, and parallels the river downstream for three miles to its confluence with the Río Chimehuin. Below this point, the river becomes the Collon Cura, described below. Pull-offs from the paved road are plentiful, and since the river is usually in sight, you can pick your water according to preference. Because this portion of the river lies along a heavily-traveled route and is so accessible, it receives substantial pressure from lure fisherman. You can offset this pressure considerably by stopping at La Rinconada.

La Rinconada leads to an off-the-beaten-path stretch of the river. It occupies a prominent spot on all Argentine road maps, but really comprises nothing more than a bridge, modest motel and restaurant, gas station, and streamside camping area. The motel is quite inexpensive, the restaurant serves plain but adequate meals, and the rooms (no private baths) are basic and comfortable. It is a perfect base from which fishermen willing to walk may explore the lower Aluminé or the Collon Cura. No public roads lead upstream along the Aluminé from La Rinconada, but fishermen who walk up from one to

three miles will pass a score of fishing spots that have yielded many of the largest trout I have caught in Patagonia. (Walk up the northern shore of the river, not the same side as the motel.) Floaters fish these waters, of course, but they seldom fish with the patience and deliberation of fishermen who have hiked for an hour or two upstream. In any case, there is plenty of room, and there seem to be plenty of fish to go around.

Río Collon Cura (coh-zhohn-COO-rah). The name means "stone mask" in Mapuche. It refers to the remains of a legendary man-eating giant that once inhabited the region, and outwitted by a Mapuche girl and her brother, was torn to pieces by his own dogs. Rocks strewn about the valley bottom are the petrified remains of this gruesome monster. Every visiting flyfisherman should fish this stream, not because of the legend, nor because it has become my personal favorite of the Northern Zone streams, but for the sake of posterity, for the Collon Cura may be a doomed river.

It is born at the point where the Chimehuin plunges foaming into the Aluminé, and flows east to reach its sad end at the Alicura Reservoir, an impoundment that, like Hetch-Hetchy,

Río Collon Cura.

Río Collon Cura. Guides often float their clients down this broad, easy-going stream.

should live in infamy. The surviving Collon Cura flows 20 miles through a parched, empty valley bottom that varies in width from one to three miles. In a few places, the highway passes next to the river, and a few dirt tracks lead to its banks, but for most of its length the river lies on the opposite side of the valley from the road, a long, hot walk from the car through scrub and gigantic tufts of pampas grass toward the distant willows. For this reason the stream receives little fishing pressure on a stream-mile basis. Indeed, it is not uncommon to drive the entire length of the river without seeing a single fisherman.

The valley of the Collon Cura runs roughly north/south, and apart from a few spectacular views of Lanín Volcano, 60 miles miles away, the scenery is uninspiring. Do, however, take note of the outcrops on the hills that line the

valley, for they provide clues to the region's volcanic origins. Prominent basaltic lava flows alternate with weathered layers of brown tufa-like volcanic ash. These ash-layers are 60 feet thick and erode so as to form steep, sculpted cliffs on both sides of the valley. Near the river, freshly eroded ash deposits are whitish and give rise to a widespread Patagonian fishing adage: *busquen las toscas blancas,* "look for the white cliffs." (Where ash has slumped into the river, the newly-exposed cliffs are white and the slumps usually occur on the deep outside edges of river curves, i.e. good fishing holes.)

The Collon Cura is simply a wonderful river, easy to wade on small cobbles and gravel from midsummer on, full of pleasant surprises. It is big water, but has such a gentle gradient that it does not feel big and dangerous as do the

Limay, Carrinleufu, Santa Cruz, or Río Grande of Chubut Province. Late in the season, if you pick your place, you can wade across the river in braided areas, necessary maneuvers when the wind howls down the flat, exposed valley.

One trick of the trade on the Collon Cura is to arrive early in the morning. It will be cool then, the river is certain to be empty of other fishermen, and the wind will be light or absent. A second trick on this river is to carefully fish the long, slow, boring-looking stretches between riffles. There is just enough current in these quiet waters to work a fly and some truly giant fish (in my experience, to 12 pounds) seem to prefer these placid stretches. Fly fishermen who enjoy long casts with nymphs and streamers will particularly love these waters. You must be patient and alert, for there are small fish in these runs and action can be slow between strikes, but Egad, there are some monsters in this delightful river.

Occasionally, absolutely windless and cloudless days come along—beware of the sun. Such days are highly unusual, but when they occur, it is great to be alive and fishing the Collon Cura.

Black-necked swans and neotropic cormorants are abundant all along the river; it is not unusual to see a dozen or more in a day on the river. Ninebanded armadillos are especially common along the braided portions of the river below the boca of the Río Caleufu. Fish the river to the last riffle above the bridge where Highway 237 crosses the Collon Cura; the lowest reaches with current are productive.

A new, higher bridge under construction (1990) bodes ill for the Collon Cura. About one hundred productive miles of this river have already been converted into a bleak desert reservoir. If another dam is indeed constructed, it would not only destroy the 20 remaining miles of this fabulous river, but also inundate much of the lower Caleufu, Chimehuin, and Aluminé Rivers, the rough equivalent of destroying, at one stroke, sections of Montana's Madison, Big Hole, Beaverhead, and Yellowstone Rivers.

The Aluminé/Collon Cura system ends, alas, at the most dismal of destinations for great streams—a reservoir. Let us now head back upstream to several tributaries to this system, safer, it is hoped from the dam-builders. We will begin with the uppermost tributary, the Río Ñorquinco.

Río Ñorquinco (nyor-KEEN-co). The Ñorquinco—"place of wild celery"—is the first important tributary to the Aluminé south of Lago Aluminé. It is a short, small river, about 20 miles long, varying in width from 20 to 40 feet, which enters the Aluminé from the west, 16 miles north of the town of Aluminé. Its significance to visitors is that it is one of the best streams in the region on which to see Patagonian birdlife and it is one of the two good dry fly streams in the Northern Zone.

The river flows to the Aluminé from Lago Ñorquinco, a typical regional lake which stretches into the Andes toward the Chilean border, and is surrounded by high mountains clad in a mixed araucaria/beech forest. The Ñorquinco River and Lake are on an 80-mile dirt road which makes a loop passing by Lago Nompehuen, Lago Moquehue, Lago Aluminé, the lower Río Litrán, the upper Río Aluminé, and back to the mouth of the Río Ñorquinco. The loop is scenic as well as interesting for fishing explorations.

The unusual productivity of the lower Ñorquinco is immediately apparent to fishermen. The river is uniformly lined with dense willow thickets and though the lower stream sustains a moderate flow, the streambed is loaded with long clumps of elodea, algae, and chara—in places so thick as to completely obscure the bottom. The willows and thick aquatic vegetation have several important effects.

First, they provide habitat for more aquatic insects than I've seen anywhere in Patagonia. Small caddis flies are in the air most of the day, and evening hatches are often thick enough to provoke significant rises. You may also see mayflies and small stoneflies.

Second, they provide outstanding cover for trout. This is one of those streams on which fishermen who wade very carefully may find themselves on the opposite side of a dense tress of elodea from a feeding trout, perhaps a rod's length away.

Third, the aquatic vegetation is so dense in many places as to limit fishing. Streamer or nymph fishing is discouraging, and fortunately, lure fishermen are out of luck on most of the lower river. Here, dry fly fishermen come into their own.

Finally, the continuous bands of dense willows force fishermen to wade. Luckily, the stream is easily waded. Footing is good and it is seldom necessary to exceed hip-depth to reach any portion of the stream. The river lends itself to wading against the current in center-stream.

The Ñorquinco is gin-clear and the fish can be quite selective, so light tackle and light touch are called for. As on all Patagonian streams, you must stay alert. There are lots of foot-long fish in the lower Ñorquinco, but the weedbeds also hold browns and rainbows to several pounds.

The lower several miles of river are readily accessible—no fences, and plenty of roadside turnouts. As you proceed upstream, the character of the river changes. Vegetation thins out and the river evolves into a boulder-studded freestone stream, with occasional deep holes. But about 12 miles above the Alumine, the upper Norquinco takes on a meandering, lake-like character—very deep, and once again filled with weed-

The small Ñorquinco is one of the Northern Zone's more productive dry fly streams. Note the abundant riparian vegetation.

beds, lined with tall bulrushes, and teeming with birds.

The only significant hatches I've witnessed on this reach have occurred in late evening, but look nevertheless for rises in these calm, but difficult-to-reach waters and keep an eye out for coypú (nutrias) swimming along with mouths full of grass. You are also likely to see swans, teros, bandurrias, and several species of sheldgeese, grebes, coots, and ducks. At least a few very large fish live in these meandering waters, but there are many dues to pay for them: it is very difficult to cast because the stream is too deep to wade in most places and careful casting from within the tall bulrushes is an exasperating experience, to say the least. Among other drawbacks in this area are an overabundance of chacay and spiny thistles—many now adorned with my flies—and rare in Patagonia, a healthy population of biting black flies.

Upstream, the Ñorquinco regains its freestone character, but access becomes a serious problem as the road grows distant from the river, now on the far side of fenced private property. Just below Lago Ñorquinco, however, the road enters Lanín National Park, and the stream is again readily accessible. (If driving, be wary of the *vados*—dips—in the road; they are marked with road signs, but many are abrupt and quite steep.) Several side roads lead to pleasant, undeveloped campsites at streamside. The campsites are in dense woods usually full of squawking austral parakeets. Black flies are troublesome here, too. The upper river is now small and shallow, with a streambed comprised of silver dollar-sized gravels.

The trout (mostly rainbows) in the upper river rise readily to dry flies, but are uniformly small in my experience. They are also surprisingly selective; I have had to go to size 20 dry flies on very light tippets to provoke strikes.

More nice campsites lie along the two-mile road to the park ranger station along the south side of the lake.

The nearest overnight accommoda-tions to the Río Ñorquinco are at the town of Aluminé, 16 miles south of its mouth. Junín de los Andes, about 65 miles south, is about a two-hour drive from the river.

Río Quillen (key-ZHEHN). The name means "strawberry" in Mapuche, but for visiting fishermen, its significance is not fruit, but dry flies. The Río Quillen is the second of the Northern Zone's dry fly streams and my own favorite. Slightly shorter, but similar in volume to the Norquinco, it arises in Lanín National Park, the outlet stream from Lago Quillen. The Quillen enters the Río Aluminé ten miles south of the town of Aluminé, from which point a dirt road follows the stream 12 miles west to the lake.

For most of its length, the Quillen is also lined with a solid phalanx of dense willows, but although its streambed is covered with a thick layer of slick algae, it lacks the dense communities of elodea and chara that characterize the Ñor-quinco.

The lower few miles of river are accessible; the road is often a few feet from the water and no fences intervene. In its lower reaches, the Quillen is often broad and shallow, and the willows force fishermen into the stream itself. Upstream wading is recommended, though the rocks are very slippery.

Residents of the town of Aluminé consider the Quillen far superior to the river that flows right through their town, and it's not hard to see why. The lower Quillen supports a large popula-tion of rainbows and browns from one to four pounds, and occasional browns in this river reach 10 pounds. Several species of caddis are plentiful on the stream and the fish are often so eager to take flies that a careful fisherman can hook three or four in the same run. Like the Trocoman, nearly every spot that looks as if it would hold fish indeed does hold fish. Terrestrials as well as caddis imitations are effective on the Quillen; I have had good luck with black ants fish-ed wet or dry. As on the Malleo, trout tend to feed right beneath the willows

The small and fertile Río Quillen is, in the author's experience, the best dry fly stream in the Northern Fishing Zone.

right next to shore, so risk losing some of your flies and make some of those Hail Mary casts into the shrubbery.

The reason the Quillen is so much fun is that action is nearly continuous.

Several age classes of fish are well represented; in short order, you may hook a sixteen-inch, ten-inch, and twenty-four-inch fish on the same fly from the same riffle. Lose your concentration on this river and you will lose your fly to these occasional eye-openers.

Several miles upstream from the Aluminé, the Quillen drops through a narrow canyon and the road winds high above the river to negotiate the canyon. The river is rocky, but productive through the canyon—more two to four-pound fish. Physical access is a problem, however, because the river flows well below the road at the bottom of steep, scrubby slopes.

Above the canyon, the Quillen flows through a broad, flat valley and is inac-

cessible in most places, since it lies on the opposite side of the valley from the road. The valley is cultivated and several pine tree plantations lie between the road and river. In some places, the distant river meanders like a spring creek over the valley floor, but near the tree farms it plunges through a streambed of round one- to three-foot boulders. Fish strike readily in these reaches, but wading is extremely tough through the algae-glazed boulders. The current is strong and flat spots in the streambed in which to take a breather are practically nonexistent.

Two miles below Lago Quillen, the road passes the tiny hamlet of Quillen, a charming village scattered through the woods in which the school, dispensary, town hall, and other municipal buildings are constructed of half-logs stained chocolate brown. Forested mountains now hem in the valley, with nires nearest the river, then robles, and finally tall coihues. Just beyond Quillen village, the road crosses a decrepit bridge and enters Lanín National Park. Lago Quillen, whose eastern end lies a mile from the Chilean border, soon comes into view.

Several beautiful campsites are situated in dense beech woods and grassy meadows along the shore of the lake and the long boca of the river. A typically picturesque park ranger station lies along the road near the eastern end of the lake. Beyond the ranger station, the road grows rough, rocky, and narrow and leads through dense woods of beech and bamboo to small Lago Hui Hui (closed to fishing in the 1989-90 season).

The upper half-mile of the boca of the Quillen is more like a lake than a river. Access and casting is difficult because of brush and the unwadeable depth of the river. I have seen but a few fish rise to half-inch mayflies that flit among the bulrushes and purple-berried calafate that line the lake's outlet. The boca has current too slow for working flies well, but look the water over carefully, for the park rangers insist that brown and rainbow trout to nine pounds are taken every year. In the top mile of the river, there are only two good riffles, in which small rainbows rise to caddis flies. The stream doesn't acquire good current until downstream of the decrepit bridge, where access is difficult because of private, fenced property.

In my experience, the Quillen does not receive excessive fishing pressure; I have spent many days on the river in recent years without seeing other fishermen. Unlike the Ñorquinco, however, the lower Quillen lends itself to fishing with lures and in 1990 a reliable friend reported seeing long strings of fish hanging in willows along the lower reaches of the river. They were victims of apparently local poachers completely disregarding catch or size limits. This small river will not long withstand that kind of pressure and unless provincial authorities quickly come to grips with this problem, the fishery of one of Neuquen's best dry fly streams will decline abruptly.

The mouth of the Quillen lies ten miles south of the town of Aluminé, about a two-hour drive from Junín de los Andes on a safe, but somewhat rough gravel road. Several kilometers of the Río Quillen flow through lands of Estancia La Ofelia, a ranch which has belonged to the Lagos Marmol family since 1907 and which now offers accommodations to fly fishermen.

Río Malleo (mah-ZHEY-oh). The Malleo has long been among the best known of Patagonia's trout rivers. It is a is a long stream, not nearly as large as its reputation would imply—not a Yellowstone, Madison, Bighorn, or Snake River, but rather a Beaverhead, Firehole, or Silver Creek. The Malleo is a subtle stream that yields its fish to stealth and cunning rather than force or dogged persistence. I have found the quality of fishing to have declined in the Malleo over the past few decades, yet the river's popularity among fishermen has persisted if not increased over that interval; this river, as few others, seems to inspire enormous loyalty among those fish it, myself included. Up to a few years ago, the Malleo was my favorite trout stream in the world. It has since been displaced by other streams, yet I cannot conceive of taking a trip to Patagonia without fishing the Malleo.

Why?

Well first, it is so nearly a perfect trout stream that a few fishermen I know would happily wade it for hours knowing full well that it supported not one single fish. The stream has solid character, a well-balanced diversity of water types ranging from hip-deep boulder-studded runs to deep, dark pools, plenty of classic pool-riffle series, and just the right amount of riparian vegetation to provide cover for fish, habitat for flying insects, and shade for relaxing fishermen. In certain reaches, it has those deeply undercut banks that you know in your bones and cells shelter a gigantic brown trout or cautious rain-

Lanín Volcano, the Río Malleo, and a busy fisherman is a typical Patagonian combination.

bow that no one has yet been clever enough to hook. And that certainty and anticipation give you an adrenalin rush that makes your hands shake as you tie on The Fly and prepare for The Cast that will at last take The Fish. . .

Second, the Malleo somehow inspires tremendous and unwonted concentration. I have watched a normally careless compatriot study currents, guage winds, and plot a single cast with the same hushed intensity as a golf pro studies a green in preparation for a critical putt. Another fishing friend was so intent on a rising fish that he had no recollection whatsoever of a party of three American fishermen who rather rudely passed within a few feet of him while leap-frogging to the next run. On the Malleo, lunch often becomes a routine formality simply forgotten until a fisherman's stomach forcefully reminds him that it is an obligation, not

a privilege.

Third, the river and its landscape invite contemplation. The Malleo is a stream on which harried executives and uptight bureaucrats or businessmen can truly abandon their troubles to apprehend their surroundings. Cormorants, streamside flowers, otters, torrent ducks, shifting cloud-shapes, passing gauchos, and above all, brooding Lanín Volcano which dominates the horizon, demand attention, and it is a rare fisherman who does not take time out to pay careful heed to these features.

The waters of the Malleo arise near the Andean divide from two spectacular sources: the ice and snow of Lanín Volcano and the broad reaches of Lago Tromen.

Lanín Volcano, a border peak with the classic symmetry of Fujiyama, reaches 12,390 feet, and towers over its neighbors. The volcano is dormant, but clouds that coalesce over the peak nearly every afternoon often simulate an eruption. Those clouds are important; it is said that *cuando el Lanín no tiene copete, no hay pesca*—"when Lanín has no cap, there are no fish." Lanín's summit is perpetually cloaked in a mantle of snow and ice, a circumstance that can indirectly aggravate fly fishermen. *Lanín* is a Mapuche word that carries the meaning "sinking" and probably derives from the tendency of foot-travelers to sink into the snow or volcanic ash that form the volcano's slopes. On hot summer days, snow runoff may carry this ashy material down Arroyo Correntoso into the Malleo to render the river milky *(lechoso)* for nearly its entire length. *Malleo* itself means "white clay," and refers to deposits of clay-like ash that predominates in the upper valley. Lanín, however, is such a dominant feature of the landscape of the upper Malleo, with so striking a visual impact that even fly fishermen forgive its irritating habit of periodically roiling the river.

Tromen has two definitions in Mapuche: "cloudy" or "place of reeds." Both meanings aptly describe the scenery near Lago Tromen, the second source of the Río Malleo. The lake is large, surrounded by high forested mountains, and one of the more isolated, lightly fished of the lakes of the Northern Zone. It can be reached by narrow dirt roads that leave Argentine Route 60 near the customs and immigration station on the Argentine side of the border or just inside the east entrance to Lanín National Park. The lake contains rainbows and some very large brook trout; no browns (yet). Beware of the big, persistent horseflies around the lake, and keep an eye out for condors. Estancia San Huberto, the only fishing lodge on the Malleo, maintains a small cabin on the lake.

From Lago Tromen to its end at the Río Aluminé, the Malleo flows through about 50 miles of diverse countryside. It is most easily described in two sections: upper and lower.

The productive upper reaches of the Río Malleo.

Upper Malleo (from headwaters to Hostería San Huberto). The top 20 miles of the river flow through a mile-wide valley that runs straight southeast from the spine of the cordillera. A dirt road, Argentine Route 60, enters the valley just north of Junín de los Andes and climbs steadily 33 miles to the head of the valley. At Paso Tromen, a low (4,110 feet) pass, the road crosses into Chile and continues to Pucón and Villarica, small towns in the heart of Chile's lake district. Paso Tromen is one of a handful of passes across the southern Andes and because it is a short and scenic route, international traffic, including public buses, is relatively heavy.

Descending eastward from Paso Tromen, the road enters Lanín National Park, and crosses the northern flank of Lanín Volcano, passing through extensive pure stands of araucaria trees. The river, which comes into view about three miles east of the Argentine border post, is freely accessible for its short run through the park. Several undeveloped streamside campsites lie in araucaria groves along the road. This reach of the Malleo is relatively steep and the river cascades swiftly through a streambed of small weathered boulders. Footing is treacherous. This is plunging water in which fishermen must seek trout in sheltered pockets, not easy fishing.

Just within the well-marked east entrance to the park, a side road branches north and crosses the upper river. A gate *(tranquera)* across the bridge is sometimes locked, but if necessary you may obtain the key at the park ranger station a few miles back toward Paso Tromen. This side road leads six miles to a tiny lake in dense woods called Huaca Mamuil (closed to fishing in 1990) and a mile beyond, Lago Tromen.

Outside the park, access to the river becomes an immediate problem, for it flows into lands of private estancias and the road is often well out of sight of the river. In order to fish most of the rest of the upper Malleo, you must either be guided or obtain permission from private landowners.

The next spot at which a public road crosses the Malleo, from which point

you may hike up or down the river is at the *Puente Amarillo* (Yellow Bridge), on a side road about six miles east of the park entrance. Between these points, however, is one of the most popular portions of the river. Look north across the river as you leave the park and you see a mountain with three prominent outcrops at its summit. The mountain is called *Tres Picos* (Three Peaks) and has given its name to the portion of the Malleo at the foot of its slopes.

Tres Picos is the "spring creek" section of the Malleo. It is not really a spring creek, for it lacks the glossy sheen, crystal clarity, and silent, almost slithering quality of waters that flow through true spring creeks. But it is indeed much different than the rest of the Malleo, downright pleasant water to fish. For nearly a mile, the Malleo—normally a moderate energy stream—practically comes to a full stop and meanders slow-

The author releases a Malleo rainbow into a pool formed by a ledge of columnar basalt.

Lanín Volcano, the Río Malleo, and guachos make up another typical Patagonian combination of sights.

ly over the valley floor as if it had lost its way. Long, slow, deep pools predominate and it is possible to see a fish rise a hundred yards off on these slick waters. Not even the Malleo has the enormous hatches of North American streams, but fish do rise here to the midges and small caddisflies that are usually drifting along the breeze. There are many small fish in the Tres Picos section and a few very large fish, but they are *not* easy to catch—to stealth and cunning, add very light tippets and tiny nymphs. Wading is easy where depth permits, but dense clumps of michay alternate with grassy meadows on both banks and you must pick your way carefully through these spiny thickets to reach your next position with unpunctured waders.

As with most famed streams, arguments rage late into the night over which portions of the Malleo are "best." Some fishermen prefer the placid waters of Tres Picos, others like the confined surges in the "canyon," and yet others are happiest on the diverse, open waters of the lower Malleo. My own favorite area, the reaches near the *Puente Amarillo,* is held in mild disdain—perhaps for good reason—by most devotees of the Malleo.

Here the river is fast, exhausting to wade because of the jumble of boulders. Getting around often requires painful brush-beating through thickets of willows and michay. Worse, I have occasionally fished this section for hours, pawing desparately through fly boxes that seemed more inadequate by the hour, in hopes of getting at least a single strike for my day-long effort. Yet in notes twenty years old I have described one spot in this section, rather to my present embarassment, as "the most beautiful pool I have seen in any river, any place."

Lone araucarias—their dramatic

George Mitchell and a Malleo rainbow.

four-pounder which took a muddler very hard, jumped several times, zipped out all of my line. Tiny midges hatching, but little else. Ratio of rainbows to browns here about 20:1.

In the days before the Malleo was a catch and release stream, now and then I kept fish for my dinner. One of these, a two-pound female rainbow, taught me why small dark muddlers were so effective, for the fish was crammed with 15 pancoras ranging from one to three inches in length and nothing else—a spiny fistful of chitin and protein. Flip over a few rocks to see them, or leave a scrap of meat in shallow water overnight, and you'll find a small pancora convention in the morning.

This part of the river is not only for fishing. Some of the small caves at the foot of the lava flows hold strange bones, bats, and objects that might have been implements of some sort. On one brushy curve is a cluster of limespattered rocks and snags favored by a colony of neotropic cormorants. Over the years I have spent hours, camera in one hand, rod in the other, stalking a pair of torrent ducks that make this reach their home—pleasant but futile exercises. And on a sunny afternoon a mugful of ice-cold water from one of the tiny springs that leak from the bottom of the basalt cliffs—either poured down your throat or over your head—will bring a fresh outlook to the hottest Patagonian day.

About eight miles downstream from the turnoff to the *Puente Amarillo* is the entrance to Hostería San Huberto. The intervening water—long riffles and pools, mainly—is inaccessible without permission.

San Huberto is the quintessential Patagonian fishing lodge. Whitewashed walls and exterior woodwork gleam. The main building is nearly surrounded by a large tract of tall pines and is trim, functional, and attractive; no foolishness here. It is a man's building and looks like a lodge, not a housewife's dream. The grounds are green, flowered,

silhouettes accentuated by isolation—are scattered along the benches above the river. Uncommonly lush meadows grow near the water's edge. The river has exposed ancient lava flows here and winds along the edges of the flows, first on one side and then down the other. At a few places the dark basalt has tumbled into the river and the heavy hexagonal blocks are difficult to clamber over. Here and there, the river runs straight into 60-foot cliffs of basalt columns to form long pools. These pools are a long walk from the *Puente Amarillo* and nearby campsite, probably not fished more than a few times a season.

Fishing is not always poor here. Among my notes on these pools are the following entries:

> January 26: near midday caught and released 15, 17, and 22-inch rainbows, all on muddler, all very acrobatic. Just before dark, lost a five-pounder above Cormorant Pool, released 2 four-pounders in pool itself. March 23 [different year, same reach]: released 2 three-pound, very fat female rainbows, another spawning female

and immaculate, in sharp contrast to the arid hillsides. Drying waders hang beneath the portico, rod cases lean into every corner, vans and jeeps are parked in the gravel driveway, horses and colts wander about unconcerned, and big, friendly dogs greet each new arrival, tails wagging madly.

The interior of the lodge is cool and shadowed. Photos of fish, framed fly selections, boar heads, red deer antlers, pistols, and other manly objects adorn the walls. The dining room is formal yet homey—from the kitchen drift the faint sounds of maids chattering and laughing. The lounge is upstairs, a large, comfortable, and quiet room. A well-stocked self-service bar occupies one corner, a few shelves of reasonably-priced casual sweaters and shirts for forgetful guests occupy another. Books and magazines are scattered about on low tables. The estancia's fishing book contains remarks by fly fishermen both both famous and obscure; entries range in tone from dry to lyrical.

Over 20 miles of the Río Malleo flow through the estancia, which has been owned by the Olsen family for over a century. About 14 years ago, Carlos Olsen built a hunting and fishing lodge large enough to comfortably accommodate 16 guests in eight double rooms at the estancia, still a working cattle ranch. He named it Hostería San Huberto—Huberto is the patron saint of hunters. Carlos and his wife Carmen are not only gracious and affable hosts, but have worked hard in recent years to maintain quality fishing on the Malleo. On the main road just outside the entrance to the lodge is a sign:

Zona de Pesca y Liberación; libere todos los peces que capture con el menor daño posible. Ama y proteje la naturaleza.

It means "Catch and Release Zone; release all fish you catch with the least possible injury. Love and protect nature." Aware of the threat of over-fishing, the Olsen family as well as local guides and conservationists were instrumental in obtaining protection for the upper river.

Carlos' son Gustavo and family friend Ariel Semenov are the men who make most of the arrangements for clients, and who often themselves guide. They are capable young men with effervescent personalities who are quick to smile, and who clearly love their work. Their objective with respect to clients is to provide as much quality fishing action as possible, rather than to track down a few giant fish. They seek to provide a damned good time rather than trophies—an enlightened philosophy these days. Accordingly, they do not limit their guiding to the Río Malleo, but include trips to several nearby streams, including the Chimehuin, Quillen, Aluminé, Collon Cura, and others.

Surprisingly, about half of San Huberto's clients are inexperienced fly fishermen. As a result, guides often spend as much time teaching clients how to cast as showing them where to fish. But they are a cheerful lot, not likely to intimidate guests new to the art.

Lower Malleo (From Hostería San Huberto to confluence with Río Aluminé). Not far downstream from the lodge, the Malleo flows through a short canyon. I've not fished that section of the river, but am told by those who have that it is good water. It is nearly inaccessible to fishermen without guides.

Once the river leaves the canyon, however, it is accessible from the road which turns west from Route 23 (the road to Aluminé from Junín de los Andes) as well as the road which turns east to follow the river downstream. Both roads leave Route 23 just north of the bridge across the Malleo, ten miles from Junín.

For most of this section, the south side of the river is in private hands, while the north side is Indian Reserve land. The road is generally so close to the river that permission to fish is not expected and the residents of the dozen or so simple dwellings scattered along the stream are accustomed to fishermen. If you fish close to one of farmsteads, however, simple courtesy requires that you ask permission. It will invariably be granted and sign language will do nicely.

A pleasing characteristic of the lower Malleo is diversity of water types. There are slow runs that dodge around large rocks, each with good holding water below, rapids, deep pools, and shaded curves. The river frequently breaks into two or three willowed channels. With its current more moderate than the upper river, this section of the Malleo is eminently wadeable, with small cobbles for footing. You can cast across the stream anywhere.

Upstream from the bridge, the river is lined with willows for several miles. On this section I learned the astonishing importance of casting under willows on the Malleo. If you need convincing, perform a controlled experiment for yourself: fish a reach casting everywhere *but* under the willows and then later risk a few flies, and fish the same reach casting *only* under the willows, in deep draws, as close as possible to shore. Each perfect cast will almost always elicit a strike and I can almost guarantee that you will hook more and larger fish on the second effort. If this book contains a single surefire fishing tip, this is it.

The lower river holds a plague of small fish, about evenly divided between browns and rainbows, but you should also hook several fish from one to three pounds, and an occasional lunker. Do not sneer at these smaller fish; until you get a good look at one, they will snap far more of your tippets than you anticipate and you will wonder what you're doing wrong. The fish, especially rainbows, I have taken from the lower river have

A guide instructs his client on the lower Malleo.

Roland Turney and a brown trout from the lower Malleo.

been in the best physical condition of any trout I have ever seen. They are so firmly fat through the middle of their bodies as to appear deformed, very nearly round in cross section. The lower river supports enormous populations of pancoras and I suspect that these crustaceans are responsible for the peerless condition of the fish.

During the summer of 1988-89, the road downstream from the bridge was completed to the confluence of the Malleo and the Aluminé; it opens up the entire lower river. Rough and rocky, it is negotiable with an ordinary car only if taken slowly. Along this and other roads in the region, the sight of gauchos with perhaps a spare horse or two and a few dogs is a very common sight. In most of Patagonia, the horse is still as much an important means of transportation as an important tradition and gauchos garbed in flat black hat, scarf, waist sash (with sheathed dagger tucked into the lower back), baggy black pants *(bombachas)*, and soft black leather boots wandering through the hills are familiar and intimate features of the the Patagonian landscape.

These lowest reaches of the river are open waters. Most of the vegetation along the stream has been destroyed by goats herded by residents of the Reserve, a sticky socio-political problem that will need to be solved soon if the lower river is to be preserved.

Despite the depredations of the goats, the river is still productive. During a recent season, a half-hour of fishing yielded six small rainbows, one 14-inch brown, a 15-inch rainbow, and a 17-inch brown. Success with dry flies is spotty on the lower river; the flies I have found most effective are Montana nymphs, small muddlers, wooly buggers, and small unnamed eyed salmon fly nymphs tied by an Argentine named Pepe Delgado which are available in sets from one of the small fishing shops in Junín de los Andes.

The Malleo is convenient to the fishing lodges at San Ignacio or San Huberto and portions are accessible by road from accommodations in Junín de los Andes or San Martín de los Andes.

Río Chimehuin (chee-may-WEEN). Mapuches believed that forests, rivers, lakes, and their denizens were protected from heedless depredation by a fearsome creature that assumed the form of a huge bull and warned off despoilers with loud roars that preceded fierce windstorms. This creature lived in the depths of large lakes and was called a *'chime"* (CHEE-may). A *chime-huin* is a place frequented by chimes, apt title for one of the world's most notable trout rivers. Poachers beware.

The Río Chimehuin is the granddaddy of Argentine trout streams, source of fish and fish stories that will be prominent in international angling lore for as long as men cast flies to trout. It is the river that put Argentina on the fly fishing map of the world. . .

Fifty miles long, the Chimehuin arises at the outlet of Lago Huechulafquen, flows southeast through a valley reminiscent of the Big Hole or Paradise Valleys of Montana, turns south at sleepy but trout-conscious Junín de los Andes, and curves east through grassy hills to join the Aluminé a few miles south of La Rinconada. The river has been so assiduously explored by fly fishermen that nearly every important pool on the river has been given a name.

It is a large stream, about the size of the Madison or Yellowstone Rivers, but has a moderate gradient. In some sections it braids into several courses and in others it has carved long, deep channels into the valley floor.

The river and its surroundings are described below in four sections: Lago Huechulafquen and the Boca, the Upper River, Junín de los Andes, and the Lower River.

Lago Huechulafquen and Boca Chimehuin. One of the first trips a visiting fisherman should make—even before wetting a line—is from Junín de los Andes to the end of Lago Huechulafquen. The drive will give visitors a quick look at a typical cross-section of Andean Patagonia, that biological and physiographical structure so essential to understanding Argentine trout streams. The trip is relatively short—about 42 miles—and an easy hour's drive will take you from the arid hills in which nestles Junín de los Andes to the cool forests on the slopes of the spectacular mountains that form the spine of South America.

Lafquen means lake, and *huechulafquen* is the "upper lake." Huechulafquen (way-choo-LAUF-cane) lies at 3,200 feet and has an area of 30 square miles, by Argentine standards not very large. But it is a typically long narrow lake and extends deep into the mountains. The eastern third of the lake lies in grassy foothills, but on reaching the mountains proper, the road begins to dip and wind through dense shaded forests of enormous coihue trees and groves of bamboo *(chusquea)*. The entire lake is within Lanín National Park, but a few small farmsteads are scattered along its shore

Lago Huechulafquen, source of the legendary Río Chimehuin.

Hostería Paimun, a fishing lodge on Lago Huechulafquen, lies literally in the morning shadow of Lanín Volcano.

and the park service maintains a few simple campsites at lakeside.

As you drive west, the road drops onto a flat, wooded plain just above the level of the lake. To the north, the shining peak of Lanín Volcano, just eight miles distant, heaves slowly into view. This plain lies at the junction of the west end of Huechulafquen and its north arm, called Lago Paimun (Solitary Lake). The two lakes are separated by a hundred-yard-wide strait called La Angostura. Across the lake lies the entrance to the south arm of Huechulafquen, called Lago Epulafquen.

In this spectacular setting, two resorts have been built, Hostería Paimun and Refugio del Pescador. Hostería Paimun is the newer and more elegant of the two, a large terraced building of stone and varnished wood set among lawns and flowerbeds. Views from the rooms are breath-taking. A half-mile back toward Junín from the Hostería Paimun, a short side road leads to La Angostura and the Refugio del Pescador (Fisherman's Haven), a smaller and more informal resort built in a copse of beeches at the water's edge. Both lodges provide room and full pension at moderate prices.

Lagos Huechulafquen, Epulafquen, and Paimun all support trout, including very large rainbows and browns. Boats may be rented at either lodge; fishing clientele tend to be trollers. Fly fishermen usually row along shore looking for cruising fish or take boats to the boca of the Río Paimun, several miles down Lago Paimun, to try for spawners waiting to make a run up the river.

Most fly fishermen, however, are usually found twenty miles east, at the far less dramatic opposite end of Lago Huechulafquen—the legendary boca of the Chimehuin. From afar, the boca is unimposing, the rocky outlet of a large lake that winds beneath a scattering of

The boca of the Chimehuin, looking west up Lago Huechulafquen.

araucaria tree past a pair of scrub-covered slopes. But over the decades this quarter-mile of water has attracted the rapt attention of such fishing luminaries as Bebe Anchorena, Poló Bardin, Joe Brooks, Jorge Donovan, Roderick Haig-Brown, Charles Radziwell, Charles Ritz, Ernie Schweibert, and many, many others.

A few large angular boulders, left behind when the last glacier retreated up the lakebed, poke above the water just above the outlet. A few are handy casting platforms from which persistent fishermen launch flies for hour after hour into the quickening water. Some of these, such as Radziwell's Rock, even have names. As the lake steadily becomes a river, it makes a gentle turn to the north and passes under the bridge. It picks up speed, takes another turn to the east and plunges into a long set of rough cascades called *La Garganta del Diablo*, The Devil's Throat. Technically, a boca is a short section of water, the actual outlet of a lake, but the boca of the Chimehuin is considered to be all of the water between the lake and *La Garganta*.

This is trophy water; gigantic fish have been, and still are taken from this short stretch of water. Joe Brooks coined the phrase "boca fever" to describe the effect it still has on certain fly fishermen; his own boca trophy was an eighteen and a half pound brown. Jorge Donovan took a fourteen-pounder, Eliseo Fernández a twenty-pound brown, and Carlos Radziwell an eigh-

teen pound brown, but to my knowledge, the record fish taken on a fly is still in the hands of Bebe Anchorena, a twenty-four pound brown taken on a streamer in 1961.

No first time visitor can resist stopping on the bridge to peer over into the river. You see quickly why it is possible to sight-fish the boca. Its transparence is astonishing; in water well over your head you can see a dime on the bottom and tell if heads or tails is up. Old-timers would have assistants spot fish for them from slopes well above the river. From the bridge you can also see the province's Department of Ecology trailers tucked into willows on the first curve of the boca. Stop here first to get advice, to catch up on the latest fishing gossip, and to pay the modest daily fee charged by the province for "preferential waters." Then set up, and start out.

Time of day, weather conditions, and extraneous factors seem to be irrelevant. Most fishermen agree that unlike other Patagonian streams, the Río Chimehuin is a morning and evening river. My experience bears out that observation, but for some reason the axiom does not apply to the boca. Brooks caught his trophy brown at three o'clock on a sunny, windless afternoon, Bebe Anchorena caught the record fish at 10:00 p.m., just as it grew dark, and fly reel manufacturer Roberto Sacconi took an eighteen-pound brown at 5:00 p.m. Jorge Donovan caught his fish at eleven in the morning "among bathers and all sorts of tourists from other skilled

Roberto Sacconi fishing the lower Río Chimehuin.

fishermen to those incapable of building a fire."

One of several controversies with respect to the Chimehuin is what type of fly to use. Older, more traditional fishermen hold that large flies bring in large fish on the river and in the boca; Joe Brooks sometimes used six-inch-long honey blonde streamers. The hipper generation of young fisherman insists that larger fish will be taken on small nymphs and dry flies. It is likely that truth is parceled out equally between the two positions, though neither side would ever admit it. No formula, no orderly progression of steps will inevitably lead to a trophy fish from the boca. My recommendation, offered reluctantly, is to simply follow your own preferences. Fish large and small have been taken from the boca on muddler minnows, muddler marabous, wooly buggers, rubberlegs, and a host of bucktails and streamers. They have also been taken on dry flies—black ants, Wulff patterns, ginger quills, adams, and spider patterns.

I am not, alas, among that rather large group of fishermen who have taken trophy fish from the boca. My largest boca trout was an accident—a three-pound rainbow that took one of Pepe Delgado's salmon fly nymphs just above *La Garganta* while my attention was elsewhere. You will find that boca fishing requires a great deal of both patience and persistence, neither of which are strong constituents of my fishing style. Perhaps next year. . .

One word of caution: if your schedule permits, arrange your visit to the boca on a windless day or else early

Jim Sperry fishing the lower Río Chimehuin.

in the morning. Prevailing easterly winds that howl down the lake over a fetch of about 16 miles not only play hell with casting, but pile up roaring combers that can break over your head in the upper boca.

Upper Río Chimehuin (from *Garganta del Diablo* to Junín). About 16 miles of river and several tons of trout lie between *La Garganta* and Junín.

Before describing the upper river, however, I'd like to deal with another current Chimehuin controversy. Word has it that the famous Chimehuin has been overfished, that it no longer supports the populations of large fish it once held. . .

So far as I can tell, the sources of these baleful rumors are capable anglers who have fished the river for decades and have noticed in recent years that they can no longer bring several large fish to net in two or three hours' fishing. I am among those who have experienced this apparent decline. Ten or twenty years ago, it was easy to hook several fish weighing several pounds in several hours on nearly any reach of the Chimehuin; in recent years I have left the river on many days without having raised a single fish.

Everyone agrees that it is not so easy today; what they disagree about is why. Too many fishermen is the usual complaint; excessive poaching for the purpose of selling fish to restaurants is another. Both imply overharvesting. (Naturally, nobody even considers that they have become poorer fishermen.) It is true that in years past, a great many large fish were killed by fly fishermen. One famous anecdote concerns a well-known angler who walked into the kitchen of his hotel, plopped a twelve-pound brown onto the cleaning table, heaved a sigh, and announced to several onlooking fishermen, "I just can't understand why there are so few of these fish in the river nowadays."

But those days are largely past. Apart from the poachers, who are ruthless, and local residents who seek food for the family table, very few visiting fly fishermen would risk the scorn of their colleagues by marching into their hotel or lodge with dead fish. More fairly, they know better than to kill more than an occasional fish.

It takes facts, not fishing stories, to solve this sort of puzzle, but unfortunately, fishing facts are in short supply in Patagonia. Neither federal nor provincial authorities presently have sufficient funds or equipment to undertake the routine fisheries work required to determine species composition, age class structure, habitat characterization, or population studies that enable long-term trends to be identified with confidence.

But a few facts are available: first, census work done on Río Blanco, a small tributary to Lago Huechulafquen, indicates that the size and number of spawning trout are not decreasing, but actually increasing (their average size was nearly eight pounds). Second, scuba divers report seeing far more large trout in the Chimehuin than fishermen seem to be catching. The fish seem to be there, as always. Third, this decline seems to be limited to the Chimehuin; most of the rest of the zone's trout streams seem to offer the usual good fishing. Fourth, it *is* more difficult to catch fish on the Chimehuin these days. And finally, more fly fishermen work the Chimehuin than ever.

Why, then, aren't fly fishermen hooking as many large trout on the Chimehuin as they used to?

I don't know—but I have heard one quite plausible if debatable answer. Jim Sperry, a Connecticut Yankee fly fisherman who discovered Patagonia recently, pondered the question for a few days and arrived at the following explanation: The practice of releasing fish is a relatively recent development; so is the greatly increased fishing pressure on the river. As a result, says Jim, large fish, now with a second lease on life, are simply learning to avoid certain flies. I like the answer, for it explains many puzzling observations of my own, such as why flies that have *proven* effective on other nearby streams are so useless on the Chimehuin.

The explanation will lodge painfully in the craws of many fly fishermen, for it implies that while the fish grew wiser over the years, the fly fishermen failed to keep pace. It would appear that a lot of fish are — perish the thought — outsmarting a lot of smart fishermen.

Whatever the case, as you start fishing the Chimehuin, do not march into the stream expecting the fish to line up behind your fly — as you have heard they used to do. These fish have encountered the likes of you many times before.

None of this means that the Chimehuin is not still an outstanding trout stream, for many still the best river in the southern hemisphere. Indeed, it merely adds another dimension to the legend. It does mean that if you are to catch fish on this river you will need to marshall and put into practice every fishing skill you possess. Stalk carefully, avoid sloppy casts, use the lightest tippets you are secure with, study the naturals, change flies often — in a phrase, approach the river with the respect it deserves.

Well-marked public access to the river is provided at several points from the road below the boca. The first of these downstream from the bridge is a path that leads to the *Pozón de las Viudas* (Widow's Pool), an hour-glass-shaped pool favored by the widows of the owners of the estancia that was once adjacent to the river at this point. Below the Widow's Pool is the *Corredera Larga*, the Long Run, a moderate-depth reach long distance casters will love.

Next is the *Manzano* (Apple Tree Pool). There are two pools with this name, one above Junin, and another below town, so if you make plans to meet friends at the *Manzano*, be sure you have the same pool in mind. The upper *Manzano* has yielded scores of huge fish. The most recent I saw was a fifteen-pound brown lugged with loud, macho

fanfare into Junín's only restaurant. This stretch of the Chimehuin is fly fishing only water, but fish like this are often taken with what Argentines call a *moscón* (mohs-CONE) or big fly. A moscón is a large, heavily weighted fly, usually similar to a black wooly bugger or marabou that is used with spinning tackle. It is fished deep with a jerky retrieve and is very effective for large fish. Moscóns meet the letter of the law, but violate its spirit and in my view should be prohibited on fly fishing only waters.

The next two pools are *Corrales* (Corral Pool) and well-named *Piedra del Viento* (Windy Rock Pool). The second public access point below the bridge leads to the *Balsa Vieja* (Old Ferry Pool). The third access leads to *Herradura* (Horseshoe Pool), and nearing Junin, the fourth access, near the bridge over the canal, leads to *Boca Toma*.

The nearest designated public access point to Junin is near an undeveloped campground a mile or so above the turnoff to Lago Huechulafquen from Argentine Route 234. It provides access to a portion of the river known locally as *Usina*. Upstream from the campground, the Chimehuin braids into several channels which usually form very long, easily wadeable riffles. This reach is personally significant, for it was the first place I fished the Chimehuin. My first cast, made on a sunny January afternoon, yielded a 23-inch rainbow and during the rest of the day I caught and released fifteen more fish from one to four pounds on a small muddler that did not survive the experience. It was an impressive introduction. . .

West of the campground is an array of buildings that was once a fish hatchery and now houses Neuquen's Applied Ecology Center. The center is used primarily for fishery studies and propagation of llamas and coypús. If your schedule permits, take time to visit the center and inspect the animals, for the staff are friendly, patient with foreigners struggling with Spanish, and pleased to describe their work to in-

Middle reaches of the Río Chimehuin. The green patch at upper left is the town of Junín de los Andes.

---

terested visitors.

Downstream from the campground, the river passes a military installation, passes through Junín's equivalent of state fairgrounds, flows under the highway 234 bridge, and curves gently into Junín de los Andes. The last famous pool is at the northern edge of town, the *Pozón de las Señoritas* (Ladies' Pool), so named because of its proximity to the brothel, whose employees sometimes do their wash in the pool. Obviously, the waters close to Junín are all accessible, and are fished very heavily by townspeople, but they should not be ignored for that reason. In 1990, for instance, I met a Texan in my hotel who was traveling by bus to Chile. His schedule had gone awry and he had to spend an unplanned day and night in Junín while awaiting a connecting bus. He had a pack rod with him, for he had heard about Chilean trout, but he knew very little about Argentine fishing. With an hour to kill before dinner, he set up his rod and strolled four blocks down to the Ladies' Pool, where he promptly hooked (and lost) the largest trout he had ever seen. He had to leave early the next morning, but that Texan will not soon forget Junín de los Andes. . .

Junín de los Andes. Among those who fought in the Campaign of the Desert was a man named Miguel Vidal, a buck sergeant in one of General Roca's cavalry regiments. Vidal liked the looks of the country along the Río Chimehuin. The hills are studded with dramatic outcrops of basalt, and erosion has exposed the plugs of two or three ancient volcanos. The slopes are covered with sage-like nenéo, and the valley bottoms are green meadows of grass and sedges.

So Vidal decided to stay. Although the campaign had ended successfully, he was a prudent man, so the first structure he built was a small fort. He named it Junín after the Peruvian site of a decisive battle in South America's war of independence from Spain. Thus on February 15, 1883, a year before Neuquen was even accorded territorial status, Junín de los Andes became the region's first settlement.

In the century since then, other cities in the province have overshadowed Junín (hoo-NEEN). The town seemed to languish and neither acquired the commercial importance of the city of Neuquen nor became a tourist mecca like nearby San Martín de los Andes. What eventually distinguished Junín from its sister cities is indicated on a battered sign along the highway at the entrance to town. The lettering, fading and barely legible, says *Capital Nacional de la Trucha*, "Trout Capital of the Nation."

Today Junín is a ranching community of 7,500 souls with an unpretentious, distinctly frontier flavor, and small town charm. Auracaria trees line a scrupulously clean plaza. Stores and houses are small and trim. Families walk arm-in-arm to church on Sunday. Teen-agers gawk at tourists and whisper and giggle among themselves. At night, few neon lights illuminate store-fronts; and but for a few patrons of Junín's restaurant, sidewalks are usually empty and streets silent by ten p.m. Travel writers call it "unspoiled," but few travelers would give Junín a second glance were it not in the midst of some of the finest trout fishing waters on the face of the earth.

Fishermen have compared Junín to Livingston, Ennis, and West Yellowstone, towns whose principal claim to fame is their proximity to fine trout fishing. As we all know, some trout towns in the United States are not above promoting themselves and their attractions to an extent that somewhat overshadows reality. Junín, however, does not fall into this category.

Within a half-hour drive of Junín, visitors can reach the Chimehuin, Malleo, lower Aluminé, Collon Cura, Quilquihue, and Curruhue Rivers. Somewhat further afield flow the Quillen, upper Aluminé, Ñorquinco, Caleufu, Meliquina, and Filo Hua Hum Rivers. It is safe to say that several hundred miles of trout streams in which flourish several thousand tons of fish lie within a fifty-mile radius of this serene village, quite possibly site of the densest concentration of exquisite trout habitat in the world.

Junín, however, has not yet given itself over to fishermen. Its streets are not yet lined with tackle shops, parked drift boats, or neon royal coachmen. Even so, newly arrived visitors soon notice that something is up. Groups of cheerful men file into the town's only restaurant for dinner with long-billed caps, polaroid fishing glasses dangling from sunburned necks. A few pedestrians stroll by conspicuously decked out in the latest angling fashions from Orvis, L.L. Bean's, Eddie Bauer, Kaufmann's and so on. Occasionally, a fisherman in full battle dress will step from a car, gadgets arrayed across his vest like campaign ribbons. Now and then, vans pass by with big inflatable rafts in tow. Dusty rental cars are much in evidence.

Junín does have two rather unobtrusive general tackle shops, one on the south side of the plaza and another a few doors east, but more important to fly fisherman, this tiny town has the only authentic fly shop in Argentina, indeed Latin America—not a lure in sight. The shop is an adjunct to the STH fly reel factory, located a literal stone's throw from the Río Chimehuin, at the northeast corner of town, just above the Ladies' Pool. The shop has all the tools and gadgetry so dear to the hearts of fly fishermen: rods (Orvis and Loomis blanks), reels, fly boxes, boots, vests, lines (Scientific Angler and Cortland), leaders, and a large selection of quality flies tied by such skilled Argentines as Pepe Delgado, Allan Fraser, and Carlos

Trisciuzzi. If the airlines have managed to lose all of your baggage, all is not lost if you can somehow reach this shop. Fishermen should pay a visit to the shop whether or not they need anything, not only to study the fly selection, but if possible, to tour the reel factory.

STH reels is the brainchild of Roberto Sacconi and several associates. In 1975, Sacconi realized that his passion for fly fishing and his engineering know-how could be merged to create a better fly reel. He opened a small factory in Buenos Aires and quickly began to produce a series of fly reels of advanced design by combining computerized production techniques with the craftsmanship of skilled metalworkers, and by subjecting his product to rigorous laboratory and field tests (some reels have survived four *million* revolutions without failure). The world rushed to his door and the result is 72 models of fly reels designed for everything from tarpon to trout. The reels are impressive, machined from a single piece of special aluminum alloy, constructed to tolerances more commonly employed in the exploration of space than of trout streams, and imbued with a compact, anodized beauty that delights the eye as much as the hand of all fly fishermen. Sacconi eventually realized, with characteristic foresight, that it would be far more appropriate to manufacture fly reels in the heart of trout country than in far-off Buenos Aires. So ten years later he moved his factory to Junín.

The move has been a success. The factory employs residents of Junín and he and his staff can field-test his products just outside the front door. At considerable cost, Sacconi has avoided polluting processes involved at some steps in the manufacture of the reels; the factory does not contaminate the Chimehuin, which flows by a few yards away. A year ago, Sacconi decided to add the fly shop, thus converting Junín into a true fly fishermen's headquarters. Most North American tackle manufacturers and trout towns could learn a number of useful lessons from the experiences of Roberto Sacconi and Junín de los Andes.

In the center of town and on its outskirts, four hotels and inns offer accommodations to fishermen.

The oldest and most famous of these is the Hostería Chimehuin, next to the river three blocks east of the plaza. Old-timers still call the Hostería Chimehuin El Turco's—the Turk's—after its late Lebanese owner, José Julián. The inn was once the gathering place of Argentina's first few fly fishermen and when Patagonian fishing was discovered by the rest of the world, shortly after World War II, members of the international fishing fraternity joined the small aristocratic crowd that met every season at the Hostería Chimehuin to share cocktails and fishing tales. Now run by the Turk's autocratic widow, much of the inn's glory has faded; the quality of food and service has slipped and rooms in the original buildings are deteriorating, but dimming photographs and fishing memorabilia on the walls tell a good deal of the story of this angling landmark. Despite its decline, the Turk's is still popular, newer annexes are more comfortable, and the dining room still rings with fishing stories.

On the highway just north of town, the new Hotel Alejandro Primero offers room and half-pension to visitors in a comfortable building constructed along the lines of a fishing/hunting lodge. West of the highway across from town, Hotel San Jorge sits on a gentle slope overlooking Junín. Like the Alejandro Primero, the San Jorge offers room and meals to fishermen in pleasant surroundings. Prices at all three hotels are reasonable and competitive, and meals can be arranged to accommodate any fishing schedule.

Fishermen watching their budgets should stop by the Residencial Roster, a comfortable family-run hotel two blocks west of the plaza. Small and friendly, the Roster lacks a dining room and only serves a continental breakfast to its guests. Sandwiches and light snacks are available at several places in town, but a full lunch or dinner can only be obtained at Junín's one restaurant, the Ruca Hueney, on the southeast corner of the plaza.

The Ruca Hueney is presided over in Old World fashion by its rotund, mustached owner, who every few minutes makes a round of the restaurant greeting diners and their families and friends while nattily dressed waiters dart among a dozen or so tables. He is quick to identify fishermen and always asks his guests how the day's fishing went. Two or three entrees are usually available at lunch and dinner, and a meal with appetizer, dessert, and wine is a hearty experience. Unfortunately, the menu varies but little, and after several evenings of the same fare even the dullest palate grows restive.

Junín is in ranch country. While ex-ploring the nearby rivers, you often see cattle, sheep, and long-haired angora goats grazing the hillsides or being moved about by mounted gauchos. If you arrive in January or February, you are especially fortunate, for your visit will coincide with one of Junín's two celebrations at which these gauchos show off their outstanding horsemanship and other ranching skills. The first of these, called the *rural* (roo-RAHL), takes place in late January and is the rough equivalent of a combined county fair and rodeo. The second celebration, called the *Fiesta del Puestero* (pway-STAY-ro), is held in mid-February, is larger and more boisterous than the *rural*, and approximates a state fair/rodeo. A *puesto* is the seasonal home of a gaucho who tends to herds of domestic animals at great distance from the comfort and facilities of ranch headquarters. These

A parade during the "Fiesta del Puestero," *Junín de los Andes.*

Guachos at rest during the "Fiesta del Puestero," Junín de los Andes. Note the sheathed facones *(daggers) tucked into sashes.*

men live lonely and difficult lives and rely entirely on their own skills, somewhat like North American sheepherders of eras long past. They are called *puesteros* and the fiesta is both a celebration of their skills and an opportunity to have a hell of a party with colleagues they may not have seen for a year or more. Both events take place in a beautiful setting amidst tall pines, willows, and poplars on the banks of the Chimehuin near the Highway 234 bridge. Uproarious events, the celebrations are carried out for residents of Junín and Neuquen Province, not for tourists.

Even when the fishing is great, a hot day and cool night is very well spent wandering about the fairgrounds drinking beer, watching folk music and folk dance groups, eating grilled meat, looking for bargains among the handicrafts (gaucho knives *[facones]*, woolen sweaters, tack, decorative weavings, belts, sashes], watching races, roping, and sheep-shearing competitions, inspecting exhibitions, and dancing far into the night. . .

If your itinerary permits, do not fail to see these events and experience an authentic celebration of Argentine country life.

Junín de los Andes is served by nearby Chapelco Airport and has two bus stations. For train buffs, the nearest connections are at Zapala, 125 miles to the north, or at Bariloche, 140 miles to the south. Rental cars are available, but since Junín lacks a formal rental car agency you need to inquire about this service at the town's hotels (San Martín de los Andes, 25 miles south, has two rental car agencies). Obtain a fishing license and regulations at the small tourist office on the central plaza. Unfortunately, international mail service is not reliable in Argentina. Letters arrive from the United States, but only sometimes. If you choose to have mail sent to you in Junín, be sure to have correspondents use the town's complete name and the province—Junín de los Andes, Provincia de Neuquen—in order to avoid confusion with a large city in Buenos Aires Province also named Junín.

Lower Río Chimehuin (from Junín to confluence with the Río Aluminé). The lower river flows entirely through ranchland, but public access is provided at a few points. Two sizable tributaries enter the Chimehuin within a few miles of Junín, the Río Curruhue and Río Quilquihue, and this added volume alters the stream's character somewhat, allowing deeper channels to be carved into the basement rock. The pool/riffle pattern is more regular and the river divides less frequently.

The pool behind Junín's small cathedral is (of course) *Pozón del Cura* (Priest's Pool), and the first pool downstream from town, behind the lumber mill, is called *Matadero* or Slaughterhouse pool for the abattoir that once stood on the site. The next pool, *Toscas Blancas*, White Cliffs, flows beneath a prominent slope of the weathered tufa described above. Both pools are fished very hard by locals. Public access is provided to the *Confluencia Pool*, at the point where the Río Currhue enters the Chimehuin. Downstream from this reach, a long line of Lombardy poplars leads toward the river from Highway 234. This line of trees leads to *Los Alamos*, or the Poplars Pool, and not far below, at a curve in the road which overlooks the river is the Chimehuin's other *Manzano*, or Apple Tree Pool, sometimes called *La Angostura del Manzano.* A conspicuous trail along the west side of the river leads to the deep and mysterious *Marquesa* Pool, which has given up so many gigantic fish to so few fishermen. *Thompson's* Pool, named for a local landowner, lies above the mouth of the Río Quilquihue, to which public access is also provided.

The eight miles or so of river that encompass these pools is one of the most accessible reaches of the river and may also be the most productive, at least with respect to aquatic life. Now and then, for reasons I have not fathomed, the cobbled shores of this reach are littered with the carapaces of scores of dead pancoras, drying salmon-pink in the sun. On these banks I have also found many empty caddis cases of cemented gravel and tiny sticks; a few of them were two inches long. The adults, which I have never seen, must be gigantic; they may be nocturnal emergers.

Except for the overriding fact that trout are more difficult to catch today than in years past, my fishing experiences on the lower river have been so diverse that I can discern no pattern that might be helpful to other fly fishermen. I have diligently worked my way through more variables on this puzzling river than any other stream I have fished. I have fiddled with tippets, fished dry, wet, deep, with indicators, with split shot, early, midday, late, upstream, downstream, and all around stream, never confident that I had finally discovered the solution, only hopeful. I have worked through yards of tippets and scores of flies—including some truly bizarre patterns—on the lower Chimehuin. On some days I have taken several large fish on muddlers or salmon fly nymphs and on other days the only flies that would work were small humpies and royal wulffs floated high through the foam line. On an embarrassing number of days, nothing seems to work. No formulas, no familiar string of events seems to emerge.

From my notes (2/1/88—just below Marquesa Pool):

Sunny and windy. Dense hatch of large and small mayflies, also a few caddis flies. Scant rises until just before dark...took several small rainbows on muddlers (to 12 inches, very fat and strong). Got boring; long strikeless spells. Finally fished Gerry's cricket dry under willows, immediately hooked a 24-inch brown. He jumped hard; that fish was *very* surprised. . .

Gerry's cricket will not help readers, for it is a size 10 black fly tied by a friend of mine in Alaska for his own use. He uses it, with great success, for pink salmon in tidewater. Why it occasionally works on the Chimehuin (and other trout streams), I have no idea. Roberto Sacconi introduced me to an elegant locally-tied wet fly, the Chateaubriand, but even this attractive offering is not always effective.

Eight miles south of Junín, the river curves to the east, away from Highway 234. A dirt road, Provincial Route 49, leaves the paved highway and parallels the river at some distance. Convenient public access is less frequent on this lowest stretch of the river.

The road passes first through a plantation of young pines, then of older pines. About a mile down the road, look for a small sign that says *Peatonal* (footpath). This is the first access point to the river downstream from the highway. A stile over the fence on the river side of the road leads to a path which in turn leads to the *Puente Negro* (Black Bridge Pool). It is a fairly long walk and there are good stretches above and below the pool, so pack a lunch.

Four miles from Highway 234, the road passes a grove of poplars in which sits a small store housed in a charming building of native rock. The last public access point on the lower river is nearby, a long path that leads through an area called the *Bosque Triángulo* (Triangular Forest) to the river.

A few miles beyond, the road climbs up out of the valley floor away from the river. Between these points a broad meadow, the *Mallin Redondo*, lies between the road and the river. Many fishermen park near the concrete pylons that carry high tension wires, cross the fence, and hike through the grass and cattle to the stream. Best to ask permission to do so at the Estancia Cerro de Los Pinos, behind the small store.

After the road leaves the river valley, it winds through dry hills reminiscent of Montana, complete with herefords and bull thistles, for about ten miles to the south shore of the Río Collon Cura, about six miles below La Rinconada.

The lowest four or five miles of the Chimehuin are virtually inaccessible to the public without making a long hike. As a result, this is the part of the river that receives the least fishing pressure. Unfortunately, permission to hike downstream over lands of the Estancia Chimehuin is not always granted. Fishermen determined to wet a line in this portion of the river should drive to La Rinconada, follow the Aluminé downstream for about two miles until they are across the river from the mouth of the Chimehuin, seen easily from the highway. Park the car, carefully wade across the Aluminé above the confluence, and hike up the Chimehuin (it may not be possible to wade across the Aluminé early in the season). Start early, when the day is cool, for it can be a long, tough hike along sunbaked slopes. The Chimehuin has gathered considerable momentum near the end of its journey from Lago Huechulafquen and the big boulders that comprise its streambed in these reaches make for tough wading. The fishing, however, can be extraordinary. . .

Río Curruhue (coor-WAY). Two miles south of Junín, Highway 234 crosses the Curruhue River. At the bridge, a dirt road follows the stream west toward its source, lower Lago Curruhue, lowest in a long chain of clear lakes. The Curruhue ("dark place") is a short, small stream, ten to twenty feet wide, for most of its 12 miles a merry riffle through clean, polished boulders—a good fly stream

for light tackle. At times well-hackled, easily visible dry flies that will float high through its turbulence are very effective. The Curruhue, however, has fishing characteristics that vary dramatically through the season, an attribute that can be very frustrating for fly fishermen.

One acquaintance, for instance, who habitually fishes dry flies upstream on a short line with very short drifts, was astonished by the number of fish from 18 to 22 inches (rainbows and browns) that this technique brought to net four miles above Highway 234 in December of 1988. When we fished the same reaches in February, 1990, the stream was a good foot lower than its spring flow level and our largest fish was six inches long. . .

The Curruhue is an early season stream, fished with most success in November and December. The river is well oxygenated, but in late season its flow is so low and the albedo of its rocky bed so high that its temperature rises considerably and I am sure that all but the smallest fish then move upstream to the lakes or downstream to the Chimehuin. If you arrive in Junín early in the season, by all means explore the river with a light rod and a pocket full of dry flies. But if you have not arrived until after New Year's Day, drive out to the bridge and peer at the stream. If it appears to be filling its banks fairly well and is clear, fish it; if the stream appears to be low, direct your attention elsewhere if good fishing is your objective for the day.

If the river is fishable, drive up the road, and have at it. But even if the river is too low, give a day over to driving up the Curruhue Valley, for the road nearly reaches the Chilean border, passes no fewer than five lakes, leads to a delightful hot springs, and is one of Patagonia's least known scenic drives, well off beaten tourist paths.

For the first ten miles, the road passes through valley farm and ranchland—cultivated fields, meadows, long "curtains" of Lombardy poplars, and pine plantations. Access to the river is spotty in the valley bottom, but here and there the road passes within a few yards of the Curruhue and there are several places in which you can clamber into the stream from roadside without risk of trespassing.

Ten miles from Highway 234, a road from the south joins the dirt road from Junín. This road, reopened in 1990 on repair of a bridge across the Río Quilquihue, leads to San Martín de los Andes. Drive straight on. A few trees begin to appear on the hillsides, and ahead the densely forested cordillera comes into view. Fifteen miles from the highway, the road enters Lanín National Park and a forest of low ñire trees. A mile beyond lies lower Curruhue Lake.

Lago Curruhue (or Curruhue Chico) holds landlocked Atlantic salmon, but is a difficult lake for fly fishermen. The boca is too small and brushy for quality fly fishing and unless you see rises within casting range along the lake's margins, pass the lake up.

The road gets rough at the lake, for it is hewn out of rocky cliffs well above the water. A park ranger's office lies along the road on the moraine that separates Curruhue Chico from the much larger upper lake, Curruhue Grande. Here, 20 miles from the highway, you are negotiating a narrow winding road up an alpine valley with high peaks on both sides. Lago Curruhue Grande, eleven miles long, glimmers through the trees below the road. Soon the road becomes a cool, green tunnel through a forest of gigantic coihue trees and dense bamboo thickets. Keep an eye out for the sign that identifies the 200-year-old coihue.

Twenty-five miles from the highway, the road descends to the west end of Lago Curruhue Grande. A short side road leads to several forested campsites at the edge of a lovely beach of sand and gravel. At this point, the forest shelters the lake from prevailing westerly winds and the water is usually glass-calm. Be certain to inspect the beach-edge for rises. On my last visit to the lake, I hooked a six-pound cruising rainbow from this beach on a Joe's Hopper.

The fish was rather stupid. No grasshoppers were in sight; I was in a hurry and it was simply the first fly I saw when I popped open my fly box. The fish ignored my rushed, sloppy casts, but when I finally put the fly within range, the experience became a textbook operation.

A half-mile past the end of the lake, the road forks. Take the left or southern fork for 200 yards to the shore of Lago Verde, a small lake that opens an excellent view of high Andean scenery and stark, black lava flows of recent origin.

Take the right or northern fork to continue westward into the heart of the mountains. At 35 miles from the highway, the road crosses *El Escorial*, a steep flow of glassy, black scoria several miles long that has spilled north from nearby Huanquihue Volcano. The lava reaches the edge of yet another lake, Lago Epulafquen, actually the southwest arm of Lago Huechulafquen. Epulafquen *(epu* means "two," and *lafquen* means "lake")* holds eight to ten-pound rainbows, but spots from which to cast a fly from shore are rare. The road passes the south shore of the lake and a mile further on passes the last lake, Lago Carilafquen ("Green Lake"). Just south of Lago Carilafquen, a sign marked *Cascada Carilafquen* indicates the trail-head for an easy 20-minute walk to a small waterfall on the short stream that flows from Lago Carilafquen into Lago Epulafquen. To combine a short hike through a pleasant forest with a bit of boca fishing, tote your rod down this trail.

Just past Carilafquen, about a two-hour drive from Junín, lie the *Termales Lahuen-Co.* The road first passes a park ranger office, and a hundred yards further, a well-developed campground. Drive past the campground and keep right to reach the thermal area.

The hot springs have changed considerably over the decades. A ferry from the west end of Lago Huechulafquen once provided service to Puerto Encuentro on Lago Epulafquen, from which it is a short drive to the thermals. Free lodging for reasonable periods of time was

Boca of the Río Quilquihue at Lago Lolog, near San Martín de los Andes.

provided in rustic cabins not far from several hot pools. But the ferry service has been discontinued, and during the most recent dispute between Chile and Argentina, the military occupied the zone and the cabins were torn down, presumably to deny shelter to an occupying force. Abandoned for several years, the area was finally donated to the Province of Neuquen by national park authorities. It is now in administrative limbo, but an enterprising family has since tidied up the site and reconstructed a bathhouse which contains six big tubs in separate rooms, clean and comfortable.

Lahuen-Co means "medicinal or miraculous waters" in Mapuche, and devotees of these springs have abiding faith in the therapeutic powers of the waters. Not many Argentines visit the springs regularly, but those who do have made the pilgrimage for years, even decades. The waters are fervently believed to relieve or cure just about any ailment that afflicts mankind, from bone diseases to skin problems to digestive disorders. While I cannot verify these claims from personal experience, I always steep for a spell in one of the tubs, just in case. And I can definitely confirm that after a couple of hours on a dusty winding road, a soak in the piping hot spring water is a very pleasant experience indeed. . .

Río Quilquihue (keel-KEY-way). Only five miles south of the Río Curruhue, Highway 234 crosses the Río Quilquihue, last of the Chimehuin's principal tributaries. From midseason on, the river at this point is tiny, a broad trickle of water through polished stones and shallow pools. I suspect, however, that much of the stream's flow is bled off for irrigation somewhere upstream, for the Quilquihue seems larger at its source, Lago Lolog, than near its mouth.

Jim Sperry casts into the martini-clear waters of the Río Quilquihue.

All twelve miles of the river flow through private lands and the middle reaches of the stream are nearly inaccessible for lack of nearby public roads.

Quilquihue means "place of *quilqui*," a small fern *(Lomaria chilensis)* that flourishes in bogs and wet meadows. The name applies to conditions long since changed, for I've observed no such places along the river. Like the Curruhue, the Río Quilquihue is a low priority stream for fly fishermen during low flows. Fish seem to be uniformly small in the Quilquihue; the largest trout I've taken from this stream over several years has been a one-pound rainbow.

It is, nevertheless, a pleasant stream to explore and on good days the river provides lots of action on light tackle. The most convenient stretch of the river is near the Highway 234 bridge, where you can fish a quarter-mile of shallow riffle downstream to its confluence with the Chimehuin.

The next easily reached section is five miles down the highway toward San Martín de los Andes, just behind Chapelco Airport. Drive into the airport, park your car, and walk—as inconspicuously as possible—around the airstrip to the river. In this area, the stream is paved with clean but awkward-sized cobbles that floor a series of riffles and waist-deep pools. You can wade across almost anywhere. No trees line the banks, only a few willows and lots of spiny shrubs. But for a few steep banks, there is no shelter on this reach of the river. For that reason, I do not fish here on windy days and I suggest that you do not, either. Some odd feature of terrain turns this zone into a virtual wind tunnel on breezy afternoons.

The upper Quilquihue is a much different river. The banks are thickly forested and the river is larger, divided into more distinct freestone riffles and long, hip-deep runs and chutes. Most of the fish are still small here, but it is an even more pleasant reach to fish than the lower river.

To reach it most directly from Junín, drive toward San Martín de los Andes on paved Highway 234. About a mile before reaching town, a sign indicates Lago Lolog to the right (west). The side road is paved for a mile or so, then turns to dirt just beyond a military base (ignore the well-armed guard on the road unless you are actually flagged down). Continue six miles, winding uphill, until the lake comes into sight. The road forks; take the right (north) fork and you soon reach the bridge across the river, just below the boca. Stop and park here (the road continues ten miles to join the Junín route to Lahuen-Co Hot Springs).

About 100 yards of smooth enticing water lie between the bridge and lake. A typically narrow and very long lake, Lago Lolog is oriented east-west and prevailing westerlies kick large waves into the boca on a normal day. Fish downstream from the bridge to escape the wind. Trails follow both banks of the river; take the trail down the northern shore. A quarter-mile below the bridge you will find a wide, lake-like spot in the river ringed with reeds. Casting is difficult here because of obstructions and deep water, but small fish rise in this pool—along with a few large ones I have been unable to fool. Below the pool, the river breaks into its more characteristic rapids. Look for torrent ducks in the

Río Quilquihue, near San Martín de los Andes.

river and austral parakeets in the beeches.

At this point, we leave the drainage of the Río Collon Cura, into which all of the rivers described to this point drain. The next series of streams, with a few exceptions, eventually drain into the Río Limay. Both series ultimately reach the Río Neuquen, but those which follow are more easily reached from the town of San Martín de los Andes, a few tiny villages, and in a few cases, from Bariloche. We'll start at the town of San Martín de los Andes.

San Martín de los Andes. San Martín, an attractive town nestled in wooded mountains at the foot of Lago Lácar, lies 24 miles southwest of Junín. If you are flying to San Martín or Junín, book passage to Chapelco Airport, which lies about halfway between the two towns. San Martín is considerably larger than Junín and has more tourist facilities, but is still small enough to explore afoot. Central European architecture prevails, and many hotels, restaurants, shops, and coffee houses are decorated in alpine motifs. Because San Martín is a gateway town to two Argentine national parks as well as a growing ski resort, it is more of a bustling tourist center than Junín, and is somewhat more expensive, but it is nonetheless a charming town and well located with respect to certain trout waters.

Fly fishermen who prefer a somewhat more bustling ambience than somnolent Junín are likely to find San Martín to their taste. All of the streams north of Junín are accessible from San Martín and are only about a half-hour's drive further than from Junín. San Martín, on the other hand, is the logical base for reaching several rivers to the south: Meliquina, Filo Hua Hum, upper Caleufu, and Traful.

Your first stop should be the tourist office on the central plaza. San Martín's tourist office is exceptionally well-organized and helpful. Staff are courteous, efficient, and some are bilingual. Names, addresses, rates, and snap-shots of hotels, inns, and homes of families who accept tourists are prominently posted, and accommodations for every budget are available. At this office you may also obtain fishing licenses and regulations, local and regional maps (also try the ACA office for maps), and information on car rental agencies, currency exchange, and so on. If you are news-starved, you can buy the English language Buenos Aires Herald at the Ateneo bookstore and coffee house, on San Martín's main street.

San Martín has at least two dozen hotels and inns which range from comfortable modern facilities to extremely charming lodge or chalet-style accommodation. Breakfast is usually included in the room charge and most of the hotels have a dining room. The town also has at least two dozen restaurants and

cafes. Many restaurants are on the single main street, but San Martín is a great town to explore, so do not ignore the many smaller, often cheaper restaurants and coffee shops on the back streets. Meals can be exquisite. I'll not soon forget one such dinner of hot bread served with a buttery cheese sauce, a baked chicken breast with rice, nuts, raisins, and curry, washed down with ice water and a light white wine, and followed by fresh raspberries in cream, and expresso.

Two tackle shops have been opened in San Martín which carry some fly fishing equipment, but the only place you can now buy quality flies is in the small boutique next to the lobby of the Hotel La Chemineé. The boutique carries a line of lovely handicrafts that happens to include a large selection of flies tied by or under the supervision of Pepe

San Martín de los Andes, on the shores of Lago Lácar.

An upscale hotel in San Martín frequented by fishermen.

Delgado, one of Argentina's premier fly-tiers; everything from big streamers to dry flies to nymphs to English salmon fly patterns are available.

San Martín de los Andes is the northern terminus of one of South America's most heavily traveled but beautiful scenic drives, the so-called Seven-Lakes Route *(Ruta de Siete Lagos)* to Bariloche through Nahuel Huapi National Park. The route is a spectacular succession of sparkling lakes set in dense forests amid mountains that extend well above timberline. A few good fishing places described below lie along the route, but fishermen should take a day to travel the route whether they plan to fish along the way or not, for it is a splendid sightseeing trip through the heart of the east-slope Andes.

Río Meliquina (may-lee-KEEN-uh). First of a trio of small trout rivers south of San Martín, the Río Meliquina is a small jewel that is the outlet stream for the lake of the same name. It was once one of the finest landlocked salmon streams in South America and though the number of salmon in the stream is today small, it still holds a good population of rainbow and brown trout.

To reach the stream, drive south from San Martín on Highway 234, start

of the Seven-Lakes Route, which becomes a gravel road on the outskirts of town. Sixteen miles from town, the road forks. Take the left (southeast) fork, provincial Route 63, and continue. Two miles from the fork, the road reaches the northern end of Lago Meliquina and winds down its southern shore. A mile down the lakeshore, the road passes the entrance to the Club Norysur, one of Argentina's oldest private fishing clubs. Although the club is private, brief visits by fly fishermen are not discouraged by the present manager. Decades ago, this was nearly the only place in Patagonia to obtain flies tied by an Argentine, Jose "Pépe" Navas, a carpenter who became the club's chief guide and general factotum, and at that time nearly the only Argentine who could tie flies. Navas is now retired, but it is often possible to obtain a few of his flies at the club.

Club Norysur, once called *Asociación de la Pesca en los Parques Nacionales* (National Park Fishing Association), and its nearby streams and lakes occupy an important place in Argentina's fishing history, for it was the nursery for many Argentines who have since become dedicated fly fishermen. The club's lounge and dining room were the first places that many young men heard of this curious endeavor called fly fishing and the nearby streams were the first waters into which they made those first doubtful and awkward casts.

The club's fishing records, kept since 1946, offer a detailed and fascinating glimpse at changes in fishing attitudes and fish species over nearly a half century. A sharp fisheries student will one day learn a great deal about the mechanics of trout and salmon interactions as well as earn an advanced degree by subjecting these records to rigorous statistical analysis.

One of the surprising facts that can be gleaned from the club's records is that the Río Caleufu once consistently yielded larger fish than the much more famous Chimehuin. The records also indicate that although many club members were already fly fishermen, in the early 1970's the popular trend in fishing style shifted dramatically from trolling in lakes to fly fishing in rivers. The trend is confirmed by records of other fishing clubs and resorts; fly fishing was catching on throughout Argentina. Finally, the records reveal what happened when brown trout arrived on a scene dominated by rainbows and landlocked salmon. The first brown to appear in the area, a two-pound youngster taken from the Río Meliquina, was taken in 1953. Ten years later, the largest brown caught outweighed the largest rainbow. By 1973, six rainbow trout over four pounds were caught, but during the same interval *fifty-six* brown trout over four pounds were landed—in this region, at least, the browns had apparently won the struggle.

And that is one reason to keep your wits about you on the small, unlikely-looking Meliquina. The river flows south for nine miles from the south end of the lake, where it is joined by the even smaller Río Filo-Hua-Hum to form the Río Caleufu. If it is late in the season, walk upstream to the boca from the bridge below the lake to see if you can spot large fish in the glassy waters. A prior generation of fly fishermen once used twelve-foot greenheart rods to cast Hardy-tied salmon flies to shoals of salmon to twelve pounds in this pool.

Except for a few inholdings, the west bank of the river lies within Lanín National Park; the east bank, as well as the land around the lake is in private hands. There are, nonetheless, several points of public access to the river over the next several miles. Most of the Meliquina flows through woodlands, a jumble of boulders that pile up every so often to form deep swirling pools. Expect to beat brush and clamber over rockpiles. The river supports rainbows, browns, and a few brook trout, and on some days these fish will rise as readily to dry flies as to nymphs and wet flies. Most of the fish you raise will probably weigh a pound or two, but stay awake on this stream, for as soon as your concentration flags, a six or seven-pounder is likely to glide out of the shade or drift from behind a boulder to correct your lapse, and carry away your fly to boot.

Río   Filo   Hua   Hum (fee-lo-wah-OOM). It means "Snake Basin River", but do not let the name scare you; I have only seen two or three snakes in the years I've wandered through Patagonia and none of them on this river. The stream drains the lake of the same name and is only about two miles long below the lake.

Nine miles south of the south end of Lago Meliquina, a dead-end dirt road (provincial route 64) forks right (west) from Route 63, and heads toward Lago Filo Hua Hum and the east end of Lago Falkner. The Filo Hua Hum first drains Lago Falkner, flows about five miles to Lago Filo Hua Hum, drains that lake and then flows two more miles to join the Río Meliquina. I have not fished the upper five miles of the river simply because I don't like its looks, but I manage to fish the lower two miles regularly. I park the car near the boca at the east end of Lago Filo Hua Hum, fish the boca, wade into the river, fish downstream all the way to the Meliquina, and hitch a ride back to the car. It's hard work, but can be a long, pleasant day of fishing.

The lake, deep glacial blue, is about three miles long and is restricted to fly fishing. Grebes, geese, mergansers, and ducks are usually plentiful. The boca merges into a series of gin-clear meanders with beds of sand and mud, and reefs of elodea. The bottom at the boca is firmer than it looks; with waders, a fly fisherman can wade far into the lake and cast in every direction. In 100 yards of the meanders below the lake I once counted over two dozen trout from two to four pounds, mostly rainbows. The fish are spooky and long fine leaders are required in the boca and meanders. The first fish I hooked in this river was the most emaciated trout I have ever seen; it was two feet long and

The shining Río Caleufu, at its confluence with the Río Collon Cura.

weighed just over two pounds — practically an eel. But I was relieved to find that it was a fluke catch, for all other fish, about three rainbow trout to each brown, have been in normal condition.

The first part of the river below the boca is grand wading — gravel and small cobbles — but the lower mile is treacherous, full of huge, irregularly-shaped rocks. Do not forget your bug dope, for black flies and big horse flies can be bad along the lake and river. The stream holds lots of small fish, but my notes also indicate fish at nearly every stop on a tape measure — 13, 15, 16, 17, 19, 21, 22, and 23 inches. Montana nymphs, muddlers, and on some days, dry flies can be effective on the Filo Hua Hum.

Río Caleufu (kah-LAY-oo-foo). Last of the three streams in the Meliquina zone, the river is formed at the junction of the Río Meliquina and the Río Filo Hua Hum, and flows about 30 miles east to the Collon Cura. The Mapuches called it simply *Caleufu*, "the other river." It holds browns, rainbows, and in its uppermost reaches, brook trout.

The Río Caleufu has been another of those enigmatic Argentine trout streams in my experience. On some days I have hooked one fish after another from three to five pounds with such careless ease that I have grown bored; other days have ended with fruitless, increasingly frantic searches through fly boxes for something that might provoke a strike. Hiking along high banks during midday hours, when the sun is high and visibility good, I have seen more large trout hovering like small barracudas in clear, still shallows of the lower Caleufu than in any other Patagonian stream of similar size. Hooking them, however, can be a good deal more difficult than catching sight of them on those bleak, exasperating days...

Access is a serious problem on the Río Caleufu. The river is only accessible from public roads along its upper four miles and its lower four miles. The intervening 22 miles of stream flows through an enormous estancia owned by Mr. Douglas Reid, one of Patagonia's earliest professional fishing guides and a man closely associated with the early development of fly fishing in Patagonia. Access to the river, and accommodation at the estancia can be arranged through Northern and Central Zone guides.

The upper Caleufu is accessible at several points along Argentine Route 63 south of the bridge across the Río Filo Hua Hum. About four miles below the bridge, Route 63 leaves the river valley and climbs toward Paso Córdoba. Park the car along the road in any of several pull-offs and make your way to the river, but don't forget that it can be a long uphill walk back to the car.

The lowest few miles of the Caleufu are accessible by a different, distant route. The quickest way to reach the lower river from Junín is to take paved Highway 234 north from Junín to La Rinconada and continue on Highway 40 southeast to the intersection with Highway 237, the main paved route to Bariloche from the north. Drive south on Highway 237 and cross the Collon Cura bridge. Just south of the bridge, turn right on a dirt road, Route 49, which heads back northwest. Approximately ten miles from the paved highway, Route 49 passes a couple of remote estancias and crosses the Río Caleufu about two miles above the point at which it enters the Collon Cura. Park the car and fish upstream or downstream.

The lower river is not forested like the upper river; dense thickets of brush and willows line its channels. The going is easy, however, once you reach the river proper. Long sand and gravel bars provide easy passage for fishermen, and wading is easy. Near the bridge, the river has formed a few small, spring creek-like side channels that are worth exploring with tiny flies on light tippets. On its long, exposed passage through the steppelands, the Caleufu warms considerably. My notes indicate that the lower river is usually several degrees warmer than the Collon Cura. The temperature of the lower Caleufu makes for comfortable wet wading, but I suspect that it also drives many of the larger fish into the Collon Cura late in the season, a surmise I have tried to exploit on the latter river.

If you drive south from the upper Caleufu on Route 63, or drive south on paved Route 237 from the Collon Cura bridge near the lower Caleufu, you will eventually reach a small stream with a huge reputation, the Río Traful.

Río Traful (trah-FOOL). Ask any Argentine fly fishermen to name their five favorite Patagonian rivers, and the lists are likely to include the Chimehuin, Correntoso, Malleo, Río Grande (Tierra del Fuego)—and the Río Traful. The order of the rivers may change in accordance with individual tastes, and like most fishermen, they may have a particular fondness for a stream avoided by others, but a great many of them will say that the Río Traful is the finest fly stream in South America.

About 12 miles long, the river is one of the storied streams of Patagonia,

Estancia La Primavera, on the Río Traful.

The lovely Traful Valley, from Estancia La Primavera.

notable not only for its fish, but for the extraordinary scenery of the countryside through which it winds. A moderate-sized river, from 20 to 40 feet wide, it has long riffles with distinct heads, centers, and tails, waist-deep runs, rocky pocket water, and in its short canyon a few of those long, alluring pools in whose shimmering depths every fisherman expects the monster fish-of-his-life-time to lurk. The Río Traful is the outlet stream of Lago Traful, an unspoiled twenty-mile-long lake in the north section of Nahuel Huapi National Park. Like the Collon Cura, the Traful ("union of rivers") reaches an ignominious end when it flows into the Embalse Alicura, the same reservoir that destroyed the lower Río Limay. So die rivers. The lower half of the Traful is readily accessible from roads that parallel each bank, but the upper half flows through private lands. The north bank of the upper river comprises Estancia Arroyo Verde, owned by Mauricio Lariviere, while the south bank lies on lands of Estancia La Primavera, owned by Mauricio's brother, Felipe.

The upper Traful River Valley has been in the hands of the Lariviere family for over fifty years. "Pim" Lariviere, late father of the two brothers, was one of Argentina's first well-known fishermen and one of the founders of the Club Norysur on Lago Meliquina. He passed his passion for fishing on to his two sons, gracious and cultured men who with their families have been exacting stewards of this peerless river for decades.

Fly fishermen traveling on their own in Patagonia may bristle on learning that they have no practical access to the upper Río Traful. True enough, the issue here and elsewhere in Patagonia (and parts of the United States) merits serious debate. The other side of the coin, however, is apparent on the Río Traful. Unlike many other landowners, Felipe and Mauricio Lariviere have worked tirelessly for decades to maintain and enhance a quality fishery on an extraordinary river that happens to flow through their lands. As a result of those efforts, fly fishermen the world over owe a debt of gratitude to these two men.

The Traful supports hefty browns and rainbows, but the principal reason for its fame is not trout, but landlocked salmon, *Salmo salar sebago. . .*

Legend holds that near the turn of the century, an ox-cart drover noticed that salmon eggs were beginning to hatch several days before they would reach the safety of their intended destination, the new hatchery near Bariloche. Rather than lose the precious cargo, the panicked drovers unloaded the eggs from the wagons, and put them into the nearest water, which happened to be the Río Traful (or say some, Lago Traful). Many plantings of salmon failed in those days, but this serendipitous planting succeeded wildly, and decades of legendary fishing have resulted. Mauricio Lariviere, an enthusiastic historian, doubts the truth of this widely told tale, but the event is at least plausible, for the mortality rate on a number of shipments that included sebago eggs made in about that time was exceptionally high.

In the Northern Zone, the only waters in which salmon have survived the decades are Lago Meliquina, Lago Nahuel Huapi, Lago Curruhue Grande, and the Limay and Meliquina Rivers. But the only system in which they have not merely survived but flourished is in Lago and Río Traful.

This fish, called "the Rolls Royce of freshwater sport fish" by Felipe Lariviere, attracts and puzzles fly fishermen like no other fish. Despite a plethora of theories, no one really knows why the fish does not eat when it makes its spawning run, nor why, since it does not eat, it strikes—or for that matter, fails to strike—certain flies. It is a wonderfully powerful fish; nearly all fly fishermen who have hooked landlocked salmon have from time to time galloped downstream in sudden panic when they realize that their backing might run out. It is a beautiful fish, and in the days when fishermen kept fish, they found that no streamside meal could compare with grilled salmon.

It is likely that salmon were first introduced to the Traful between 1903 and 1908. The first good evidence that the plant succeeded appeared in 1914, when they were first discovered to be spawning in the river. For several decades, the only sport fish in the Traful were salmon and brook trout; the first brown did not appear until 1937. In that year the largest Traful salmon Felipe Lariviere recalls—24 pounds—was netted. In 1938 Estancia La Primavera began to keep careful records, and a 23-pound, 6-ounce salmon was entered in the book. Rainbows and browns have become the predominant fish since those days. The maximum size of the salmon has declined in intervening years—a large fish is now from about nine to eleven pounds—but they still average a respectable five pounds or so. The Traful is today a fly fishing only, catch and release stream.

On my first trip to Argentina, I anticipated fishing the Traful, and carefully packed a handful of English salmon flies I had collected as a teen-ager, oddly named ornate flies tied on heavy hooks that had moldered in fly boxes for years. They didn't look much like anything I ever saw in a river, and would raise eyebrows and provoke smirks in certain circles in the western U.S.: Jock Scott, Black Dose, Lady Caroline, Black Doctor, Green Highlander, Durham Ranger,

and so on. I loved these gaudy and complicated creations, of course, but had absolutely no faith in their ability to catch fish. I was astonished to discover that at least two of them—the Jock Scott and Black Dose—actually worked. I eventually found, however, that such mundane patterns as Mickey Finn streamers and Muddler Minnows could also provoke salmon to strike on the Traful.

Do not step into this river assured that you will hook a salmon. For each trip on which I have managed to hook salmon, there have been about two salmonless trips. Conventional (and logical) local wisdom holds that timing is all important. Since the salmon move down from the lake in May and June, the river is considered to be a late season stream—March and April are the likeliest months. I have had good luck during these months, but have also hooked salmon in the Traful in mid-January (two six-pound fish on No. 8 muddler minnows) and in early February (a five-pound fish on a Mickey Finn); they were probably flukes. More important, unless you are one of those rare fly fishermen who has solved the riddle of landlocked salmon, you may not hook one even if the river teems with them. As Jorge Donovan observes, hooking salmon seems to require an instinct that stems from stream experience rather than the experience one gains from books. Don't get your hopes too high; there are some dues to pay. . .

The Traful is not only a salmon stream. From my notes of January 10 and 11, 1981:

Hard downstream wind just below hatchery. Light sprinkle. First fish 17" brown on No. 6 Mickey Finn. In five hours released 15 fish (six browns, eight rainbows, one small salmon). Six were over 20", one was 24". No one else on stream, fish in every type of water. Second day: Near Piedra del Viento ["Windy Rock"]. Day clear and sunny, water warm: 62° F. Caught 12 fish, three over 20", largest a corpulent 22". Most are

Dunstan gets his Traful salmon.

rainbows in excellent shape. No salmon. Streamers good, bucktails bad. Big rocks, hard work wading. No other fishermen. Wind blowing very hard.

And from January 24, 1978:

Two miles above Río Limay. Sunny; water temperature: 60° F. Got two 19" rainbows, two 18" rainbows. Two four-pound fish escaped. Trout I kept was crammed with ten to twelve pancoras. Took five-pound, 22" salmon. Also caught several rainbows 12-15 inches. Incessant downstream wind.

The valley of the Traful is spectacular. The lower valley is scrubby and dry, but wind and water have carved monolithic outcrops of limestone on both sides of the valley into fantastic formations. Columns, sculpted spires, and fenestrated rock walls jut from the slopes everywhere you look. The river itself lends the impression of sparkling cleanliness, like a great flowing martini. Rocks are scoured smooth, except in slow stretches, and pink roots of willows shine from eroded banks.

The lower six miles of the Río Traful are easily accessible from Route 65, a dirt road that leads west into the park along the south bank of the river from paved Highway 237. Undeveloped roadside campsites are plentiful along Route 65. The point at which the Traful enters the Río Limay (just downstream from the point at which the Limay changes from a river into a reservoir) is called Confluencia. Despite its prominence on maps, Confluencia is not a town, but a road and river junction, and site of an ACA gas station, which has a bar and restaurant but no sleeping accommodations. On a bluff across the Traful from the gas station, however, lies the Hosteria La Gruta de las Vírgenes (Virgin Grotto Inn), a moderately-priced hotel which serves all meals. It provides the nearest accommodations to the lower Traful and Limay rivers.

Estancia Arroyo Verde and Estancia La Primavera both offer accommodations to fly fishermen, which of course includes access to the upper half of the river. Rates are high, but service is splendid in facilities accoutered in the fashion of estancia grandeur and traditional fishing lodges. In keeping with this tradition, pools on the upper river are given wonderful names: Allenby's Pool, Nelly Blood, Pool of Plenty, Paris Pool, Federico's Pool, and so on. On signing the guest book, you join distinguished ranks; Joe and Mary Brooks, Mel Krieger, Carlos Radziwell, Ernie

Bizarre but beautiful formations of weathered limestone characterize the valley of the Río Traful.

Schwiebert, Dwight David Eisenhower, and Bebe Anchorena are only a few of those who have sought salmon and otherwise enjoyed themselves on the Río Traful.

Route 65, a dirt and gravel road, heads west into the park from Confluencia, parallels the lower Río Traful, and eventually the southern shore of Lago Traful. It eventually links with Route 231/234, the Seven-Lakes Route between San Martin de los Andes and Bariloche. About 21 miles west of Confluencia, Route 65 reaches Villa Traful, a tiny and charming village on the shore of Traful. Pleasant log cabins may be rented at Villa Traful, and boats are available. Campsites are plentiful along the lakeshore. The road west to the Traful River from Villa Traful is steep, winding, and narrow, so village accommodations are not recommended for those intending to fish the river. This road, however, is one of the longest good dirt roads through dense forest that I have found anywhere in Argentina, and the campsites on and around Lago Traful are among the most pleasant in the entire park. The scenery is remarkable, and the area is neither as developed nor as crowded as most other lakes in the park.

Río Limay (lee-MY). The Limay River flows from the eastern end of enormous Lago Nahuel Huapi north to Confluencia, where it slides into the backwaters of a hydroelectric reservoir, Embalse Alicura. Virtually every inch of the river is easily accessible—a mixed blessing—for it is paralleled by paved highway 237, the main highway from the north of Argentina to San Carlos de Bariloche, one of the country's principal year-round resorts.

Limay means "limpid, transparent" in the Mapuche tongue and fly fishermen are cautioned never to forget that fact. One of the most noteworthy attributes of the Limay is its extraordinary clarity. It is also a very high energy stream. Because of its transparence, however, it does not *look* very powerful, and therein lies a hazard for fishermen.

The Limay, one of the largest rivers in Patagonia, forms fairly classic riffle/pool patterns, with long reaches of smooth water between. At a host of spots along its 30-mile length, the river appears to be easy to cross at low water, and many a fisherman has learned to his regret that this appearance is an incredible and dangerous deception. The current is extremely powerful, and the river kills a few careless souls every year. You *must* wade this stream with great care; take no chances.

Fishermen will note the almost total lack of benthic flora and fauna in the river; there is practically nothing on the bottom but clean cobbles. It is an easy stream to wade—with respect to footing—for this reason, but at first glance it looks as though a fish would starve to death. Look carefully, though, and you will find small caddis cases near willows, large numbers of chironomid larvae, lots of pancoras and on this river as well as the Traful, big, biting horseflies.

Most of the fish in the Limay are rainbows, but a few very large browns do move into the lake from Lago Nahuel Huapi and perhaps from the reservoir. The trout in the Limay are not easy to catch and I have not had much luck on the river. Trustworthy fishing friends, however, have reported excellent fishing on this river as recently as the 1989/90 season, days on which they have hooked from twenty to thirty fish two pounds and over. The Limay is one of my problem streams; I have not even been able to determine if the fish are highly selective or simply have not been on the feed when I step into the river. Perhaps next year. . .

On the strength of my friends' experience, I recommend that readers head for one the following places for their first attempt at the Limay: the boca, Villa Llanquin, or the Valle Encantado.

The boca lies just ten miles east of Bariloche on Highway 237. It is easily visible from the highway bridge which crosses the river a hundred yards or so east of the lakeshore. Drive across the bridge slowly, and check it out for other fishermen and for waves. Crowds are not likely to be a problem on the boca except in the fall, when the big browns are moving into the river. Waves, however, can be a major problem, for the prevailing easterlies have a fetch of over 30 miles with which to build up huge, rolling combers. Save yourself a lashing from the wind by getting up quite early, and getting to the boca before the wind picks up. Righthanded casters will want to head for the the south shore on most days. The river is wide and deep at the boca, so you will need heavy tackle on a breezy day. I suggest a floating line with a fast-sinking tip. Wear a good windbreaker; the lake is cold, and the spray will chill you on the sunniest of summer days.

Since busy Highway 237 parallels the entire east shore of the Limay and access is easy on most of the stream, fishing pressure is uncommonly heavy on this shore; it is not unlikely that several tons of lures are cast into the stream each season from the many turnouts along the highway shore. You can offset 95 percent of this pressure by driving to Villa Llanquin (zhan-KEEN), a cluster of houses 14 miles north of the boca bridge. A currentpowered ferry at Villa Llanquin swings one vehicle at a time across the river to a rough road that leads to some estancias in folds of the dry hills east of the river. Do not take your car across the ferry, however. Reach the opposite shore by using the suspended foot-bridge and hike a mile or so up or downstream to reach waters that are seldom fished. A few rafting companies float clients down this portion of the river, but they are rarely fishermen. Good fly water lies in both directions and several sections of river can be waded safely, so pick a sunny day, pack a hearty lunch and a rod with

The boca of the Río Limay, near Bariloche.

some oomph, and enjoy yourself.

About ten miles north of Villa Llanquin, the Limay enters the *Valle Encantado* ("Enchanted Valley"), an area of bizarre rock formations that foreshadows the spectacular valley of the Río Traful. Dense willow thickets line this section of the river and during low water (only) shallow gravel bars permit fly fishermen to maneuver into good casting positions for some of these banks of willows. At the north end of the Valle Encantado, a short distance upstream from Confluencia, the river slows as it approaches Alicura Reservoir and on calm evenings cruising fish occasionally dimple the river.

Good luck on this lovely, puzzling river.

Río Correntoso ("Swift River"). The Seven Lakes Route between San Martín de los Andes and San Carlos de Bariloche is one of the premier scenic drives in South America, and is highly recommended for all visitors to Patagonia. Fishermen, however, should take special note of one of the lakes the route passes—Lago Correntoso—for its outlet has long been one of the premier fishing holes in South America: the Boca Correntoso.

Río Correntoso. The entire length of what Argentines fondly call the world's shortest river appears in this view.

Virtually all of the Seven Lakes Route passes through densely wooded mountains, and Lago Correntoso is typical of the lakes of the area—long, narrow, sparkling blue, ringed with shaded forests, and full of fish. The lake empties into Lago Nahuel Huapi by means of a very short stream, the Río Correntoso. Every year hordes of spawning trout make their way through this aquatic corridor between the two lakes, and every year hordes of fishermen try to intercept them at the boca.

Argentines love to claim that the Río Correntoso is the shortest river in the world. Actually, Guiness gives the title to the 54-foot Roe River in Montana, but the Correntoso is certainly among the shortest, for the entire river comprises a narrow, foaming, riffle indicated by various authorities to be from 494 to 787 feet long. Because of steep, brushy banks and swift currents, the river itself is nearly impossible to fish; it is the boca that attracts the interest of fishermen.

Arnold Gingrich once observed that fishing is the least important thing about fishing, and the maxim holds true for the Correntoso. As I will explain, most North American fishermen will become bored to distraction with the fishing at the boca. But the lacustrine scenery in the immediate area is splendid, and the inn overlooking the boca is imbued with the tradition and sense of fishing history that makes for grand fishing lodges. The combination of these factors is absolutely irresistible to fishermen.

Like the boca of the Chimehuin, the Boca Correntoso is one of Neuquen Province's special fishing areas *(zona preferencial);* you must pay a daily fee to fish there. Obtain a permit at the provincial offices in the village of Villa La Angostura, four miles south of the boca on Route 231. If you can afford this book, you can afford the permit.

The boca is also a special management area. Only fly fishing is permitted and while trolling is permitted in the lakes, it is prohibited in the vicinity of the boca. Regulations are rigorously en-

Hotel Correntoso, overlooking the famous boca.

forced. A fishing warden is usually working at the boca or nearby, and in 1990 I watched him chase encroaching trollers from the area on two occasions.

The style of fly fishing the boca is a bit bizarre. The boca is about 50 feet wide at the lake and the energy the river has accumulated in its short plunge from Lago Correntoso pushes the current far out into Lago Nahuel Huapi. A short, gravelly delta extends into the lake, but the bottom drops off quickly beyond. Most fishermen wade onto the delta along the edge of the current, make the longest cast they can manage straight across the current, and madly strip line from their reels as the river carries it far out into the lake. By the time the drift ends, their entire fly line and at least half of their backing is usually in the lake and a long, long, long retrieve ensues.

I have watched fishermen repeat this process for hour after hour, taking occasional breaks only to sit down for a few minutes or to grab a bite to eat.

Most fly fishermen scorn the method. Fly-tier Allan Fraser calls it *trolling a pie* in Spanish, roughly "trolling afoot," and most stream fishermen I know couldn't stand it for more than a quarter hour or so. As unappealing as it

must sound to confirmed stream fishermen, it is something every fly fisherman should experience once in his life, for the single overriding, redeeming characteristic of this phenomenally boring method of fly fishing is that it works. . .

Every season an astounding number of large fish are taken at the boca by this means, and for decades fishermen have traveled to the Correntoso from all over the world to try their luck. Part of the appeal of the Correntoso is that the boca is one of the few places in the world that fly fishing becomes a true spectator sport, where a fly fisherman who hooks a good fish can for a few minutes bask in the same glory that a quarterback or a bullfighter enjoys on a Sunday afternoon, an opportunity few fishermen can resist.

The Hotel Correntoso, situated on a bluff overlooking the boca, is a picturesque, European-style inn that serves three-course meals with wine at moderate prices, and caters largely to fishermen. Architects wisely constructed the bar, dining room, and terraces so as to provide unobstructed views of the boca and on a calm sunny day it is possible to watch large fish enter the river as you sip your wine or stir your tea. One of life's sublime pleasures is to enjoy a fine meal while watching a fly fisherman work the Boca Correntoso. When the bar or dining room is crowded and someone sees that a fish is on, a mad rush to the windows results and every moment of the episode is subjected to detailed and critical analysis. Woe to the fisherman who makes a stupid mistake. If, however, he succeeds in landing a nice fish, he invariably holds it up for the hotel crowd to see, and graciously accepts the hearty applause and bravos that follow. It is a unique experience in fishing, and I have actually seen smiling fishermen bow to a crowd of clapping onlookers.

Nice fish are taken throughout the season, but the best time to fish the Correntoso and other nearby waters is early and late season, November/December

From the dining room of the Hotel Correntoso, fishermen watch their colleagues fish the boca.

for rainbows and March/April for browns. In mid-summer, the river can be as much as 6°-7° F. warmer than Lago Nahuel Huapi, little incentive for trout to enter the river. Most of the fish are large rainbows; about half as many are even larger browns. Streamers and Matuka-style flies are popular, but Wooly Buggers, Rubberlegs, and Bitch Creek Specials have also proven effective. A few large cruising fish are taken on dry flies.

The place to start your visit to the Correntoso is at the hotel. Rates in 1990 were high but not exorbitant. It is an elegant four-story structure decorated with boar heads, antlers, and sporting scenes in the Currier and Ives style. A twenty-five-foot Mapuche dugout canoe — remarkably similar to those used by Pacific coast tribes of the U.S. and Canada — sits in the lobby. Motifs are otherwise mixed or distinctly Old World. My room was adorned with a reproduction of a Romney portrait of Lady Hamilton as well as a drawing of a fossil ammonite. An enormous silver antique expresso machine dominates the dining room. Rooms are spotless, and the tiled bathrooms have the best showers I have found in South America; plenty of pressure and plenty of hot water.

The dining room is charming, intimate, and bright. Meals are excellent and cheap. A meal comprising an appetizer from a tray with a dozen selections, the usual fresh rolls, a pasta dish with pesto, and fresh fruit salad, lubricated with a half-bottle of wine and a fresh expresso, cost an incredible three dollars in 1990.

The decorations of the dining room foyer are of great interest to fishermen, for ceiling and walls are covered with information that memorializes exceptional fishing events of the past: names, dates, weights, and even national flags are among the memorabilia. The largest fish among them is a 22-pound, 7ounce fish taken by "A.J." in 1968. Of the 50 or so fish identified, twelve exceed 17 pounds! The earliest fish recorded in the foyer was caught by "Fritz" on November 1, 1964, a 13-pound fish, and the most recent was also a 13-pounder caught on December 14, 1984. The Count of Chateaubriand caught a 17-pound fish in April, 1973, and marked the event by having his crest painted on the wall. American Mike Konak apparently lacked a title, so he celebrated his 14-pounder with the stars and stripes. The record fish for browns and rainbows caught on fly tackle in Argentina were both taken at this boca—a 25 pound brown caught by Luís Peirano and a 19-pound rainbow caught by Luís Aracena.

A number of years ago, the Hotel Correntoso fell upon hard times and was falling into ruins when it was purchased recently by the present owner, Hector

Fishermen memorialize their notable catches on the walls of the dining room lounge of the Hotel Correntoso. Weights are in kilograms.

Pedro Vérgez. Señor Vérgez, new to fishing, restored much of the hotel, but had tentative plans to paint over the fishing information described above. He has noted the great interest in the information, however, and may yet change his mind about covering up these scraps of history.

Among the casualties of the hotel's bankruptcy are the fishing records, which have disappeared. In 1988, Vérgez started a new fishing book, however, and these entries will give readers insight into the size and species of Correntoso fish, productive dates, and fishing methods of recent years:

Date	Species	Weight (nearest pound)	Method
November, 1988	Rainbow	7	Fly
November, 1988	Brown	9	Fly
February, 1989	Brook	2	Trolling
February, 1989	Rainbow	4	Trolling
February, 1989	Rainbow	2	Trolling
February, 1989	Rainbow	3	Trolling
February, 1989	Rainbow	7	Trolling
February, 1989	Rainbow	5	Trolling
March, 1989	Brown	12	Trolling
April, 1989	Rainbow	8	Fly
April, 1989	Rainbow	8	Fly
April, 1989	Rainbow	10	Fly
April, 1989	Rainbow	7	Fly
November, 1989	Brown	3	Trolling
November, 1989	Rainbow	6	Trolling
November, 1989	Brown	9	Trolling
November, 1989	Rainbow	8	Fly
November, 1989	Rainbow	7	Fly
November, 1989	Rainbow	8	Fly
November, 1989	Brown	12	Fly
November, 1989	Rainbow	10	Fly
November, 1989	Rainbow	9	Fly
November, 1989	Rainbow	9	Fly
December, 1989	Brown	12	Trolling
December, 1989	Rainbow	7	Trolling
December, 1989	Rainbow	7	Trolling
December, 1989	Rainbow	9	Trolling
December, 1989	Brown	12	Trolling
December, 1989	Brown	9	Fly
December, 1989	Rainbow	9	Fly
December, 1989	Rainbow	10	Trolling
January, 1990	Brown	13	Trolling
February, 1990	Brown	7	Trolling

A few entries in the book merit special mention: December 6, 1989 — Alejandro J. Buchanan released seven-pound and eight-pound fish.

February 7-9, 1989 — NADA! (nothing!).

In a 1989 entry, Bernie L. DeMerchant of Manaus, Brazil said, "Caught one nine-pound brown on a black leech, released four fish and lost six. Also lost a 90-foot fly line." On the next day, DeMerchant hooked two fish, released one, and caught another nine-pound rainbow on a black leech. On the morning of the following day, he hooked eleven fish, and kept one ten-pound rainbow. On the afternoon of the same day, he released four fish and lost six. He closes his entry with "Wild Fishing!" Wild, indeed. . .

The Hotel Correntoso is not the only place to stay near Río Correntoso. Three or four new lodges have been constructed nearby and rapidly growing Villa La Angostura, a few miles away, has several inns and restaurants. Bustling Bariloche, with its scores of hotels, is just over an hour's drive distant. Check out the other facilities, but if you are a fisherman with a deep appreciation for tradition, you will be most comfortable at the Correntoso.

There are other places to fish nearby and you don't have to drift a nine-weight line a quarter-mile into a lake to enjoy them. Boats are available on both Lago Nahuel Huapi and Lago Correntoso. I've not fished in Nahuel Huapi, but fishing dry flies to rising fish along the bands of bulrushes that line portions of Lago Correntoso is most rewarding on calm evenings. It can be done by boat or in a few places from shore. The bottom is solid in the rushes, except where tiny brooks enter the lake.

On one trip many years ago, I took four rainbows from two to four pounds from the edges of the bulrushes on No. 6 muddlers fished dry. The fish were in good if not excellent condition and the fish I kept was stuffed with pancoras, large adult dragonflies and damselflies, and what at first glance appeared to be a huge mass of twigs. On closer inspection, I found that about half of the twigs had been invaded by caddis fly nymphs. The twigs were real enough, but to be certain of getting protein, the poor trout had to ingest every twig that was the right size; half the time, it got nothing but indigestible cellulose.

Fly fishermen who tire of the boca and have a day to spare should drive to nearby *Ruca Malen* (roo-kah mah-LEN). Drive six miles north on Route 231 — a good dirt road — from the Hotel Correntoso to the junction of Route 231 and Route 234. Keep to the right and stay on 231, heading toward San Martín de los Andes, or you'll wind up in Chile. Eight miles north of the junction, 234 crosses a small, sparkling stream and on the other side you will see a cluster of attractive log and wooden buildings on the shore of the northernmost tip of Lago Correntoso — the Hotel Ruca Malen.

Like the Hotel Correntoso, the *Ruca Malen* ("house of the girl child") was once an elegant hotel that went bankrupt and was nearly abandoned when the present owner, Tony Koloszyc, took it over ten years ago. Mr. Koloszyc has transformed it into an informal, charming inn with comfortable rooms and fine meals. He takes great pride in the fact that then-retired President Eisenhower stayed twice at the inn to ride, fish, and relax.

The lodge attracts trollers, and rental boats are available. As with most other waters of the region, the best time to fish here is early and late in the season — November and April. One reason for the timing, of course, is proximity to spawning runs, but another reason is temperature. Although the lakes are relatively cold, they do warm up during the summer, and streams that flow into the lakes are usually colder than the lakes. During the austral spring, lake temperatures will be about 50° F., but inlet stream temperatures will be about 40° F. So fish the bocas. As summer progresses and the lakes begin to warm, trout either ascend the tributary streams or go deep in the lakes. In fall, trout begin to congregate at tributaries for spawning runs and to seek the cooler, more comfortable temperatures near the tributary streams. So fish the bocas again in the fall.

Although Ruca Malen is primarily a lake resort, there is some action for fly fishermen. The stream that flows into Lago Correntoso alongside the hotel is the outlet of Lago Espejo Chico ("Little Mirror Lake"). A powerful little stream, it has pushed a delta into Lago Correntoso which is bordered by a pair of long, low, brushy, spit-like peninsulas that jut far into the lake from its nominal shoreline. A somewhat overgrown trail leads from the hotel out to the end of one of these spits and a similar trail from the other side of the bridge leads to the end of the other spit. Wear boots, walk to the end of either spit, relax, and keep eyes open and ears alert for rising trout. Cruising fish feed along the shorelines in this area, including within the stream current, and they will take dry flies. In two hours on one exceptional evening, I lost two five-pound rainbows and released two three-pounders. A jungle of bulrushes covers the ends of the spits and casting is difficult, so if fish are rising along shore, rent a rowboat from the hotel, and have at it.

Even if your schedule does not permit you to fish at Correntoso or at Ruca Malen, make an effort to travel the Seven Lakes Route between San Martín de los Andes and Bariloche. Pick a sunny day and at least take a good look at these fishing landmarks. The trip takes between four and five hours by automobile and I believe you will agree that the journey will be well worth the investment of your time.

Bariloche (bah-ree-LO-chey). Its full name is San Carlos de Bariloche, but nobody ever uses the full name. Founded in 1898, Bariloche has a population of about 70,000, and is the largest city in the interior of Patagonia. It is the gateway to the heartland of Argentina's temperate zone national parks, and the

San Carlos de Bariloche lies along the southwest shore of immense Lago Nahuel Huapi, where the forested Andes merge eastward into the dry Patagonian steppes.

destination of hundreds of thousands of tourists.

While Junín de los Andes is a town of great interest to fishermen through which pass occasional tourists, Bariloche is a town of great interest to tourists through which pass occasional fishermen. While Junín is small, quiet, and rustic, Bariloche is large, boisterous, and glitzy. San Martín de los Andes lies somewhere between the two extremes.

People come to Bariloche to ski, hike, climb, sunbathe, sail, swim, shop, gamble, sightsee, flirt, dance, get married, and simply be seen. They wear mating plumage, preen at sidewalk cafes, and crowd into sidewalks, coffeehouses, shops, discos, restaurants, and the single seedy casino. The town is an international tourist center, busy night and day.

Despite the bustle, Bariloche is an interesting city and easy to reach from Buenos Aires by daily direct flights or thrice-weekly trains. Situated along the south shore of Lago Nahuel Huapi, the town has scores of hotels, dozens of restaurants, and several fishing shops, rental car agencies, and currency exchange houses *(casas de cambio)*. The tourist office on the central plaza is helpful, though often jammed, and you will probably be able to get a list of accommodations at the office. While at the plaza, look in the Museum of Patagonia *(Museo de la Patagonia)*, which takes up the northeast corner of the plaza and has exhibits on history, geology, anthropology, and wildlife. If you arrive just before midday, you'll be able to watch the four statues emerge from the tower of the civic center, directly above the tourist office as the clock tolls noon. You'll see, in turn, an Indian, a priest, a soldier, and a peasant.

Bariloche has four or five fishing stores, but most have overpriced, poor quality flies. It is clear that shop owners have little knowledge of flies as products or tools. A small shop one block west of the centrally located Bariloche Hotel does have some quality flies, but also has a big selection of junk flies. The stores are more like sporting goods shops than fishing shops; most specialize in spoons and lures. The one true fly shop in Bariloche is hidden in a small shopping gallery at Mitre 125, Local 18, a few paces off the city's main street. Fly fisherman and guide Ricardo Ameijeiras and his wife have squeezed a small fly shop and a retail clothing business into one small location.

Boating is understandably a popular pastime in the Bariloche area, and perhaps as a result, trolling is a popular fishing method. Argentine trollers are well aware that the world's record brown trout, a 35-pound, 14-ounce giant, was taken by Eugenio Cavaglia in 1952 just off the shore of Victoria Island, not far from downtown Bariloche.

Experienced fly fishermen are likely to establish headquarters at some town other than Bariloche—Junín or San Martín to the north, Esquel or El Bolsón to the south. But some fly waters are within relatively easy reach of Bariloche. The boca of the Limay is a fifteen-minute drive east and the rest of the Río Limay is nearby. The Río Traful at Confluencia is a forty-mile drive on a good road, and the Río Correntoso is about an hour's drive from the city. My personal preference for waters near Bariloche lies to the south, the Río Manso.

Río Manso (MAHN-so). The first matter to consider with respect to the Río Manso is *which* Río Manso we are discussing, for there are at least four rivers of this name south of Bariloche.

The first, Río Manso Superior (upper Manso River), flows east into the western end of Lago Mascardi and parallels the road to the foot of Mount Tronador, a popular day-tour destination. This river is too fast for my taste, and is not a recommended stream for fly fishermen.

The second, called simply Río Manso, flows west into Lago Hess, then into Lago Roca and on into Chile. This is the river I will describe.

The third river, also called Río Manso, flows south into Lago Steffen and is virtually inaccessible.

The fourth, Río Manso Inferior (lower Manso River), drains east from Lago Steffen, then reverses its direction and flows across the border into Chile and empties into the Pacific Ocean. Most of this river is also inaccessible and is not recommended.

Fishing the Río Manso—and nearby Lago Hess—is a high energy proposition. Because of features of landscape

The Río Manso, near Bariloche.

The lower Río Manso is glassy, challenging dry fly water.

and vegetation, it requires a good deal of walking, wading, and brush-beating if you get lost, but it combines a day's fishing with a scenic drive and has given me some of the finest dry-fly fishing I've ever had in a small lake. The Manso is basically a rainbow stream and the the fish are not very large—about two pounds, but they are larger in the lake and a few big browns are usually in the neighborhood.

To reach the river, drive south from Bariloche on paved Highway 258 for 22 miles. At the village of Villa Mascardi, a dirt road, Route 81, heads west from the paved highway and parallels the south shore of Lago Mascardi. This road is narrow, and to accommodate tour buses, traffic is one-way toward the mountains (west) in the morning, and one-way away from the mountains (east) in the afternoon. Drive defensively and with particular care on this road. Six miles from the highway junction, the road forks. Take the left fork and head east toward Lago Hess. Two miles from the fork, the road passes south of Lago Los Moscos and continues west into a forested valley. For the next seven miles, the road parallels the Río Manso, usually hidden from sight by dense woods.

Along these seven miles between Lago Los Moscos and Lago Hess, you will see a number of crude tracks that lead north into the trees from the road. The tracks lead through thick brush to various stretches of the river. Park your car and go exploring. Whenever possible use a trail, for the brush-beating is very hard work in this area.

The river is gorgeous water, with big deep holes, long rapids, and considerable variation in water types—something for everybody. It is difficult to overstate the clarity of the stream; some holes that look to be a yard or so deep are practically chin-high water. It is relatively easy to wade, but only in low water stages. The streambed is spotless, almost sterile in appearance. Waders are necessary, for the river is cold.

Fish the river at any spot that affords easy access, but my recommendation is to enter the river a half-mile or so above Lago Hess and fish downstream to the lake. This section of the river is but lightly fished because of the difficult access, dense brush, and long drive. Serious fishermen walk upstream from the mouth at Lago Hess, which they reach by boat, but they don't go far. At one hole on this stretch I once tapped a two-foot brown trout with my rod tip after the damned fish declined all other offerings.

When you reach the boca, get out your dry flies. The lake is beautiful and provides a full view of Mount Tronador. It is surrounded by woods and thick bamboo, bad brush for waders. As on most lakes in the area, the shore is lined with bulrushes, but the bottom is firmer than it looks and it is usually possible to wade to the edge of the reeds.

I once fished the boca on the last day of fishing season, April 9, 1978, and had terrific fishing. A hatch of large caddis flies was under way and large fish were rising steadily to them and to flying ants and adult dragonflies that now and then fell buzzing into the water. Virtually any fly that floated high worked, and in the two hours before dark I released several two to three pound rainbows and lost two that might have reached five pounds.

The Manso pauses for a while in Lago Hess, and then continues on to Lago Roca. This stretch of the river is very slow, somewhat like Idaho's Silver creek, and on a still day is also good dry fly fishing—*if* fish are rising. Wading and casting is difficult because the stream is deep and reed-lined, but it can be fished. At the end of the road is a small hosteria/bar called Hostería Cascada Los Alerces. Food and drink, but no overnight facilities are available. At this point, you are a few miles from the Chilean border.

At this point my description of the streams of the Northern Zone ends, but Patagonia's fishing grounds do not end just outside of Bariloche. Distances, however, begin to become intimidating. To the south, seldom fished trout waters flow in the vicinity of El Bolsón (80 miles), Esquel (180 miles), Perito Moreno (500 miles), Calafate (900 miles), Río Gallegos (1100 miles), and at many points between these scattered settlements. And on Tierra del Fuego, trout waters flow near Río Grande (1300 miles), and the southernmost city in the world, Ushuaia (1400 miles).

As you travel south in Patagonia, however, the land becomes increasingly austere—the harsh, nearly deserted landscape that has intrigued travelers and adventurers for centuries. Roads and airports grow scarce. Cost of food, lodging, and transportation increases significantly while facilities diminish in quality and frequency. Public transportation along the few roads becomes more expensive and less dependable. Though the countryside is interesting and fishing can be outstanding, conditions are often rugged for tourists, and travel delays are sometimes unavoidable in this remote and fascinating region. For these reasons, this area is not recommended for do-it-yourself fly fishermen, unless you are under no serious time constraints—at least for the first trip.

In truth, you could easily spend the rest of your life exploring the trout streams in the Northern Zone, and seldom fish in the same places twice. I suggest that you first fish these waters, and *then* begin to wonder about those remote, mysterious rivers to the south.

CENTRAL ZONE

The Central Zone comprises the province of Chubut (choo-BOOT), and Los Alerces National Park. Most of the streams in the zone are within the watershed of the Río Chubut, which flows into the South Atlantic, or the Río Grande, which flows into Chile and on to the South Pacific. The principal settlements of interest to fishermen are El Bolson (bowl-SOWN) and Esquel (ehs-KEHL).

The Northern Zone is in Patagonia, of course, but it is a rather civilized version of Patagonia. On entering the Central Zone, however, you are on the threshold of the remote land that so firmly grips the imagination of anyone who has ever dreamed of adventure, the northern edge of a thousand miles of untamed terrain. How fortunate are fly fishermen that fate has seen to it that this far-off corner of the world is blessed with an abundance of fish. . .

Río Chubut. Chubut Province is shaped roughly like a rectangle, about 250 miles north to south and 300 miles east to west. It has three distinct landscapes—on the east, the wave-battered South Atlantic coastline; on the west, the forested Andean Cordillera, a narrow band of exquisite scenery; and in between, arid, empty plains reminiscent of the Great Basin of the western United States, but without the people. The Río Chubut, one of Patagonia's longest rivers, flows 500 miles through these parched plains, and is one of the handful of streams that manages to cross the steppes and reach the sea.

The Río Chubut is one of the few

The Río Chubut, a lovely fly stream in the steppes, well off the beaten tourist path.

The lakes of Los Alerces National Park are nurseries for some of the largest trout that have ever been caught.

significant Patagonian rivers not born in a large lake in the lap of the Andes. Its headwaters are in the hills of the southwest corner of Río Negro Province, where it somehow gathers enough water to evolve into a real trout stream. The uppermost section of the river, some 35 miles long, is too small for quality fly fishing and soon after it begins its eastward run across the desert it becomes too warm and alkaline to support trout, but in between are about 30 miles of good water. This productive reach of the river lies downstream from the village of El Maiten for about 20 miles and then east from the Estancia Leleque for about another 10 miles.

Because of its remote steppeland location, the Río Chubut is a long way from overnight accommodations. The nearest town is El Bolsón (bowl-SONE), a small attractive community in a valley whose lovely surroundings have drawn a large number of Argentines who live what we describe as alternative lifestyles. A major destination of university students during vacation periods, many of its 8,000 residents are artisans, operate small farms, or work in cottage industries. A half-dozen small hotels and inns and twice as many restaurants are available. Go to the tourist office on the main plaza for information on rates and locations.

El Bolson lies 80 miles south of Bariloche on Highway 253. About half of this road has been under construction for several years and will doubtless be under construction for several more, so it can be slow and dusty going. If you are driving, plan on a four hour journey.

To reach the Río Chubut from El Bolsón, head south on paved Route 258 for 30 miles to the junction with gravelled Route 71. At this junction, Route 258 veers east, while Route 71 continues south toward Los Alerces National Park. Stay on Route 258 and head east for 12 miles to the junction with Route 40, a dirt road heading north. The tiny village of El Maiten (my-TEHN) lies 21 miles north of this junction on Route 40, which parallels the river for that length. It sounds complicated, but the road is excellent and you can reach the river in about an hour from El Bolsón.

Fences lie between Route 40 and the river for most of the drive to El Maiten, but this is empty country, and so few houses are in view that there is no place for a wandering fly fisherman to request permission to cross the fences to reach the river. If you cross the river at El Maiten, however, and drive south on Route 45, which parallels the other side of the river, access is no problem along 14 miles of the stream.

Once the river swings east, no public roads lie nearby. To reach it, you must ask permission at the Estancia Leleque (lay-LAY-kay), just south of the village of Leleque on the old, graveled Route 40.

The Chubut flows through a somber, treeless range studded with jagged parapet-like formations. The landscape is dry but dramatic. You can reach the Chubut from Esquel by a circuitous drive along Routes 12, 35, and 4, but while the trip is an interesting journey through an empty desert, it is long and not recommended for fishermen in a hurry. Do not make the trip after recent rains, for some roads may be impassable. Two small streams along this route, Arroyo Lepa and Río Ñorquinco, are not suitable for fishing.

The Chubut is fairly small, about the size of the Malleo, and lined with a solid phalanx of dense willows. It is an easy stream to fish, however, for it has just enough gradient to create a sequence of short riffles that flow into deep pools. There are lots of slow, waist-deep runs and wading is effortless on a substrate of firm sand banks and gravels ideal for spawning fish.

You will hear the familiar piping of fío-fíos in the willows and note a conspicuous absence of trails along shore. The river is rarely fished; there are virtually no tracks but those of sheep, goats, and cattle on the stream. The only other sounds you are likely to hear are the hiss and murmur of the river, the wind in the willows, the splashing of your fishing companions, and the rattle of an occasional truck passing by.

The Río Chubut is primarily a rainbow stream, although you may catch a few brook trout. You are not likely to catch trophy fish on the Chubut; the fish are not large by Patagonian standards, at least in my experience. Don't fish this stream for big fish, but for sheer pleasure. In 1977 I caught a rainbow near the railroad crossing that weighed four pounds and I've not caught one as large since then, but I nevertheless return to the river at every opportunity. That fish, incidentally, was taken on a muddler and contained no fewer than 26 pancoras!

Turn over a few rocks and you will find caddis larvae that form a black, half-inch case shaped like a long, thin tooth. Populations of this caddis— somewhat similar to American *leptoceridae* or Australian caddises—are so dense that they appear to be colonial. Small adult caddis flies are on the wing during most of the day and a very few inch-long pale green adults flit by occasionally. On the bottom, you'll also see small, sculpin-like prey fish dodge into crevices. The fish feed on floating insects, but dry fly work is frustrating unless the fish are actually rising to a hatch. Attractors will work, but you will do better drifting nymphs through the riffles and pools.

Like the Chimehuin, the Chubut is a more productive stream in early morning and late evening than during midday hours, an obvious problem unless you are camping nearby. The wind can also be troublesome during midday hours, but the willows usually provide welcome shelter.

Because it lacks the moderating influence of a large headwater lake, the Chubut is a fairly warm stream, which accounts in part for its productivity. Fishery biologists inform me, however, that the temperature occasionally gets *too* high for trout. As a result, the stream is periodically stocked with fish from the Baglitt Hatchery near Trevelin.

No matter, it is a delightful trout stream right out in the middle of nowhere...

Río Carrileufu (kah-ree-LAY-oo-foo). The Carrileufu is the northernmost of a series of rivers that link a chain of splendid mountain lakes, most of which lie within Los Alerces National Park. Although the rivers are all part of the same drainage system, each has its own name, and merits its own description. For the sake of orientation, however, I should first describe the entire system.

The Río Carrileufu drains Lago Cholila and flows into the north end of Lago Rivadavia. Lago Rivadavia is in turn drained by the Río Rivadavia, which flows into tiny Lago Verde. The

outlet of Lago Verde is the Río Arrayanes, which flows into the northern end of Lago Futalaufquen. This lake drains into a hydroelectric reservoir, Lago Amutui Cuimei, by means of the Río Frey. From the reservoir, the waters enter the Río Grande and make their way through the mountains and across the border to the Pacific Ocean. It is a complex system, but when you see the region's tangle of lakes and mountains, you'll understand why it is difficult to tell if you are on a Pacific or an Atlantic watershed.

The *Carrileufu* ("Green River") and the rest of the rivers in this system are more typical of the streams of the Central Zone than the Río Chubut. They are characterized by forested banks and cold clear water, each a shaded corridor through breathtaking alpine scenery. It is often difficult to fish these rivers continuously, simply because around each

The upper Río Carrileufu, Butch Cassidy country and trout and salmon country.

bend may be a spectacular new vista that demands careful inspection, if not contemplation.

You need waders for all of the mountain rivers; they are significantly colder than the rivers of the Northern Zone, far too chilly to wade wet for a full day.

The Carrileufu has two distinct characters. Its upper five miles are narrow—40 to 60 feet wide—and have a relatively high gradient with lots of riffles and swift runs; the lower seven miles are much slower, with long, wide, and very deep reaches, and only occasional riffles.

The upper river drains southeast from Lago Cholila (cho-LEE-lah), and is a nearly ideal stream for fly fishermen from midsummer on. The current is swift, but many riffles are only hip-deep and in many places it is possible to wade across the stream. Footing is firm, and unlike the lower river, most reaches of the upper section are wadeable.

The Carrileufu is primarily a rainbow stream, but it holds other species as well. It is not a productive dry fly stream (for me, at any rate), but I prefer to use streamers, muddlers, and salmon flies on the river in any case, because they not only attract rainbows, but also occasionally interest the landlocked salmon the river holds. Yep, this river and the Río Rivadavia are salmon as well as trout streams. The same caveats apply on these rivers as on the Traful: you won't always hook them and late season (March and April) is better than early or mid-season. I once hooked a small salmon in February on the Río Rivadavia, but that was an exceptional event. Biologists inform me that the salmon in these rivers do not reach the size of the Traful fish, and my own experience confirms their observations. It is possible that the colder temperature of the lakes and streams limits their growth.

I have not discovered a sure-fire formula for catching fish (trout *or* salmon) on the Carrileufu or its sister rivers. The most important lesson I have learned is

This Carrileufu salmon took a muddler.

to fish very late, right up until dark; the last half-hour of light can bring the hottest fishing of the day. Nevertheless, for me these rivers run hot or cold; there is no middle ground. On some trips, I have hooked over a dozen fish a day from two to six pounds without half trying and on other trips—mostly midsummer—I have not been able to get as much as a strike for three days running. But I'm working on it. . .

To reach the upper Carrileufu, you must get to the village of Cholila. A mile west of Cholila, an ACA gas station sits at the junction of Routes 71 and 15, both dirt roads. Drive north from the gas station on Route 71 for just over a mile to a road that heads west; a sign at this road is marked "Lago Cholila." The road leads eight miles to the lake and skirts the north bank of the upper river for most of its length. No access problems. The road is rough and rocky, but can be negotiated with a normal car if taken very slowly. Undeveloped campsites are plentiful at streamside.

Cholila is 56 miles south of El Bolsón. Take paved Highway 258 south for 30 miles to the junction with Route 71, a dirt road. Take 71 south into Cholila. Accommodations closer to the river are described below.

Not far from Cholila, the Carrileufu takes a ninety-degree turn, and veers from southeast to southwest at the point locals call *la curva*, the curve. The portion of river downstream from the curve is the lower Carrileufu.

The lower river has created a bottomland about a half-mile wide, bordered on the northwest with towering peaks and on the southeast by somewhat lower wooded mountains. In between is a lovely valley green with neatly-tended farmsteads and cultivated fields divided by long lines of Lombardy poplars. Oxcarts haul firewood and sheaves of hay to and fro, and farmers and courting couples ride about on horses. But for the mountains and utility lines, the countryside looks more like eighteenth century New England than modern Argentina.

As if enjoying the scenery, the Río Carrileufu flows slowly through this green countryside. It is broad and deep, and riffles and chutes are widely separated. Most of the rivers and lakes in and near the park are fed by glacial runoff, and like the Carrileufu have the turquoise-tinted clarity that rock flour imparts to glacier-fed streams. You can see fish from high banks, but not in large numbers.

Banks of elodea and chara flourish in the slower currents of the lower river and the bottom is usually firm. It is easy to move along shore, but because of deep water and the many fallen trees, wading is difficult. The lower river is not easy to fish with a fly rod. To solve this problem, local guides have begun to arrange float trips for visiting fly fishermen. It is a good solution, for with an inflatable and small motor it is possible to float and fish several rivers and traverse several lakes without getting out of the boat. Contact the tourist office or guide Raúl San Martín in Esquel for information.

Not all fishermen have the problems I have on the Carrileufu or require a boat. One Saturday, returning from a fruitless morning on the lower river, I ran into a farm boy fishing in a hole behind a giant fallen tree. We exchanged greetings, and like fishermen everywhere, inspected each other's equipment. He had a great deal more to inspect than I did, for I was in full regalia: fancy rod, waders, vest, a few doodads hanging here and there—the works. His gear comprised a tin can and a length of monofilament. . .

I felt like a member of a SWAT team in full battle dress confronting an unarmed civilian. Fairly certain that I was the first foreign fly fisherman this boy had seen at such close quarters, I made a few casts to demonstrate that my gear was not merely decorative, but had something to do with fishing. No fish (of course) showed the slightest interest in my fly. Unimpressed, he then made two casts, and beached a pair of two-pound rainbows. I congratulated him and smiled, he tried hard not to smirk, and we parted company.

The boy was using a *latita*, a tin can that is a deadly fishing instrument in the right hands. You will see poor people using latitas throughout Patagonia. You can make your own by finding a number 8 tin can, stripping off the paper, and firmly wedging a short stick inside the can in such fashion that you close your fist around it. You now have a sort of spinning reel. Tie one end of several yards of monofilament onto the can, and wind the rest on just as the bail of a spinning reel winds line on the spool. Put a hook and weight on the business end of the monofilament, twirl it about in tight circles with one hand, let fly, aim the hand holding the can in the direction of your cast, and you're fishing.

The retrieve is hand over hand. The equipment has obvious limitations, but you can't beat the price and with practice you can make long and accurate casts with bait or lures. My farm boy colleague was using live grasshoppers with his latita; I've no doubt he went home with a heavy string of fish.

Visitor accommodations are scarce near the Carrileufu. At this writing—1990—Cholila has one small restaurant and a small bed-and-breakfast style inn, El Trebol. Six miles south of Cholila is a small group of farms called Villa Lago Rivadavia. The Suarez family rents comfortable cabins on the edge of this hamlet in January and February of each year. Not far from the river, the cabins have all facilities and are tastefully appointed. You must provide your own food. The cabins, called Cabañas Carrileufu, are among the most charming rural accommodations I have found anywhere in South America. Look for a sign along the road. Several hotels and lodges lie to the south of this area, but they are over 20 miles from Cholila on a narrow, winding, dirt road, too far for convenience if you are doing the driving.

Río Rivadavia (ree-vah-DAH-vee-uh). Ten miles south of Cholila on Route 71 lies Lago Rivadavia. The lake, ten miles long, is the northern boundary of Los Alerces National Park. Its southern end is drained by the Río Rivadavia, the four-mile river that flows into Lago Verde.

The Rivadavia is a fly fishing only, catch and release stream. It holds mostly rainbows and a few brooks, browns, and salmon. The river is large and powerful, reminiscent of Neuquen's Río Limay. Like that river, it must be waded with great care, for depths and current strength are deceptive. The whole river can be fished in one day, but a long, hard day. Three spots are favored, especially when the salmon are running: the upper boca, lower boca, and boca of Arroyo Calihual.

About a mile south of the southern end of Lago Rivadavia, Route 71 crosses the Arroyo Calihual, a small stream that cascades from the mountains to the east of the road. The Calihual is itself closed to fishing, but on both sides of the bridge that crosses it, rough tracks along its banks lead about a quarter-mile west to the banks of the Rivadavia. These tracks offer the only easy access to the river from Route 71. Walk or drive (beware of soft sand) down the tracks to the river, and start fishing. The Lago Rivadavia boca lies about a quarter-mile

upstream from the mouth of the Calihual.

Both banks of the river are wooded, but the trails are easy to follow. Beware of the bamboo; you'll freeze if you puncture your waders. Considerable walking is required because much of the river is too deep to wade, and you must often come ashore to get around the many deadfalls that line the stream. Good runs and riffles are widely separated. Your best fishing positions will be on long gravel bars that lie upstream from deep pools, but be careful—the pools are well over your head.

When the sun is high, you can sometimes see fish in these pools. They are not all large, of course, but you have to keep your wits about you. I have lost fish in these pools when flies at the end of eight-pound tippets were snapped off before I could react.

Lots of small brown caddis flies flutter along the river, and fish do rise for the adults, but I have had no luck on this stream with dry flies, primarily because of the difficulty of getting into good casting positions.

Fío-fíos are common in shoreside brush and I have seen and heard more kingfishers on the Rivadavia than on any other stream in South America. These are ringed kingfishers, *Ceryle torquata*, big gray and white birds—a foot long—with creamy white collars.

To reach the Lago Verde boca of the Rivadavia without fishing all the way down the river from Arroyo Calihual, drive to the commercial campground on the peninsula that juts into Lago Verde from the east side of the lake. Park and hike along the northeast shore of the lake to the boca—about a half-mile.

This is one of several developed campgrounds in the park. Usually called "autocamping something-or-other," they are exactly what they sound like. For a modest fee, they provides travelers with a campsite, clean sanitary facilities, hot water showers, a place to wash dishes and clothes, and often a small store or snack bar. If you have a tent and sleep-

Rare, twisted arrayán trees line the banks of the Río Arrayanes.

ing bag in your car, you can camp in them. Their owners are usually good sources of local information.

Río Arrayánes (ah-rah-ZHAN-ehs). If you continue south on Route 71 past Lago Verde, you shortly reach what is surely one of the most beautiful rivers in South America, the Río Arrayánes. This gem of a stream is only some three miles long, but it has a little bit of everything—a turquoise translucence, interesting wildlife, breathtaking surroundings, and fish. . .

One of the nicest things about fishing in the Central Zone is the simple act of fishing in wooded streams, a sharp and pleasant contrast to the streams of the Northern Zone. All of the mountain streams in this region are forested, but the Río Arrayánes is rather special, for it is lined with the twisted, fragrant Arrayán trees from which its name is derived. Though they grow in dense groves, Arrayán trees discourage the proliferation of undergrowth and form a shaded, park-like forest in which one half-expects to see elves or leprechauns dart about.

The Río Arrayánes is large, but has spring creek-like characteristics: a relatively slow current, luminous transparence, and abundant streambed

vegetation. Route 71 is carved into the mountainside high above the river for its entire length, but the southern end, including the boca of Lago Futalaufquen, is accessible down a steep slope. This reach of the stream is slow for working a fly, however, and steep drop-offs inhibit wading. In the middle reaches of the stream are sand bars that are wadeable late in the season, but there are many deadfalls to maneuver around. The best place to start on the Arrayánes is on its upper reaches, near the Lago Verde boca. Near the north end of the river, a short, steep road veers west from Route 71 and ends at a parking lot on the river's edge a hundred yards below the boca. Park here to fish the boca and take along your binoculars, for there is much to see.

Fish often rise at the boca. On my last visit, I released a four-pound rainbow that took a Rubberlegs at the edge of the reeds. While I fished, six black-necked swans watched nervously from across the river and a pair of four-foot river otters *(lobito de río)* swam by unconcerned.

The main path from the parking lot leads to a suspended footbridge that crosses the river and leads to a dock from which bused-in tourists take launch trips on Lago Menéndez, a huge,

Fish on! The fishermen released a four-pound rainbow at the boca of the Río Arrayanes.

Y-shaped lake just out of view. From the boca, you can see another river entering the Río Arrayánes from the west. This is the outlet of Lago Menéndez, Río Menéndez, and it is highly recommended. The Río Menéndez is big, but very short, and has more current and riffles than the Arrayánes. Very nice fly water. Cross the bridge, take the pleasant walk to Lago Menéndez, and fish downstream.

The Río Arrayánes is a rainbow stream, but it also holds, at least from time to time, brook trout, landlocked salmon, and brown trout that move into the river from Lago Futalaufquen. It is such a lovely river, however, that it really doesn't matter if it contains fish or not.

Once you have reached the vicinity of the Río Rivadavia or Río Arrayánes, you are within reasonable driving distance of overnight accommodations within the park or in the town of Esquel. If your schedule and budget permit, try to stay in the park, for it is a remarkable area, in my view much more attractive than Nahuel Huapi National Park. It is much less developed, less crowded, and more isolated; with the exceptions of the damned cows that range freely through the park and the hydrolectric reservoir in the southern part of the park, its

The Hostería Quimé Quipán, a fishing lodge on Lago Futalaufquen.

Hotel Futalaufquen on the lake of the same name is a fishermens' hangout in Los Alerces National Park.

pristine character has been successfully maintained. It is nearly an ideal national park; though not highly developed, its road system is sufficient to permit a thorough look at its terrain, and facilities are comfortable and do not clash with their surroundings. Campsites are well laid out, lush, shady, and spotless.

Park headquarters *(intendencia)* are in the village of Villa Futalaufquen, at the southern end of the lake of the same name. (Take an hour to visit the regional museum near the intendencia for a brief orientation to the park's geology, wildlife, and history.) About a half-dozen inns and hotels are located in and around Villa Futalaufquen, but fishermen who do not camp in the park or who drive there from Esquel usually stay at one of three inns: Hotel Futalaufquen, Hosteria Quimé Quipán, or the Hostería Cume Hue.

The Hotel Futalaufquen (foo-tah-LAUF-cane) is the oldest and most elegant of the three inns, but is furthest from the rivers. It lies at the end of the road that leads along the west shore of Lago Futalaufquen, two miles north of Villa Futalaufquen. A large stone and log building in a grove of tall beeches at lakeside, the hotel has a comfortable bar and sitting room reminiscent of English pubs. Guest rooms and dining room are appointed Old World style.

The Hostería Quimé Quipán (kee-may-kee-PAHN) lies directly across Lago Futalaufquen from the Hotel Futalaufquen. It is five miles north of Villa Futalaufquen on Route 71. A two-story white stone and stucco lodge, it is comfortably appointed as most of area's fishing lodges. As at the Hotel Correntoso, fish caught by guests have been memorialized on enameled wooden plaques since 1968. Any old fish will not do; to qualify for the plaque, one's catch must weigh more than nine pounds. Data are missing from some years, but sizes of a few fish taken since 1978 are 11, 13, 14, 15, and 21 pounds. Of 128 fish recorded, five are landlocked salmon, 28 are rainbows, and the rest are either brown trout or not identified. The Hosteria Quime Quipan lies about 15 miles south of the Río Arrayánes and about 23 miles south of the Río Rivadavia.

The Hostería Cume Hue (koo-may-WAY) lies 15 miles north of Villa Futalaufquen (10 miles north of the Hostería Quimé Quipán) on Route 71. It is about three miles from the Río Arrayánes and 11 miles from the Río Rivadavia.

All three hotels are on the lakeshore. They cater primarily to trollers, although more fly fishermen have begun to arrive in recent years. Boat rentals and guide services can be arranged at each lodge.

Arroyo Pescado (ah-roe-zho pes-KAH-though). Jorge Donovan indicates that while the first settlers of southern Patagonia were predominantly of British extraction and those of northern Patagonia predominantly latin, the area in between, central Patagonia, was once a refuge for a class of people who lived outside the law.

Well-named Arroyo Pescado—Fish Creek—the name of the body of water as well as the estancia through which it flows, is a testimonial to that grim period of history. It is the only true spr-

ing creek I've found in Patagonia and is as interesting for its history as for its fishing. It is in an unlikely location, within sight of the distant Andes, but on a flat surrounded by parched hills that look as though they don't receive rainfall more than once every decade or so.

The nearest town to Arroyo Pescado is Esquel, a town of about 20,000 that is literally nestled in a valley carved out of high mountains by glaciers. To the east, the hills are dry, treeless, and colorful, to the west rise the high, forested peaks of the Cordillera. Southernmost of the interior Patagonian cities, it was originally an offshoot of the coastal communities settled by Welsh immigrants between 1865 and 1914. The town is also the southernmost terminus of Argentina's railroad system. In 1989, train service was available from Buenos Aires, but even dedicated train buffs should be advised that it is an arduous, 42-hour trip through countryside that many would regard as monotonous.

The town has over a dozen hotels, and several mediocre restaurants. The one restaurant that provides both excellent food and excellent service is the Jockey Club. The tourist office at the bus station is very helpful. Villa Futalaufquen and Los Alerces National Park lie 29 miles west.

Arroyo Pescado lies 32 miles the other way, southeast of Esquel. To reach the estancia by road, drive eight miles east to the junction with paved Highway 40, then south on Highway 40 for 14 miles to the well-marked junction with a dirt road, Route 25, the old road to the coast. Drive further east on Route 25 for ten miles toward the heart of the desert—the last place on earth you would expect to find a spring creek teeming with trout. But you suddenly round a corner and see a line of willows on the valley floor, and soon long rows of Lombardy poplars come into view. The road enters the poplars and a little further on is a driveway into an estancia. A nearby sign reads, *pesca con mosca solamente*—"fish with flies only."

Walk—do not drive—through the

Cold springs in the steppes. Arroyo Pescado flows through an arid grassland.

trees down the driveway, knock on the door of the main house and, in English, ask permission to fish. You will most likely be greeted by Mr. Trevor apIwan, owner of the Estancia Arroyo Pescado, and will not be charged for fishing in the arroyo.

Mr. apIwan, a retired surgeon, is an elderly man, courteous to visitors and employees alike. Though happily settled in his modest home, he enjoys meeting foreigners and hearing news of the wider world and generously shares his extensive knowledge of the area and its history with strangers.

The estancia was established in 1865, and has been in his family for well over a century; his grandfather was one of the original founders of the Welsh colonies of Patagonia. Mr. apIwan is bilingual, of course, but his English falls quaintly on the American ear; over cups of strong black tea, he explained that the estancia was once twice its present size—one by two "leagues."

I later learned that a "league" is equivalent to about three miles.

The year of 1909 was a season of high hopes and tragedy for the apIwan family. Trevor was eight years old. His uncle, Lloyd apIwan, had opened a store, the Mercantile Company, at the estancia primarily to trade with the Mapuches, with whom the Welsh had traditionally enjoyed excellent relations. The store did well, and news of its success traveled to Lago Cholila, where under assumed names, Butch Cassidy, the Sundance Kid, Etta Place, and three other men had been running an estancia for two years.

On the night of December 28, a torch was tossed through a window onto the bed in which Lloyd lay asleep. He fired several shots, and drove the marauders off, but in putting out the resulting fire, he burned his hands bad-

A Welsh victim of the Butch Cassidy-Sundance Kid gang sleeps alongside the Arroyo Pescado.

ly. The next day, the gang—five men and a woman—attacked again and overpowered Trevor's uncle. As the looting proceeded, Cassidy's spurs became entangled in a rug and he fell down. Lloyd leaped on him, grabbed his pistol, and tried to shoot the outlaw. But the weapon lacked a trigger, having been modified to be "fanned," and with his burned hands, Lloyd could not manipulate the gun quickly. Before he was able to use the weapon, the Sundance Kid entered the room and gunned him down with a Winchester 45. The gang cleaned out the store's valuables and quickly rode off.

Efforts by the territorial police to deal with the gang had been indifferent in the past, but the entire Welsh community was outraged by the murder and they forced the police to mount a vigorous pursuit. From this point forward, facts merge into legend, but the best evidence indicates that the police indeed caught up with the gang within a few months near the Chilean border. Only the woman is said to have escaped and she disappeared into the mists of history, and the myths of the Old West.

Lloyd's tombstone, a plain brown slab on a rocky hillside, lies about 50 yards from his nephew's house, visible just south of the road that leads to the arroyo. Pause as you head for the fishing and reflect for a moment on immigrants, outlaws, and legends.

The history of the fish as well as the people of Arroyo Pescado warrants mention. In 1920, only pejerrey and perch were found in the creek. At about that time, an Englishman who owned a ranch near Tecka, a village 30 miles to the south of Arroyo Pescado, planted brook trout in the Río Tecka, a sluggish tributary to the Río Chubut which is tenuously connected to the Arroyo Pescado. The brook trout made their way down the Río Tecka to the Arroyo Pescado and eventually eradicated the native species. For decades thereafter, the arroyo contained nothing but giant brook trout and the first fish Trevor caught as a boy was a brook.

Rainbows, however, had been planted in the Río Chubut in 1904 and they eventually made their way up the Tecka and into the arroyo, where they quickly displaced the brook trout. So far, no brown trout have appeared, but they are in the Río Tecka and may eventually find their way into the arroyo. For now, at any rate, the Arroyo Pescado is a pure rainbow stream. And what rainbows they are. The largest fish measured in 1989 was over 30 inches long and weighed *over* 13 pounds. It may

Big rainbows cruising in the shallows of Arroyo Pescado.

still be there, for the arroyo is a catch and release stream. Perhaps because its temperature and flow are nearly constant year around, the trout have developed atypical spawning seasons. The major season is rather late, in November and December, and a second smaller spawn occurs in about May. For this reason, fishing is not permitted in the stream until January first of each year.

From a distance, the arroyo is unimpressive, a reedy patch of flat water winding through a flat sheep pasture. The only jarring sight is the line of concrete pylons that carry high tension wires from the Futaleufu Dam all the way to the coast. But up close, your first impression will change. Head down the road to which you will be directed and turn south toward the pylons. As you near the stream, geese, ducks, black-necked swans, flamingos, and cormorants may come into view and it is hard to stay calm as you watch three to five pound rainbows glide over the smooth, chalky bottom of the arroyo.

The Arroyo Pescado may be the best place to fish in Argentina for those fly fishermen who like nothing better than sight-fishing for large rainbows. It does not have the tamed character of some western spring creeks, in which a fisherman feels vaguely as if they he is casting flies into an aquarium. It is not a long stream, but fish seem to be more or less uniformly distributed over its two to three mile length. A fly fisherman could easily spend an entire day exploring its many nooks and corners, so pack a hearty lunch.

As you would expect, the water is as clear as air. Though the fish do not seem to be particularly selective, sloppy casts or big tippets are not tolerated; these fish are not stupid. The current is very slight and filamentous algae is abundant. You will have to take care not to lose fish and fly in the masses of elodea or tough stems of bulrushes. The pasture is so flat, firm, and brushless that you can fish most of the creek in a pair of bedroom slippers if it suits you,

but waders help to get to good positions. The bottom is muddy—firm in some places, but soft in others. The water is too cold to wade wet for long; I once measured its temperature at 45° F.

Dry fly fishing is best in early morning and late evening, when the wind is light and the surface unruffled. I have found nymphing to be better during midday hours. These days it is fashionable to use microscopic flies on spring creeks in the United States. I find that technique thankfully unnecessary on the Arroyo Pescado, and do well enough using dry flies up to size 12 and stonefly imitations to size 8. Big attractor flies are not effective. Very small caddis flies are present, as well as dragonflies, damselflies, and crane flies.

Río Grande. First, do not confuse this river with Tierra del Fuego's Río Grande; the two rivers have little in common.

The Río Grande of Chubut Province is the southern boundary of Los Alerces National Park. At its nearest point, the river lies 25 miles southeast of Esquel. To reach it, drive on paved Route 259 south of Esquel to the small town of Trevelin. From Trevelin, either drive west toward the Futaleufu Dam at the end of the Amutui Quimei Reservoir to reach the upper river, or continue south on Route 259—now a dirt road—for about 17 miles toward the Chilean border to reach the lower reaches of the river.

The road from Esquel to the Río Grande passes through a pastoral valley of the type depicted on rural travel posters: well-tended farmsteads bordered by stately poplars are surrounded by lush green meadows full of cattle, sheep, and horses. The valley is full of lovely maitens, round trees like lollipops in silhoutte; in the background, sculpted peaks full of small glaciers tower well above timberline.

Trevelin (tray-vay-LEEN) is another of the communities founded by Welsh immigrants. Welshmen who arrived at the coast of Patagonia on the sailing vessel "Mimosa" in 1865 wasted no time in establishing their presence in this valley. A granary and mill were built and a town quickly grew up around the facilities. *Trevelin*, in fact, means "milltown" in Welsh. The town is small (5,000), and has only one small hotel at this writing, but it does have several tea rooms, so stop on your way through for an English style tea hour.

The Río Grande, called Río Futaleufu on some maps, runs southeast for a few miles, then suddenly veers west and flows across the border into Chile and on to the Pacific Ocean. Its source is a 30-mile-long reservoir created when industrialists won a battle with conservation interests and were permitted to build Futaleufu Dam within a national park — the equivalent of building a huge dam in Yellowstone or Glacier National Park. The dam supplies power primarily for an aluminum smelter at Puerto Madryn, a port on the Atlantic coast. Its cost to the fishery resource is not yet clear, but four separate lakes and scores of miles of prime spawning habitat have been inundated by the reservoir. The dam is a clear example of the type of development that can not in my view be permitted to recur in the prime fishing grounds of Patagonia.

As its name implies, the river is a *big river* — a true daughter of glaciers. At least three times the size of the Río Limay, 200 feet across in most places, it is likely to be the largest river a fly fisherman will encounter in Patagonia. The river is dangerous. It is cold and deceptively clear, carries a huge volume of water, is deep, and has a slow but powerful current. Look for gravel bars and wade with extreme caution. Do not fish this stream alone.

Because of the large number of farms in the river valley, access is a problem on the Río Grande. All you can do is ask permission from the local landowners; it is generally granted. Wading is a problem not only because of depth, but because of streamside willows and

deadfalls. In a few places, however, meadows extend right to the edge of the river; casting is easy at these spots.

The Río Grande is primarily a rainbow stream. They can run from four to eight pounds, but some have reached 15 pounds! The river also holds browns, a few brooks, and salmon.

Rising fish are almost as common on the Río Grande as on trout streams of the western U.S, especially during evening hours. Because the stream is so smooth, you can see rises at great distances. I have taken fish on dry flies on the river, but it is often difficult to get into position to reach them on this huge stream. Guides are beginning to deal with this problem by floating the river in inflatables. I usually fish the stream wet, with muddlers, streamers, and large wet fly patterns. As on the Rivadavia, unseen fish have snapped off my flies with appalling regularity on this stream.

The salmon the Río Grande holds are not Atlantic salmon, but Pacific salmon and their arrival is cause for great excitement among Argentine fishermen. Pacific salmon have been observed since 1985 in the Río Corcovado, another river to the south that also drains into the Pacific, but until recently, none had appeared in the Río Grande. In 1988, the first Pacific salmon — believed to be a silver — was taken by a fisherman from the Río Grande and since the species is rare in Argentina, the news spread like wildfire in fishing circles. You will recall that between 1905 and 1910, fry of silver, sockeye, and chinook salmon were planted in many Argentine lakes and rivers. All of these efforts failed, but more recent plantings in Chile have been successful, and it appears that Argentine fishermen will soon have the opportunity to fish for anadromous salmon in its few Pacific-flowing drainages.

About 17 miles south of Trevelin on Route 259 lies the Arroyo Baggilt Fish Hatchery, Chubut's only provincial hatchery. It lies about 100 yards south of the main road and is well marked.

Visitors are welcome and a brief tour of the hatchery is worthwhile. About 80 percent of its production is rainbows and the balance are brook trout and browns. The hatchery maintains a vigorous stocking program and virtually every drop of water in Chubut Province that will support a trout eventually receives them from this hatchery. Their most successful fish is the Shasta River strain of rainbow, which they received from the Bariloche Hatchery in 1978. According to Teddy Griffiths, the affable Welsh-Argentine hatchery manager, they have put these fish into barren waters and have returned three years later to find a few fish weighing as much as eight pounds!

Not long ago, Griffiths was shocked to find a strange fish busily building a spawning redd in the tiny stream that flows from the hatchery facilities to the Río Grande. It turned out to be a fifteen-pound coho salmon. . .

A few other nearby streams offer dry fly fishing. The Río Corintos, four miles south of Trevelin, and the Río Desaguadero, halfway between Esquel and Villa Futalaufquen hold small rainbows. But for my money, the best show in town in this part of the world remains the big, brawny Río Grande.

Points South. The Río Grande is the last of the streams I will describe in the Central Zone. The next major fishing zone does not even begin for 600 air miles south of Esquel, not far from the Strait of Magellan. That fact does not mean, however, that there are no trout streams between Esquel and the Southern Zone—quite the contrary.

But as you move south from Esquel, Patagonia undergoes a dramatic qualitative change from the perspective of the traveler. South of Esquel, an austere Patagonia becomes even *more* austere. Trees disappear; eventually the brush disappears—grass covers the flat terrain. Signs of human habitation dwindle and finally vanish for intervals of a hundred miles or more. A lone, sunbleached boulder becomes a notable landmark as the road disappears into the horizon with the curve of the earth. Route 40 changes from a lightly traveled highway to one of the loneliest roads on earth...

Fishing trips can be made to this part of Patagonia in ordinary cars, but only cars in good mechanical condition. Four wheel drive helps, but is not required. Good tires and spares *are* required. Travel is recommended during summer months only, and only on dry roads. You must be prepared to camp in most places and must carry ample food and drinking water. And you must be prepared to graciously accept long delays that may result from a myriad of causes. The Peter Principle is as operational in Patagonia as elsewhere. And you must be prepared to deport yourself and be treated as an ordinary human being, not as a monarch from some far-off country. You will attract more attention, but get no better service in a tiny crossroads tavern than the gaucho at the other end of the bar. This is the real world, where your smile is more important than your dollars. . .

Fishing becomes chancy in this region, for accurate information is scarce, and inaccurate information is overabundant. On a tip, you may endure several days of discomfort to reach a stream that has poor to mediocre fishing or is running muddy because of distant rainstorms.

On the other hand...you may happen upon waters which hold, as I firmly believe, world record brook trout.

From the point of view of fly fishermen, the law of diminishing returns is bound to come into play. The quality of fishing simply may not warrant the effort and expense required to get to the more remote streams in this in-between part of Patagonia. If you are like most fishermen, however, you are convinced that the the most remote streams have the best fishing, the largest fish, the nicest campsites, and so on. And I have no doubt that a few of you are going to wander this in-between country in search of those remote streams, no matter what warnings I pass on in these pages.

I am still exploring this part of Patagonia and have not been to all of its trout streams, but I have fished some of them, so in order to help you to avoid driving a hundred miles of murderous roads to reach a barren stream, I will briefly list the main waters between the Central and Southern Zones and will pass on what little I know about them.

Río Corcovado (cor-co-VAH-do). Called Río Carrenleufu on some maps, this is one of the rivers into which Pacific salmon are making their way. It holds large brook trout—up to seven pounds. To reach the river, drive four miles south of Trevelin on dirt Route 259 to the junction with Route 17. Head southeast on Route 17 and continue for 37 more miles to the village of Corcovado. Head west, and in a few miles you will cross the river.

Lago General Vintter. This large lake lies south of the Río Corcovado, but is accessible only by a 60-mile dirt road that heads toward the Chilean frontier through desolate, empty countryside. It is reputed to hold nothing but brook trout, which are reputed to be very large indeed. Be advised that I do have not first-hand information on the region or its fishing.

Río Senguerr (sen-GEHR). About 180 miles south of Esquel, a dirt road—Route 56—joins paved Route 20. The road leads west to the village of Alto Río Senguerr (Upper Senguerr River). Thirty-five deserted miles west of Alto Río Senguerr lies Lago Fontana, from which flows the Río Senguerr. Lago Fontana is almost never fished and its boca is reputed to hold immense brook trout. The lower part of the river is small (from 10 to 20 feet wide), has plenty of good fly water, and usually flows clear. Near Facundo, I have taken small brook trout, but nothing worth making a special visit for.

Río Mayo (MY-oh). Near the town of Rio Mayo, the river is a murky little stream unworthy of attention.

Río Los Antiguos and *Río Jiménez* (ahn-TEE-gwose and hee-MEN-ehs). Perito Moreno is the gateway town to Lago Buenos Aires, a huge freshwater inland sea fed by runoff from the southern Andean ice-cap. It is a fascinating area, but has little of interest for fly fishermen. Two rivers enter the lake near Los Antiguos, a lakeside village near the Chilean border: Río Los Antiguos and Río Jiménez, the border stream between Argentina and Chile. Brooks, browns, and rainbows have been planted in Lago Buenos Aires and its tributaries, and both streams hold trout, but are subject to intense spring flooding and braid through broad gravel bars in their lower reaches. They lack well-defined channels and are unappealing and unsuitable for fly fishing. Pass them up.

Río Chico (CHEE-coh). If Patagonia had an area named The Empty Quarter, it would be the lands drained by the upper Río Chico. Between the villages of Bajo Caracoles and Tres Lagos lie 200 miles of practically nothing but swirling, black, 400-foot dust devils. Farther north, scattered herds of angora goats somehow find sustenance on the steppes, but on the upper Río Chico, domesticated animals give way to wildlife—guanacos, rheas, tinamous, foxes, and armadillos. Hilltops and the road disappear into shiny, shimmering mirages. A crumbling rock structure about halfway between the two villages is actually a dark and dingy bar named Las Horquetas, which serves gin and warm beer to the occasional passing truck driver.

The Río Chico lies nearby. Rainbows and brooks were planted in the river as recently as 1978. It is not as small as its name suggests—40 to 60 feet wide—but carries an enormous load of sediment. I have never seen the river clear and is not a suitable stream for fly fishermen. Pass it up.

Río Chehuen (shay-WANE). On some maps, the Río Chalia. A small, murky stream near Tres Lagos. Not worth fishing.

Río Las Leonas (lay-OWN-ahs), Río Santa Cruz. Río Las Leonas ("Tigress River") and Río Santa Cruz, outlet streams for Lago Viedma and Lago Argentino, respectively, are nearly 500 miles south of Esquel. The westernmost sections of both lakes lie within Los Glaciares National Park, described in Chapter 6. Access is no problem; Route 40 parallels the entire length of the Río Las Leonas and further south crosses the Río Santa Cruz.

The two rivers are similar in character—milky-blue, but quite turbid with glacial rock flour for most of the year. They are enormous, deep rivers, in places several hundred feet wide and they surge smoothly but powerfully from these huge lakes. Their gradients are relatively steep, and they have scoured impediments from their paths, so they form few riffles. Essentially lakes in motion, they form strong eddies, whirlpools, and upwellings as they slide down their canyons.

The lakes of the upper Río Santa Cruz are one of the few systems in Patagonia in which lake trout have flourished. Locals call lake trout *bocones* for their large mouths, or *truchas canadienses*, "Canadian trout." Sport fishermen scorn the fish for its lack of fighting spirit and consider it a plague. Both rivers hold these lake trout and are reputed to hold rainbows and landlocked salmon as well. I have seen 24-inch lake trout caught by locals, who use latitas and hooks baited with large chunks of meat, but have not seen either of the other fish taken from the rivers.

In my view, neither river is suitable for fly fishing, and I don't fish in them. When asking around about other fishing waters, I was once directed to a tributary of the Río Las Leonas called Río Turbio (sometimes called Río Matas Negras) for trout, but when I arrived—admittedly late in the season—the streambed was bone dry.

In general, then, this is not an area to which I would direct fishermen. Other features of the park and its surroundings, however, are most interesting indeed—the Mount Fitzroy chain, Perito Moreno Glacier, and so on.

Just north of the Southern Fishing Zone, the powerful turquoise, Río Santa Cruz carries glacial runoff to the sea.

Lago Roca, in Los Glaciares National Park, site of a river that appears and disappears about every four years.

If these attractions draw you to the park, I suggest that you bring along your fly rod and take the trouble to fish in one place, Lago Roca, the only real fly fishing waters in the area.

Lago Roca (ROW-kah). Lago Roca lies within Los Glaciares National park, 28 miles southwest of El Calafate on dirt Route 15. Calafate is the only town in the region. With its dusty, disheveled look and its somewhat predatory character, the town is reminiscent of Fairbanks, Alaska. Residents are helpful to strangers, but a large proportion of its 3,000 inhabitants are devoted to separating the many tourists who come to visit the park from their dollars. There are several hotels and inns in Calafate, but you must shop around, for some are outrageously over-priced; many handicrafts are also far more expensive than they should be. Restaurants are reasonable, and some serve excellent meals.

There are three ways to reach Lago Roca from Calafate. The best route is the direct, southernmost of the roads, Route 15, which will give you a view of Perito Moreno Glacier. Lago Roca comes into view at the marked park entrance. Just inside the entrance, one of many side roads leads to the lakeshore. Keep driving, however, for about two miles to the campground, and then another mile or so beyond the campground to the western end of the lake.

The western end of Lago Roca is connected to the Brazo Sur ("South Arm") of Lago Argentino by a very short, unnamed river and it is this river that is the fly fishing water. There are a few slight problems with the river—sometimes it flows east to west, sometimes it flows west to east, and sometimes it disappears altogether. . .

The river's condition depends entirely upon Perito Moreno Glacier, which forms a dam whose four-year cycle is described in Chapter 6. If you arrive not long after the glacial dam has broken, the water level in Brazo Sur will be low, and the river may be a half-mile long. If you arrive just before the dam is ready to break, Brazo Sur will be high enough to merge with Lago Roca, and the river will be gone.

If your arrival coincides with correct conditions, the river will be from a quarter to half-mile long, clear (unlike the turbid Brazo Sur), very cold, and teeming with large rainbow trout. Clean gravel beaches and exposed creek deltas are perfect for casting. In four hours on one December evening years ago, I released 15 rainbows from 15-22 inches and kept one for dinner, all taken on flies from shore. The fish are not selective; dry flies (No. 12 mosquito), size 8-10 dark stonefly nymphs, muddlers, and streamers are all effective from time to time. The fish are in superb condition, strong fighters for their size.

Fishing is best in the morning or during the long austral summer evenings, when you can cast to rising fish until 11:00 p.m. Winds can be strong during midday hours, so either take fairly heavy tackle or spend the windy hours inspecting wildlife or the wonderful scenery. Birdlife is abundant—in the lake and meadows, geese, chimangos, black-necked swans, caracaras, bandurrias, and Andean gulls; in the woods, Magellanic woodpeckers; and in the clouds, if you are lucky, condors.

Campers should note that the nearby campground is cheap, nicely located in a grove of huge lenga trees and so quiet that you can hear icebergs fall from glaciers in the mountains across the lake. The campground now has a small store and coffeeshop, and there are no biting bugs.

Río Coyle (COY-lay), sometimes called Río Coig. South of Calafate, Route 40 passes through gently undulating countryside in which herds of nervous sheep begin to appear. Forests mottle distant mountainsides, but the steppes through which the dusty road winds are treeless; here and there sprout lonely bushes—never more than waist-high, usually knee-high. All the rest is grass and gravel. The basically flat terrain in combination with the dramatic cloud formations common so far south lend the region that feeling of endless, empty spaciousness so characteristic of southern Patagonia. Big sky country, indeed.

A hundred miles toward the coastal city of Río Gallegos from Calafate, Routes 40 and 5 cross the mossy, tea-colored Río Coyle. The upper river holds brook trout, but in most places it braids so many paths through the grasslands that it lacks a distinct, fly fishable channel. If you are exploring the area, do fish the upper river wherever you can find a deep-cut, coherent channel, but be warned that there are not many such reaches. Have plenty of bug dope; black flies can be bothersome right on the steam. The lower Río Coyle, near the sea, usually holds no more than scattered, stagnant pools during the late summer.

Río Turbio (TOOR-bee-oh). Southwest of the upper Río Coyle, the terrain undergoes a gradual but significant change. Clumps of beeches begin to appear and sere, scrubby grasslands give way to lush and green meadows full of thousands of sheldgeese. By the time Route 40 nears the town of Río Turbio, it is passing through a beech forest. A few miles north of town, the road begins to parallel the upper Río Turbio—"Turbid River." The river is small, clear, and clean. It holds brown trout, but the fishery seems to be declining. Prior to 1985, the river was full of fat, 8 to 15-inch brown trout, but in 1990 I was only able to hook a few six-inch fish rising to a small brown caddis.

Unfortunately for fish, Argentina's largest coalfields underlie the rolling hills near the town of Río Turbio and effluent from the mines enters the river east of town, ruining it for many miles downstream.

No matter. If you are close enough to this part of the world to fish the upper Río Turbio, however, you are close enough to fish in a number places that offer much better fishing, for finally—nearly 600 miles south of Esquel—we have reached the northern edge of Patagonia's Southern Fishing Zone.

SOUTHERN ZONE

Patagonia's Southern Fishing Zone begins at Latitude 48° South, about the same position of Seattle or Winnipeg in the northern hemisphere. The zone includes the extreme south of Santa Cruz Province and extends to the southern edge of the island and Province of Tierra del Fuego at 55° South, at about Copenhagen or Ketchikan, Alaska. It is near the end of the continent, and trout streams are crowded into a steadily narrowing wedge of mountains and rolling plains. Roads are empty in this region and settlements scattered, but wildlife is notably abundant and fish are notably big.

The climate is essentially cool, and seasons distinct. The mean annual summer temperature is about 50° F., and mean winter temperature just above freezing. The infamous winds—these latitudes are the "Roaring 40's" of sailing lore—are strongest in spring and summer and somewhat more moderate in fall and winter.

Río Gallegos (gah-ZHEY-gohs). With its tributaries, the Río Gallegos is the northernmost trout stream in the zone. Formed by the union of the Río Turbio, Río Penitente, and Río Rubens, the Gallegos flows east from the edge of the Andes to enter the South Atlantic at the town of Río Gallegos. It is a brown trout river, first of the great sea trout streams of South America, and typical of the steppeland streams of the extreme south.

Upper Río Gallegos, near Puente Blanco, a spawning ground for Patagonia's sea trout.

Long stretches of the Río Gallegos are almost never fished and for good reason: except at or near its mouth, almost no facilities exist for visitors.

Trout were introduced into a few rivers in the extreme south of Chile as early as 1905, but not until 1927 were they planted in the headwaters of the Río Gallegos system. More trout were introduced the following year, and in 1941, 1942, 1973, 1978, 1980, and 1982. The trout were all browns, and the results have been spectacular.

The Gallegos, which freezes over every winter, appears to be a relatively unproductive river; in many reaches the current is sluggish and aquatic life is sparse. At some point in their history, however, some of the browns began to run to sea, returning fat and silvered from salt water to spawn in the gravels of the Gallegos. They had become sea trout. . .

The Gallegos browns are not as large as those of Tierra del Fuego's famed Río Grande, but they are large enough. According to fishery biologists, the Gallegos sea-runs average about seven pounds, while the Río Grande fish average about nine pounds, an observation that conforms to my own experience. The largest Gallegos sea trout caught in 1989, however, taken on spinning gear, rivaled the largest sea trout caught in the Río Grande that year; it weighed 26 pounds. The Río Gallegos flows through Santa Cruz Province, in which the fishing season lasts from November through mid-April. The browns begin to enter the river in September during spring runoff. They move relatively slowly, however, and the best time to fish is from late December through March.

When the browns are fresh from the sea, they are silvery, and are called *plateados* (plah-tey-AH-thos) or "silver-plated ones" by Argentines. They adopt normal coloration soon, however, and by the time they reach the upper river—my favorite area—they are difficult to distinguish from resident fish.

I prefer the upper river, despite its isolation, simply because it has more character than the lower stream and is less windy. The best base of operations is a lonely spot on Argentine Route 40 called Puente Blanco (White Bridge). The nearest town is 28 de Noviembre, a small settlement of pastel-colored houses 31 miles west of Puento Blanco, but decent accommodations lie even further west at Río Turbio, a grim, unappealing mining town on the Chilean border. The road between the towns of Río Turbio and Río Gallegos is so lightly traveled that no gas stations lie between the towns.

Puente Blanco comprises nothing more than a bridge, a decaying wooden hotel, a few outbuildings, and an undeveloped streamside campsite. The hotel offers very basic rooms, but at this writing provides no meals for guests. It is a strategic location for fishing the Río Gallegos and Río Penitente, however, for the two streams join just downstream from the bridge.

Both streams are classic brown trout waters: slow to moderate current, occasional riffles, abundant clumps of elodea, easy wading on sand, silt, and small gravel, large streams but not unwieldy for wading and no part out of casting range. From mid to late season, the rivers are clear, not with the sparkling clarity of the northern streams, but quite clear enough for fly fishing. Fish to eleven pounds are reported to reach Puente Blanco, which is 120 miles from the sea, but the largest sea trout I have caught this far upstream weighed seven pounds.

Apart from dense mats of elodea and filamentous algae, the Gallegos and Penitente appear to be poor in food for fish. Typical riparian vegetation is sparse; grass grows to the water's edge. The grass is cropped so short by the ubiquitous sheep that one is given the impression of fishing in a stream that meanders through a putting green—great for backcasts, but not so good for insect life. A few fish rise to tiny midges, and biting black flies can be bothersome, but there is practically no sign of caddisflies, mayflies, stoneflies, and most important, pancoras.

One is not inclined, therefore, to tie on standard insect imitations. I have experimented with various nymphs near the weedbeds, which look as though they should harbor hordes of aquatic insects, but have consistently done better with dark streamers, bucktails, and salmon fly patterns.

Like many of the streams of the Southern Zone, the Gallegos is flat water; from afar it seems to have little character. It looks like a homogeneous stream that meanders all too calmly through an endless expanse of grasslands. It has a great deal more character than meets the casual eye, but you must get on the stream to find it. Variations in current are not apparent at a distance, but once on the river, you can find plenty of reaches with current strong enough to work a fly. Occasionally, as at the boca of the Río Penitente, short boulder-studded riffles have formed.

Puente Blanco marks the edge of the beech forests. To the east, Route 40 passes through gently rolling grasslands. The landscape is essentially without feature; not a tree or shrub interrupts the gentle sweep of the horizon. The most distinctive visual features are the occasional road signs and the succession of ruined tires along the roadside.

The road parallels the river, but at distances that range from one to three miles. Access roads from Route 40 are very scarce and usually comprise no more than a pair of faint tracks heading north through the grass from the main road. As a result, scores of miles of the middle river are rarely fished.

Finally, about 50 miles east of Puente Blanco, a few basaltic outcrops appear, and the road passes the trim buildings of Estancia Bella Vista and a police post. Just beyond, in a grove of trees, lies the Hotel Bella Vista, the only overnight facility on the middle reaches of the Río Gallegos.

By standards of the Northern and Central Zones, indeed the few coastal towns in the region, accommodations at Hotel Bella Vista are rough, but they are adequate, and the owner plans several improvements, including private baths. Prices are moderate and meals are plain but filling. The hotel has been owned and operated by the Van Heerden family for about ten years. Son Orlando Van Heerden speaks no English and is new to fly fishing and guiding, but he is the local fish warden, knows the river, and is making a game attempt at developing a fly fishing business. In 1989, he had only a few poor quality flies on hand, but kept a 14-pound plateado in a tank behind the hotel to show to doubting Thomases.

When the wind is not strong, the middle reaches of the Río Gallegos are fascinating waters to explore. The river is easily negotiated, and wading is easy in fine gravels. Much of the stream is flat, but it is usually a short walk to currents fast enough for flies. The only signs of invertebrate aquatic life are tiny black periwinkles. If the wind is blowing, the river is too cold for comfortable wet wading; take waders.

With respect to backcasts, brush is no cause for concern—there isn't any—but on occasion you do have to be careful not to hook a rhea. A major difference between this zone and the more northern zones is the astonishing abundance of birdlife. Rheas, called *nandús* or *charos* in this part of Patagonia, are more numerous on the Río Gallegos than on any other stream I have fished in Patagonia, especially in late summer, when they come to the river in search of water. I have counted over 50 along a half-mile of stream not far from the Bella Vista. From midsummer forward, it is not uncommon to wade into the river and be able to see rheas, flamingos, geese, ducks, and ibises without moving.

The drawback of the Gallegos is the wind. It can be murderous, and is only a foretaste of things to come further south. You must have a heavy rod and line to handle the wind; light tackle will not cut it. And you must also have good

A typically windy day on the middle reaches of the Río Gallegos.

warm clothes to handle not only the wind, but the unpredictable cold snaps that occur even in summer. I have skidded on frozen puddles near Bella Vista in February—our equivalent of August.

The wind drove me from this river for years until I learned that I could often—not always—solve the problem by fishing only early and late. The prudent fly fisherman gets up at or near daybreak—considered a barbarism by most Argentines—fishing until about ten, and returning to camp to read, nap, write up notes, or do chores rather than fight midday gales, and return to the river at 6:00 or 7:00 to fish until dark.

Gallegos Chico. Bella Vista is very close to the Río Gallegos Chico, sometimes called Río Gallegos Sur, a small tributary that enters the mainstem stream from the south. The Gallegos Chico is now closed to fishing to protect spawners, but present plans call for reopening the river in 1991 or 1992 as a fly fishing only, catch and release stream. Since the river will be reopened, I'd like to describe it, for it is one of the finest, though difficult, dry fly streams in the Southern Zone.

When I first fished the stream, I came upon an afternoon hatch of small mayflies and fish were rising everywhere. I tied on a No. 14 mosquito, put down a number of fish, and finally hooked and released a four-pound resident brown. During the rest of the day, I hooked, released, and lost 22 more fish from one to five pounds in the lower two miles of the stream, all on dry flies—one of the finest days of fishing I've had anywhere in Patagonia.

The stream varies considerably in width—from 5 to 25 feet—and is loaded with thick beds of moss and elodea. It has a slight tea tint and a slick, oily appearance reminiscent of Yellowstone's Firehole or lower Gibbon Rivers. The Gallegos Chico confronts fly fishermen with a host of technical problems, for although the fish are not usually selective, they are very wary, and long, light leaders are required. Wind and water currents are quixotic, and light is tricky. Casts must be near-perfect, and drifts quite dead. If your tippet is too heavy, the browns will ignore your fly; if it is too light, you'll lose fish and fly when they slide into the thick beds of elodea. The fish are in excellent condition, very thick-bodied. A 15-inch fish may weigh nearly three pounds.

Near the railroad and highway bridges, is a long deep pool full of big, leery fish. Ancient coal-burning trains pass by twice daily on their way between the towns of Río Turbio and Río Gallegos, and the engineer responds to a fisherman's wave with a toot from his steam whistle. Upstream, the river rushes through a short canyon. Mayflies and caddisflies are abundant near the canyon rapids. Further upstream, the canyon opens into a half-mile-wide valley in which the river has formed a series of stream benches. On both sides is black rimrock, country much like central Montana or southern Idaho. This portion of the river breaks into foam-flecked pools that meander through meadowlands, and when the rise is on, you will see familiar swirls as close as an inch from the edge of undercut banks.

The fish are big at least two miles above the highway bridge, but they are uncharacteristically spooky for Patagonian trout. Long casts are often necessary, with line falling on the grass and only a few inches of leader into water. Fortunately, the grass is closely cropped by sheep—which stare in amazement at fishermen inching along on their knees—so the ploy is easily executed and most effective. In my experience, mosquitos, quill gordons, and when light is failing, hair-wing royal coachmen work well; for some reason, gray hackle yellows and blue

uprights—good standard patterns for me elsewhere in Patagonia — do not work well on this stream.

Waders help on the Gallegos Chico, but are not necessary.

Lower Río Gallegos. The lower mainstem of the Río Gallegos is easily accessible from the town of Río Gallegos. Twenty miles west of town, along Argentine Route 40, look for a prominent water tower on a bench above the river. Trails and roads from the tower lead to the river's edge. At this point the river makes a series of gooseneck turns through the valley floor that enable fly fishermen to maneuver into favorable positions with respect to the wind. A few willow clumps offer a bit of shelter. The river is broad and deep on the outside edges of the curves, but wading is easy on broad gravel bars. About a mile north of the tower, another dirt road leads to the river from Route 40. Tidal ranges are extreme in this part of the South Atlantic—up to 45 feet—so even though the Highway 3 bridge is 20 miles from the sea, below this point the river becomes an estuary strongly influenced by tides and unsuitable for fly fishing.

The outskirts of the town of Río Gallegos (population 42,000) have the typically ragged, frontier look of Patagonian communities, but the downtown area is neat, clean, and pleasant. A half-dozen good hotels and restaurants are available to visitors. Estancia Truchaike, near the Highway 3 Bridge,

The lower Río Gallegos, near the town of Río Gallegos.

The glassy waters of brown trout-rich Río Gallegos Chico.

offers accommodations to visiting fishermen.

Railroad buffs with plenty of time may wish to ride one of the coal trains hauled by steam engines to Río Turbio twice daily. Scheduled passenger service for the general public is not available, but by obtaining special permission and signing a liability waiver, you may be able to rattle across Patagonia in a coal burner that belongs to an era long gone elsewhere. The 156-mile trip between Río Gallegos and Río Turbio takes about 12 hours.

Río Grande. Forty-four miles south of the town of Río Gallegos, Argentine Route 3 enters Chile. Further south, the route forks, leading southwest to Punta Arenas or southeast to Tierra del Fuego and the town of Río Grande. Between Río Gallegos and Río Grande lie 230 miles of atrocious roads, officious border authorities, and boring scenery. But there is also a brief trip on a converted LST across the Strait of Magellan, scores of guanacos along the roadsides, and zillions of geese and sheep. The road between the two towns is slowly being paved, but today the trip is arduous by land. But take heart, for if you have gotten yourself to Río Gallegos, you can surely get yourself to Río Grande.

The town is small (population 20,000) and neat, kept in business by sheep farming, a large military garrison, and several plants for electronic consumer products, assembled on Tierra del Fuego under favorable tax provisions. The island is a duty-free zone, and many products are indeed cheaper than elsewhere in Argentina. Fishermen who stay in town generally eat and sleep at one of two establishments: La Posada de los Sauces, on the waterfront, or the

Hotel Ibarra, on the town's central plaza. The Posada is smaller, but the more elegant of the two and serves outstanding meals. Both hotels are moderately priced, and guide service can be arranged through the management at either place.

At present, the only fishing lodge on the Río Grande River is the Kau-Tapen Lodge. *Kau-Tapen* means "House of Fishing" in Ona, the language of one of Tierra del Fuego's original Indian tribes, now extinct. The lodge is well-named; during the 1989-90 season, guests hooked and released over three *tons* of sea-run brown trout. The number and size of fish taken by guests of this lodge along is astonishing. On the following table I have summarized Kau-Tapen's data from 1985 to 1990.

they purportedly imitate (a belief widely held by those who fish the more northern zones). The problem is that there are few, if any, pancoras in the Río Grande. A few perennial guests at Kau-Tapen, including Page Brown—"Top Rod" of the 1989/90 season—have taken sea trout on dry flies (generally attractor patterns such as sofa pillows) on calm days, but the overwhelming majority are taken on wet patterns. One of Kau-Tapen's head quides, a methodical fly fisherman who constantly experiments with different patterns, insists that "any fly works." He adds, however, that "you must think in terms of the sea, not the river, on this stream." No notable pattern of behavior have emerged from my own experience on the river, and I can offer no more specific advice to readers.

Season	Number of Fish	Ave. Weight (pounds)	Number over 11 pounds	Number over 15 pounds	Largest of Season
1985/86	207	11	119	44	20
1986/87	223	8	60	25	20
1987/88	416	7	79	18	19
1988/89	614	7.6	118	19	20
1989/90*	644	9.7	240	72	25

*partial year's data

The vast majority of these fish, taken in a 20-mile stretch of the river, are sea-run browns; about one fish in fifty is a rainbow (up to ten pounds) and a small proportion are resident brown trout. The river is broad, but there are plenty of sand and gravel bars to wade, and few parts of the river lie beyond reach of a good long cast. The most effective fly has been the wooly bugger, followed by muddler, fuzzy-wuzzy, matuka, Montana nymph, Bitch Creek special, and black shrimp.

As with salmon, no one knows precisely why the sea trout take flies; their stomachs are empty when they are in the river. It is tempting to conclude that wooly buggers are effective because the trout take them for pancoras, which

Kau-Tapen Lodge is owned and operated by Jorge and Jacqueline de las Carreras, a charming and poised family who put a broadly international clientele immediately at ease, and provide five-course meals for hungry fly fishermen. The lodge is small and intimate; only eight guests can be accommodated at a time and the lodge is usually full throughout the season. Service is deluxe; one guide is at the behest of each pair of fishermen.

Sons Fernando and Jorge Jr. handle day-to-day operations of the lodge. They have laid out a complex system of roads that each lead to a different system of pools on the twenty-mile stretch of the river near the lodge, and have devised a rotation system by which each fisherman has equal opportunity to fish each beat on the river with a different guide during their stay.

Fernando is both the thinking and activist fisherman of the family. He is determined to create and maintain the finest sea trout river on the face of the earth, and has taken definite steps toward that end. The work is a labor of love for Fernando, but it has not been without cost. By limiting access to the river to casual anglers and strictly maintaining a catch and release policy, he has garnered the ill will of some local fishermen. His management philosophy is biocentric rather than anthropocentric; he puts the welfare of the aquatic ecosystem above the wishes of local fisherman, who quite understandably resent it. The proof, of course, is in the pudding, and so far his policy is proving correct; the fish are getting bigger and more plentiful. His work on the Río Grande sets an example that provincial authorities throughout Argentina would do well to study and emulate.

Kau-Tapen lies 25 miles from the town of Río Grande on Argentine Route B, about an hour's drive from town. The road passes through the colorful buildings of Estancia Menéndez, the first of the huge sheep ranches established in northern Tierra del Fuego. Half of the distance is paved, but the remainder is dirt that turns into slimy soup when wet. The lodge sits a mile from Route B on a bench overlooking the Río Menéndez, a sizeable tributary to the Río Grande. It lies at the point at which beech forests give way to the grasslands that extend to the Atlantic coast. The Chilean border lies a few miles west, and in the far distance loom the snowcapped peaks of the Darwin Range, one of the last sizable mountain ranges in the world to be explored. Do not drive to

Tierra del Fuego. A typically windy day in the open spaces on the legendary Río Grande.

Kau-Tapen without contacting the lodge first. You can contact the lodge by radio at the Civil Defense Office *(Oficina de Defensa Civil)* in the town of Río Grande.

The Río Grande is accessible from points other than Kau-Tapen. If you drive west on Route C to Estancía María Behety, for example, and request permission to fish, you will generally be directed to the river. When you reach the estancia, you will think you have arrived at a small town. Like many large Fuegian sheep ranches, the estancia is indeed a self-contained unit, with its own school, police station, social club, library, grocery store, workshops, and storehouses. This particular estancia, which once supported 300,000 sheep, is dominated by an enormous ornate sheep-shearing shed, claimed by many to be the largest structure of its kind in the world. The estancia office *(oficina)* is prominently marked; ask here for permission to fish.

The most difficult challenge for fly fishermen is not access, choice of fly, muddy roads, a foreign language, or even the vast distance between Tierra del Fuego and home waters; it is the wind. It can be incessant, and if you have not prepared yourself to accept it, can make your life miserable. At times, it is difficult to hold a camera still, to walk, stand, even to catch a good breath. Sixty-mile winds are not uncommon, and 100-mile-an-hour gusts have been recorded at ground level. The problems these nightmare gales can cause fly fishermen are not hard to imagine. The wind often eases in the evenings, and there are rare windless days, but you would be wise to prepare yourself—mentally and physically—to cast flies into the teeth of a gale.

Large fish are abundant in the Río Gallegos and Río Grande, but do not expect to step into the stream, make a few casts, and suddenly be playing a ten-pound sea trout. You need patience and persistence on these unpredictable rivers; one day you may fish hard all day long for one or two fish, and the next day you may hook seven or eight fish under identical circumstances.

These two rivers quite understandably dominate the Southern Fishing Zone, and have long overshadowed at least nine smaller streams on Tierra del Fuego that merit the attention of errant fly fishermen. These lesser known streams are short—30 to 50 miles—and similar in character to Montana's Beaverhead River or Yellowstone's Firehole River. A few are close enough to the towns of Río Grande or Ushuaia (oo-shoo-AYE-uh) to be fished on day trips, but most of them are too far from hotels to explore thoroughly on a day's visit.

Tierra del Fuego's trout fishing stems from the interest of one man in fly fishing. Between 1930 and 1937, John Goodall, an Anglo-Argentine engineer anxious to provide the island with a diversion familiar to Britons obtained trout and Atlantic salmon eggs from Chile and the Bariloche Hatchery and planted fry throughout the island. In the process, Goodall earned a prominent place in the annals of trout fishing, for the fish not only survived, but flourished.

Río Fuego (FWAY-go). The "Fire River" is the nearest of the smaller streams to Río Grande. The river lies about 30 miles southwest of town along Route F, or can be reached from Highway 3 by Route H. These dirt roads pass through semi-open country typical of eastern Tierra del Fuego. The sheep estancias are so large that headquarters buildings are separated by ten to thirty miles, so the countryside appears utterly deserted.

The lower river is often too dark for effective fly fishing, but the middle and upper reaches, in the vicinity of Estancia Buenos Aires, are classic brown trout waters. Tea-colored, gentle, and warm, the river meanders through a broad valley amidst low beech-wooded hills. Long stretches of streambanks are free of brush and other backcast obstructions. The stream was designed for fly fishermen.

Río Fuego, another Fuegian trout stream in a putting green.

Rainbows are present in a ratio of about one for every seven browns. The river is fertile, with a mossy bottom, and cut-off oxbow bends along the river provide excellent nursery habitat for the aquatic invertebrates that teem in the river. As a result, the fish are in superb condition; as in the Gallegos Chico, a 15-inch brown may weigh three pounds.

Strong winds can be frustrating in the open valley of the Río Fuego, but a succession of hairpin curves usually permit fishermen to maneuver into favorable positions.

Tributaries of the upper river offer a fishing opportunity familiar in North America but unique to Tierra del Fuego in South America—beaver pond trout. Beavers (and muskrats) were introduced into Tierra del Fuego in the 1940's, and like the trout, have flourished. The technical problems of fishing beaver ponds are as perplexing in Tierra del Fuego as in North America; approach is difficult and Fuegian browns are just as skittish as their northern cousins in these glassy waters.

The Fuego is one of Tierra del Fuego's more rewarding streams for fishermen interested in wildlife. Beavers and otters thrive along the river and guanacos are common in the area. The abundant streamside birdlife includes sheldgeese, flamingos, bandurrias, and teros.

Río Ewan (EH-wahn). Prominent among hopes of most fly fishermen is finding waters undisturbed by other fishermen. On crowded streams, we can never quite shake off the suspicion that someone may have just spooked all the fish in the pool we have so carefully approached, or worse, that the pool's prize fish was hauled out ten minutes before we arrived. This sort of anxiety is never a problem on the Ewan. On most of the days I have fished it, I was to my knowledge the only fisherman on the river.

Highway 3 crosses the north fork of the Río Ewan midway between the town of Río Grande and the eastern end of Lago Fagnano (fahn-YAH-no), about 40 miles southeast of Río Grande. Ask permission to fish the river at nearby Estancia Viamonte or at the police station near the highway bridge.

The Ewan is an interesting trout stream, a fly fishing grab bag. It supports browns, rainbows, and brook trout to five pounds which seem to have abandoned their customary habitat preferences. Deep slow pools produce rainbows as often as browns, and flies drifted through fast-running rapids are as likely to be taken by brook or brown trout as by rainbows. Ewan trout are seldom where you expect them to be, and for a few seconds after a strike even the most discerning fisherman is never quite sure what kind of fish has taken his fly. The perpetual suspense adds visceral satisfaction to fly fishing on this remote river.

The Ewan is a small stream with deep pools, a regular sandy bottom, and frequent riffles. It is usually too dark for dry flies, but lacks the filamentous algae that plague fishermen on other small slow Fuegian streams. Muddlers and small streamers are effective on the river, hit hard in the holes beneath the undercut banks.

Ewan trout are vigorous, hard-fighting fish. The rainbows jump repeatedly and routinely shake loose flies that are not well set. The brooks and browns seldom clear water, preferring to settle back against a strong current and swing their heads back and forth in a powerful, rod-jerking pulse that snaps leaders with appalling regularity.

You can follow the Río Ewan to the sea from Highway 3, fishing along the way, in about four hours. During summer months the valley floor is soft and boggy, but the effort is worthwhile not only for the fishing, but for the wildlife you will see along the way.

Río San Pablo. About 46 miles southeast of Río Grande, Route A leaves Highway 3 and leads a further 26 miles to the mouth of the Río San Pablo. The river winds through a valley bordered by low rolling hills. Dense forests of Antarctic beech cover the hills and on sunny days snowpatches glitter on slopes of distant higher mountains in Tierra del Fuego's remote interior.

The lower river ranges from slickwater chutes to rocky riffles to punch-bowl pools. If you hike upstream, you pass through meadows and peat bogs *(turbales)* that will look familiar to any reader that has been to Alaska, and which give the river a light bourbon stain. The river meanders here, and has cut deeply into the meadows on the outside of the curves. Browns to seven pounds lurk in the shadows of those curves, and the flat water is occasionally wrinkled by monstrous swirls that freeze fly fishermen in their tracks.

It is a long hike to the middle reaches of the river, and as remote as it seems, the river is periodically fished quite hard. In years past, I have watched men stagger back through the meadows under the weight of gunnysacks crammed with two dozen hook-jawed bronzed trout from three to seven pounds. I have also heard reports of fishing boats spreading their nets across the mouth of the river, in effect "corking" the stream and taking a large portion of an entire year's production.

There is an undeveloped campsite near the bridge at the river's mouth, and

Tierra del Fuego's Río San Pablo.

a small lodge, Hostería San Pablo, has been built within earshot of the booming Atlantic surf. Hopefully, the presence of a hotel at this remote river will bring to an end the illegal exploitative practices of the past.

Río Lapataia (lah-pah-TIE-uh). If you have reached Tierra del Fuego, you will probably want to visit Ushuaia, southernmost city in the world, a jumping-off point for the steadily increasing numbers of tourists who are visiting Antarctica. The city, the only Argentine town west of the Andes, has 25,000 inhabitants, and in spirit and appearance, resembles nothing so much as a small town in Alaska. Prices are high, wages are high, the climate is miserable for most of the year, and its people are friendly but highly independent, regarding themselves rightly so as residents on Argentina's Last Frontier. It has several hotels and restaurants for visitors.

If you have gotten this far, unpack your fly rod, and drive a few miles west of town to the very end of Highway 3, the Panamerican Highway, to the Río Lapataia. This short river flows through the world's southernmost park, Tierra del Fuego National Park, and empties into the Beagle Canal, the narrow strait named after the ship on which Charles Darwin undertook his epic voyage. The river is in an area of superb alpine and maritime scenery at the eastern edge of the Cordillera Darwin, the spectacular tail end of the Andes.

The river, a powerhouse, surges smooth and clear from a long deep lake, Lago Roca, to plunge through a series of narrow gorges on its short trip to the sea. Residents of Ushuaia usually fish the Lapataia with lures, but the river can produce impressive big-water caddis hatches.

It is often lashed by fierce winds that whip down the lake from the mountains, but on rare windless evenings, rainbow and brown trout to five pounds rise to emerging insects. The reach first glimpsed on arrival by road from Ushuaia is the best water for fly fishermen. This is the long reach through which the lake imperceptibly picks up speed, to gradually become a river. The bottom is firm, clean gravel, and the shore of approach is free of brush, favorable for long casting. Good boots are required to wade the stream, for the water, fresh from nearly glaciers, is frigid.

Stomach contents of trout taken from the river indicate a wide interest in foods. Periwinkles comprise the bulk of the diet, along with various nymphs, emergents, and the gammarus-like scuds that drift down from the lake. The fish are highly selective feeders on floating insects, and I have often left the stream humbled and puzzled. A correct presentation will make up for the incorrect fly on most Patagonian streams, but not this one. An impeccable presentation, absolutely dead drift, and the right fly are imperatives; sloppy technique is wasted effort on the Lapataia.

One February afternoon, in the midst of an unbelievable rise, I frantically worked my way through a dozen patterns that were steadfastly declined before discovering that blue uprights would take fish. An hour later, the rise continued, but blue uprights were worthless. After another vexing trip through my fly boxes, I found that ginger quills—and nothing else—were on the menu.

The river must be fished with great deliberation; Lapataia trout tolerate neither hasty nor lazy fly fishermen. . .

I am going to end the narrative at this point. There are other trout waters on this island to describe: the Río Olivia, site of Tierra del Fuego's only trout hatchery and a good source of information, the remote Río Claro and Río Irigoyen, and the fishy waters of Lago Fagnano. And there are intriguing rumors to follow up: big Atlantic salmon in Lago Yehuin and big browns in the Río Turbal. But these are for future trips. . .

The Río Grande, Fuego, Ewan, San Pablo, and Lapataia are a long, long way from the trout streams of Michigan and Montana. It's not easy to get to Tierra del Fuego and once you've arrived, not easy to get around. There are days when the wind howls relentlessly over the steppes, and you may wonder whatever could have possessed you to go to the time, trouble, and expense to get to this god-forsaken island, or for that matter, to anywhere else in Patagonia.

But the next day, with the sun shining and the wind calm, when you find yourself watching a guanaco that has wandered into the open, or a flock of flamingos standing in a streamside pool, or as you ponder the correct approach to a rising fish that surely weighs several pounds, you'll realize again why you have literally pursued your passion to the ends of the earth, and more likely than not, you'll be back. See you there. . .

Beaver ponds are limited to Tierra del Fuego in South America; the introduced rodents are not found on the mainland.

FLYFISHING GLOSSARY

As mentioned elsewhere, it is not necessary to speak Spanish to not only fish, but otherwise enjoy yourself in Patagonia. But it helps...

Those flyfishermen who have not cracked a Spanish book since the fifth grade or so, but who nonetheless wish to try out their Spanish on guides, storekeepers, or other fishermen, will find the following glossary useful.

agallas: gills
álamo: poplar
anzuelo: hook
arco-iris: rainbow, for rainbow trout
arroyo: brook, for brook trout; also called **fontinalis** or **trucha de arroyo**
atar: to tie (flies)
boca: mouth, short for desembocadura, river mouth or lake inlet
backing: backing
bolsa de pesca: creel
caja de moscas: fly box
chaleco de pesca: fishing vest
chusquea: bamboo
caña: fishing rod
carnada: bait
carretel: spool
clavar: to hook
co: water (Mapuche)
corregir: to correct, i.e. "mend" a fly line
cortado: cut; slang for coffee cut with cream
cortina: curtain, used to describe windbreak rows of Lombardy poplars
criadero: hatchery
cuchara: spoon; also fishing spoon
cuenca: watershed, drainage
desovar: spawn
eclosión: rise or hatch of aquatic insects
efímera: mayfly; also **mosca de Mayo**
facón: gaucho dagger, worn in sash at small of back
falso cast: false cast
fontinalis: brook trout
gringo: In Argentina, "gringo" does not mean American, nor is it a pejorative term. It means recently arrived immigrants who were not born in Argentina, and includes Italians, Germans, Spanish, and so on.
guardafauna: roughly, game warden
guardaparque: park ranger
guardapesca: roughly, fish warden
hormiga: ant

lanzar: to cast
laufquen: lake (Mapuche)
línea: line
lomo de burro: traffic hump; do not ignore; these mean business in Argentina.
mariposa: butterly (fishing spinner); also called **voladora**
marrón: brown, for brown trout
mosca: fly, insect as well as fishing fly
mosca de piedra: stonefly
mosca húmeda: wet fly
mosca seca: dry fly
ninfa: nymph
pancora: freshwater crayfish
pescador de cuchara: lure fisherman
pescador de mosca: fly fisherman; also called moscador or mosquero
picar: to bite, strike
pique: a bite, strike
plateada: plated, as in silver-plated, for fresh sea-run brown trout polilla: caddis
pozón: pool, fishing hole
punta, puntilla: tippet; also **extremo**
rebaba: barb; also **lanceta**
red de mano: hand net
reel: reel
ripio: gravel used for roadbeds; bad ripio can be appalling.
roll cast: roll cast
sacar: to catch
salmón: salmon, sometimes refers to any large trout
salmón encerrado: landlocked salmon
saltamontes: grasshopper (literally, mountain-jumper)
sauce: willow
sembrar: to plant (fish)
senda: trail
streamer: streamer
tanza, líder: leader
temporada: season
tirar: to cast

tirón: tug, jerk
termal: hot spring
tosca blanca: volcanic tuff, commonly white cliffs
tranquera: gate
troleros: trollers

trucha: trout
vadear: to wade
vado: creek or river ford
veda: closure, prohibition
villa: village
waders: waders

SELECTED BIBLIOGRAPHY

Bardin, Poló, *Hablemos de Truchas,* Achala Ediciones, Buenos Aires, 1981.

Brian, Cecilia, et. al., *Flora de Puerto Blest,* Universidad Nacional de Comahue, General Roca, 1988.

Centro Histórico Documental, *Tiempo Comunitario,* Año II, Nos. 10 & 12, Municipalidad de Río Grande, Buenos Aires, undated.

Chatwin, Bruce, *In Patagonia,* Summit Books, New York, 1977.

Dimitri, Milan Jorge, *Pequeña Flora Ilustrada de los Parques Nacionales Andino-Patagónicos,* Publicación Técnica No. 46, Anales de Parques Nacionales, Tomo XIII, Servicio de Parques Nacionales, Buenos Aires, 1974.

Donovan, Jorge, *Nací Pescador,* Signo Producciones, Buenos Aires, 1983.

Editorial Publicaciones, *Revista Patagónica,* Nos. 21, 23, and 41, Buenos Aires, 1985 and 1989.

Erize, Francisco, et. al., *Los Parques Nacionales de la Argentina y Otras de sus Areas Naturales,* Instituto de Cooperación Iberoamericana, Madrid, 1981.

Fernandez, Patricio, et. al., *Programa de Cultivo de Salmónides,* Subsecretaria de Asuntos Marítimos, Provincia de Santa Cruz, Río Gallegos, undated.

Frey, N., *Flora del Nahuel Huapi,* Sociedad de Horticultura de Bariloche, Buenos Aires, 1973.

Fuentealba, Raúl, Gomez, *Una Provincia Llamada Neuquen,* Editorial Universitaria Kennedy, Buenos Aires, 1977.

Fuster, María Luisa, *Obtención de Híbridos entre Trucha Arco-Iris y Trucha de Arroyo,* Publicación Miscelánea No. 319, Ministerio de Agricultura y Ganadería, Buenos Aires, 1949.

Fuster, María Luisa, et. al., *Salmonicultura,* Publicación Miscelánea No. 321, Ministerio de Agricultura y Ganadería, Buenos Aires, 1949.

Gomaríz, Ginés, *Pescando Truchas,* Ediciones Hoplias, Buenos Aires, 1982.

Goodall, Rae Natalie, *Tierra del Fuego,* Ediciones Shanamaiim, Buenos Aires, 1970.

Leitch, William C., *South America's National Parks,* Mountaineers Books, Seattle, 1990.

Leitch, William C., *Uttermost Trout: Little-Known Trout Streams of Tierra del Fuego,* The Flyfisher Magazine, Volume XX, Number 4, Fall 1987.

Luna, Hugo Correa, *La Conservación de la Naturaleza: Parques Nacionales Argentinos,* segunda edición, Servicio Nacional de Parques Nacionales, Buenos Aires, 1976.

Marini, Tomás, *Los Salmónidos en Nuestro Parque Nacional de Nahuel Huapi, Lanín, y Los Alerces,* Anales del Museo de la Patagonia, Tomo 1, 121-138, 1945.

Marini, Tomás, *El Landlocked Salmón en La República Argentina,* Publicación Miscelánea No. 117, Ministerio de Agricultura, Buenos Aires, 1942.

Mendez, V. M. García, *En Busca de la Trucha,* Editorial Perlidos, Buenos Aires, 1989.

Ministerio de Agricultura, *Recursos Acuáticos Vivos,* from Evaluación de los Recursos Naturales de la Argentina, Tomo VII, Buenos Aires, 1963.

Ministerio de Agricultura y Ganadería, *Cartilla para Pescadores Deportivos,* División de Protección Pesquera, No. 11, Santiago, 1977.

Mountain Research and Development, International Mountain Society, Vol. 4, No. 2 (State of Knowledge Report on Andean Ecosystems, Otto Sobrig, Editor), 1984.

Narosky, T., *Birds of Argentina and Uruguay* (English edition), Vazquez Mazzini Editores, Buenos Aires, 1989.

Pawson, Tony, *Flyfishing Around the World,* Unwin Hyman, London, 1987.

Peces de los Parques Nacionales Nahuel Huapi, Lanín, y Los Alerces, Anales del Museo de la Patagonia, Tomo 1, 121-138, 1945.

Perry, Roger, *Patagonia,* Dodd, Mead, & Co., New York, 1974.

Schad, Werner, *Los Ríos Más Australes de la Tierra,* Marymar Ediciones, Buenos Aires, 1983.

Schwiebert, Ernest, *A River For Christmas and other stories,* Stephen Greene Press, 1988.

Subsecretaria de Asuntos Marítimos, *Cartilla para Pescadores Deportivos, Provincia de Santa Cruz, Río Gallegos, undated.*

Subsecretaria de Turismo de la Nación, Argentina: Guía de la Caza y Pesca, Vol. I & II, Buenos Aires, 1988.

Shipton, Eric, *Tierra del Fuego: The Fatal Lodestone,* Chas. Knight & Co., London, 1973.

Thomasson, Kuno, *Plankton and Environment of North Patagonian Lakes,* Annales Societatis Tartuensis, IV, Uppsala, 1964.

Titcomb, J. W., *Introducción de Salmonoides en los Ríos y Lagos del Sud,* Boletín del Ministerio de Agricultura, I:107-138, I(3):253-275, Tomo 4, Ministerio de Agricultura, Buenos Aires, 1904.

Universidad Nacional de Comahue, *Atlas de la Provincia del Neuquen,* Neuquen, 1980.

Videla, Pedro Bueno, *Algunos controles efectuados sobre peces existentes en la región de los lagos,* Revista de Agronomía y Veterinaria, Tomo XI, Entrega I, Universidad de Buenos Aires, Noviembre, 1914.

Wilhelm, P. E., et. al., *Nuevo Diccionario Mapuche-Español,* Siringa Libros, Neuquen, 1989.

Fish Registers of the following establishments: Club Norysur (Lago Meliquina), 1946-1990; Hotel Correntoso (Río Correntoso), 1988-1990; Kau-Tapen Lodge (Río Grande, Tierra del Fuego), 1985-1990; Estancia La Primavera (Río Traful), 1938-1990.